EUDORA WELTY

Eudora Welty as "Powerhouse"   John Sokol © 1986

Eudora Welty

Eye of the Storyteller

edited by Dawn Trouard

The Kent State University Press
Kent, Ohio, and London, England

© 1989 by The Kent State University Press, Kent, Ohio 44242
All rights reserved
Library of Congress Catalog Card Number 88-13926
ISBN 0-87338-384-2 (cloth)
ISBN 0-87338-385-0 (paper)
Manufactured in the United States of America

Library of Congress Cataloging-in-Publication Data

Eudora Welty:eye of the storyteller / edited by Dawn Trouard.
    p.   cm.
    Papers presented at the Eye of the Storyteller Conference, held
Sept. 17–19, 1987, at Akron, Ohio.
    Bibliography: p.
    Includes index.
    ISBN 0-87338-384-2 (alk. paper)
    ISBN 0-87338-385-0 (pbk.: alk. paper)
    1. Welty, Eudora, 1909– —Criticism and interpretation—
Congresses. I. Trouard, Dawn, 1954– . II. Eye of the
Storyteller Conference (1987: Akron, Ohio)
PS3545.E6Z6727 1989
813'.52—dc19   88-13926
                                               CIP

British Library Cataloging-in-Publication data are available.

CONTENTS

CONTENTS

Acknowledgments

I wish to thank the people who participated in the Eye of the Storyteller Conference in 1987. I have expressed my thanks to the conferees and colleagues who attended, and I am pleased to acknowledge again the administrators and colleagues at the University of Akron who secured the permission and the bankroll to underwrite this conference: then-Chairman Paul Merrix of the English Department, who has always been encouraging about academic projects, and our dean of Arts and Sciences, a southerner and a gentleman, his degree in chemistry notwithstanding, Claibourne Griffin. They provided start-up funding, released time, and clerical support. Further thanks need to go to President William Muse and his wife, Marlene, for providing and fostering an atmosphere where southern literary studies are not just hospitably treated but respected. For helping make ends meet, the Stoller Fund deserves to be recognized for its financial support. And I wish to thank Kent Marsden and his staff at Foundation Support Programs for providing all sorts of planning advice and emergency service.

Among those who served above and beyond friendship, duty, or recompense are Greg Bergman, Diana Reep, Thomas Dukes, Roseanne Hoeful, Rosemary Crossland, Robin Fast, Sally Slocum, Bruce Holland, Lisa McElhinney, Alan and Judy Hart, Elton Glaser, Bob Pope, Bookie Patrick, Dan E. Moldea, Kate Marado, Giovanna Kennedy, Jim Hinkle, Paul Gallagher, Karl Purdue, Melissa Rosati, Gayle King, Sonia Smith, Judy Major, Bonnie Bromley, Marian J. Ray, and Robert Zangrando. Special thanks to Ruth Vande Kieft and Tom McHaney for their savvy suggestions and to William U. McDonald and William Bedford Clark for their generous publicity. I

ACKNOWLEDGMENTS

am indebted to Don Noble for coming and making it all so easy with his wit. I want to recognize artist John Sokol for the word portrait of Welty and his contributions behind the scene, which helped in any number of crucial ways during the project. I also need to thank Jeanne West and Julia Morton of the Kent State University Press for making the book possible. For creating order out of chaos, and generally managing the chain gang, Melissa Berry, chief miracle worker, I owe an extraordinary debt of gratitude.

And finally there are those friends and colleagues for whom I will have to live at least another life in order to cancel the debt I owe for their patience, advice, readings, and unfailing good humor. I am grateful to Carey Wall, who shared her ocean and home with me, and to Noel Polk, who keeps making me believe in guardian angels.

DAWN TROUARD

LANDING IN AKRON: An Introduction

"Where did people learn things?
Where did they go to find them?
How far?"

"First Love"

This collection of 16 essays on Eudora Welty was selected from those delivered at a 17–19 September 1987 conference on the author, The Eye of the Storyteller, hosted by the University of Akron. I suspect one of the last places, short of the bottom of a well, that a Welty reader might expect to find out things about Welty fiction would be in Akron, Ohio. But since a fortunate misattribution in an interview in 1960 where Miss Welty credits Akron and Harold Rood's little magazine, *Manuscript,* with her first literary acceptance, Akron has been waiting to make right its erroneous claim to fame. *Manuscript* was actually located in Athens, Ohio; and so Athens and Akron share a special affinity with Welty's paternal grandmother, for whom she was christened Alice, but who, Welty reveals in *One Writer's Beginnings,* was actually named Almira. She goes on to say that to be "remembered wrong" was to be rendered a kind of "orphan. That was worse to me than if I had been able to imagine dying" (*OWB* 65). In order to redeem the false credit, and to employ methods compatible with Welty's own, the goal of this conference was to be an orphan as Easter in "Moon Lake" reveals it to Nina—to exult in the opportunity. For orphaning provides access to "the other way to live": one may cease "thinking like the others. It's only interesting, only worthy, to try for the fiercest secrets" (*CS* 361).

More than 90 people attended, prepared to try for those fierce secrets. Participants arrived from France, Denmark, Utah, California, Florida; others drove in from Missouri to be shown, and some came from Mississippi to check on Yankees poaching a native resource. Mainly they came to learn of the "secret ways" (*CS* 361) that the conference was intended to reveal. The papers collected here bring together some of the most established names in Welty scholarship and introduce several new scholars. Though the official occasion of the conference was to offer an asymmetrical salute to Welty's 51 years of authorship, dating from the appearance of "Death of a Traveling Salesman" in 1936, its origin was in the idea of *power*—a topic not often linked to Welty. But power, subtle and overt, demonstrated by technique and vision, revealed itself as the hidden agenda throughout the conference. For Welty, like her creation Powerhouse, through sheer force of creative mastery "sends everybody into oblivion" (*CS* 132). The critics exercised wide license in how they chose to formulate their own view of power, but behind their disparate approaches was a common, recurring need to bear witness to Welty's formidable vision as it imposes itself on her stunningly diverse materials. Some elected to treat technical manifestations of power as revealed through her experiments in voice and style; others chose to explore power as it is exercised in communities or by the individual in conflict with that community. Sometimes intimacy—longed for, sudden, or even painful—releases power latent in the individual; or power can be discovered in the manipulations of the outsider over the insider, the interpreter over his or her audience. Power takes the form of symbol, act, and legacy.

The finest Welty criticism, of course, has always noted that her fiction defies comfortable readings; but a good deal of even the best Welty criticism, as many critics have discovered, is in fact usually partial to those relatively comfortable readings, which contentedly view Welty through the rather traditional and peculiarly focused lens of her southernness and her treatment of traditional southern themes. The Eye of the Storyteller Conference sought from the outset to deemphasize such traditional approaches to Welty, and so papers for the conference and for this volume were chosen on the basis of how successfully they opened up new approaches to familiar texts or claimed for consideration heretofore-neglected Welty texts. In one sense, then, it was felt useful to defamiliarize her a bit, in order to see her more clearly. The view was enhanced still further since the conference proved to be the first one exclusively devoted to Eudora Welty to be held outside the South. Boosted by an unconventional but unrestricted controlling theme, the essays included were marked by a kind of daring. A tacit felicity of purpose governs the critics whose work is collected in this volume: exploration—arriving together, as if at a kind of landing, determined, despite very different approaches—feminism, culture theory, frame theory, Bakhtinian discourse analysis, stylistics, and aesthetics—to plumb what they knew and to pool what still remained mysterious. Though several of the readings presented here will show contrasting methodologies brought to bear on a common subject, another kind of harmony is operative: each essay contributes to a roughing out of the fictional terrain Welty has created; there is in each "a sense of journey, of something that might happen . . . [a kind of] looking outward with the sense of rightful space and time . . . which must be traversed before she [in this case, Welty] could be known at all" (*CS* 254). Collectively, the essays demonstrate the kinds of analyses that are sympathetic to their subject. More than anything, they indicate that scholarship on Welty has come into its own, though there is still much catching up to do if scholars are to match the implicit challenge posed by her fiction.

The best way, I suppose, to approach Welty, like all great writers, is through the word. The first section of this volume undertakes the analysis of Welty's language and the cultural construction of meaning from it. Since her fictive worlds are after truthful records of time, place, and people, it is appropriate to go first to the devices by which Welty creates such vitality. So often her world depicts a struggle to communicate, to know and understand love. The author inevitably portrays this struggle in language; but in Welty's complex vision, language is only a starting place, for "all things were speech" (*CS* 194), as she affirms in "A Still Moment." Ruth Weston begins with the first story, in the first collection, *A Curtain of Green's* "Lily Daw and the Three Ladies." She examines Welty's aesthetic appropriations of folk art to create literary tableaux complete with abstract stylization and spatial perspectives—linguistic equivalents of photographs and regional folk paintings. Regional speech, counterpointed with choreographed movements, permits the story's formal structural confinement to reinforce the thematic concern with female cultural confinement. Out of homely material, Welty's fine-art methods literally capture the monumentality of Lily's *position* at the story's end.

Carey Wall's treatment of "June Recital" poses a solution to the topsy-turvy vision and mayhemic energy of this complex story. Through the lucid application of Victor Turner's culture theory, Wall discovers a coherence that accounts for the highly orchestrated methods of Morgana's systematic structuring of meaning forged from the language and necessities of communitas. The day of the story's action serves as a liminal moment whereby the necessary transformations of community can work to exorcise and reassign roles in the ever-doubled reality of Welty's vision and that of the world.

Susan V. Donaldson articulates another facet of doubleness through her Bakhtinian analysis of *Losing Battles*. Here, it is the dualism of oral and written discourses as they vie for dominance. Welty surveys the conflict between single-minded visions of truth, language, and reality in order to expose the warring strategies of discourse ideology and to calculate the familial record—written and oral—of loss.

The final essay in this unit on language accounts for the effect of style—syntax, rhythm, diction, imagery—on the tone of Welty's late story "The Demonstrators." Suzanne Ferguson details the method that most marks

Welty's style, the yoking of incompatible states of emotion. From the vision of "beauty and terror, the tenderness and violence of everyday life," Ferguson charts the methods by which Welty's art wrests consolation from despair, optimism from what seems unmitigated grief.

The second part of the collection explores the fictional treatment of women and is drawn together by a compelling phrase from Welty's story "Kin": "who had felt the wildness behind the ladies' view" (*CS* 561). In her examination of mother-daughter relationships, Elizabeth Evans raises the issue of costs exacted from this highly charged and often painful connection. Working with three respective sets of mothers and daughters, Evans demonstrates the crushing ambivalence experienced by the daughter who depends on her mother for keys to selfhood but who instead is crippled and debilitated by her attachment. The daughter can only redefine her identity when she is released by her mother's death.

Marilyn Arnold's puckish revisioning of *The Ponder Heart* reveals the complex range of Welty's female characters as she turns in her essay from the sobering analysis of loving women to death to the comic vagaries of matchmaking in her essay, "The Strategy of Edna Earle Ponder." While Arnold deftly preserves the comic design of her subject, she astutely demonstrates the power of Edna Earle's rhetorical imperialism, and she offers a cautionary tale cum critical lesson on reader response and the sexist assumptions that bind the culture and govern the casual reading.

Peter Schmidt presides over a sibyl hunt where he uncovers buried secrets about Welty's view of women in her references to these enigmatic symbols of prophecy and power. His feminist analysis demonstrates some alternative ways to read stories that have been inscribed by male culture and further links Welty as artist to literary forebears who use "sibylline prophecy as a complex metaphor for their own art and its relation to their culture."

Ann Romines raises the narrative and mythic stakes in Welty and takes this section on women to its appropriate climax with her study of Welty's triumphantly failed first-person narrators: Sister of "Why I Live at the P.O." and Circe. The issue for these grappling storytellers and victims— real and imagined—is how to assume narrative dominance, become the hero, and escape their domestic plots. For Welty, these are parts of the larger tale in which every storyteller participates, fraught with all the "flux, change, partiality, collaboration, losing battles" that Romines cites. Sister and Circe offer special insights into the ongoing struggle to achieve *herstory*.

The third group of essays takes its design from visible connections, some apparent and some more problematic; or as Welty in "Shower of Gold" puts it: "Everybody to their own visioning" (*CS* 268). The connection Jan Nordby Gretlund demarcates is Welty's affinity for Chekhov and his modes of realism. Working with Welty's own admissions in her essay "Reality in Chekhov's Stories," Gretlund notes common devices and subjects shared by the two authors. He assesses her achievement and places Welty in the international galaxy.

Daun Kendig looks not to the authorial heavens but into the Morgana woods to see if what we see and what Mattie Will thinks she sees can be resolved. Employing sociologist Erving Goffman's frame analysis as a critical compass, Kendig routes us to textual junctures where the tenuous line between perception and reality blur and the reality of desire comes into play—not only for Mattie herself but for the reader of fiction as well. Kendig demonstrates the profundity of Welty's tale "Sir Rabbit" in its exploration of the ambiguous nature of reality and the attendant psychological vulnerability of the individual.

Not even the artist is immune from the ephemeral nature of reality, and the visible connection Cheryll Burgess sees is the metafictional presence of author figures in Welty's short stories. Burgess identifies a sequence of artists who create stories through metaphoric enterprises—gardening and jazz improvising. To the degree that they fail or succeed in their creative visions, they provide clues to Welty's own conception of what is essential in the character of great artists.

Danièle Pitavy-Souques makes Lacanian connections when she argues that especially for the artist, suffering "defines us as human beings, since it is precisely *in* suffering that words originate, later language, and still later writing." Her essay accounts for the omnipresence of journeys in Welty's fiction, particularly in *The Bride of the Innisfallen,* where characters in search of understanding must leave behind the familiar territory of rationality and enter into a marginal no-man's-land where they may be transformed, liberated into the discovery of their deepest natures. Having risked this transgression into the unknown, the artist embraces the challenge of mortality and suffering.

When Welty writes in *One Writer's Beginnings* that "Travel is part of some longer continuity" (97) she is speaking again of journeys, but also of their potential to reveal connections—past, present, future. She is also speaking of rewards or, in this section, re-turns. Noel Polk's essay is the first in this final section devoted to endurance and change in Welty's fiction. He routes readers through some familiar territory in Welty, but he is engaged in an aesthetic remapping. In what ways are Welty's late stories southern? How fundamental is a sense of place to her fiction? His responses to questions like these challenge the regional Teamsterism of most critics. Polk overturns the Pavlovian response in readers who insist that any story written by a southern writer must necessarily exhibit the stylistic features of its regional drawl. Polk shows that many of the most cherished aspects of place are subverted in Welty's fictive world where she asks readers actually to *see* the world her fiction places before them with the same acuity with which it has been presented rather than through their preconceptions.

Probably no Welty story has had more readers than "A Worn Path." Nancy Butterworth takes an excursion intended to divest this story, but most particularly Phoenix, of the traps of sentimentality and polemics that have frequently marked previous analyses of it. Butterworth sees more in the character than individuality. Phoenix also provides a symbolic occasion for Welty to present the ongoing, hardly simple, and extremely real struggle of blacks for equality.

The enduring and cyclical nature of Welty's art inspires Thomas McHaney's critical pilgrimage to the genre-elusive *The Golden Apples*. For him, the multidimensional use of the cycle is method, medium, and theme. Elaborating the legendary links to Yeats, McHaney clarifies Virgie Rainey's final vision wherein mythic and personal past coalesce, as do the quotidian world and the world of imagination through "the artist's vision and the ineluctable intertextuality of language."

Finally, Ruth Vande Kieft's essay offers perspective on some dominant critical approaches in Welty scholarship. She provides insights into the pedagogical demands placed on the Welty teacher, the role criticism can play, and the dangers to the text certain critical approaches might pose in the classroom. By exploring the potential academic hazards of critical theory, she secures safe passage for students and teachers of Welty alike.

This volume, I hope, captures the diversity and energy that Welty's literature excited in the scholars. Welty has already advised readers in *One Writer's Beginnings* that writing can be a daring life. When criticism takes that dare and challenges the safe boundaries of literary approach, an editor can responsibly say only one thing more by way of introduction and that is " 'Welcome' . . . the most dangerous word in the world" (*CS* 531).

Dawn Trouard
The University of Akron

ABBREVIATIONS

CS	*The Collected Stories of Eudora Welty*
Conversations	*Conversations with Eudora Welty.* Edited by Peggy Whitman Prenshaw.
Eye	*The Eye of the Story: Selected Essays and Reviews*
LB	*Losing Battles*
OD	*The Optimist's Daughter*
OWB	*One Writer's Beginnings*

EUDORA WELTY

Language and Culture

"All things were speech"

RUTH D.

W E S T O N

American Folk Art, Fine Art, and Eudora Welty

Aesthetic Precedents for "Lily Daw and the Three Ladies"

When Ruth Vande Kieft first discussed Eudora Welty's visual imagination in her *Eudora Welty* (1962), she compared Welty's crowded scenes to Brueghel canvasses. In her recent revision of that book (1987), she shifts comparison from European to American art, and specifically to folk art, by her comment that *Losing Battles* is "more like a big brown country bucket than a Grecian urn, suited to visual display as a 'period piece' of American Literature" (164). Welty herself speaks often of her love for painting and of the folk tradition in storytelling. She knows "at least thirty . . . quilt names" (*Conversations* 55); and among her early photographs are a storefront still life, the homemade bird costumes of a Jackson church pageant, and a slave's apron on which is appliquéd a scene showing souls at various levels between heaven and hell (*One Time* 52, 88–90, 96). The apron's multiperspective design and stick figures closely resemble the primitivist paintings of Welty's fellow Mississippian Theora Hamblett,[1] as well as the more famous works of Grandma Moses. Welty is undoubtedly familiar with Hamblett's art, and she once wrote a humorous song about Grandma Moses when that artist's work was one of New York's trendy topics.[2]

Perhaps the most telling evidence of Welty's interest in folk art, however, is its presence throughout her fiction. Not only her own photography and her study of fine art but also her careful observation of the folk artifacts that decorate the lives of southerners—from beautiful handmade quilts to yard art such as grotesque bottle trees—constitute a pervasive influence in her own vision that in large part determines the way we understand her stories. Her aesthetic precedents owe at least as much to the visual arts as to the received tradition of literary arts and are the source of the abstract stylization and the spatial perspectives that add monumentality to her subjects. The result is not unlike the effect that can be achieved with a flat photograph; thus it is not surprising to find the monumental, yet deflated subjects of contemporary southern photographer William Eggleston compared to Welty's characters.[3]

Welty's own spatial bias is clear from her critical vocabulary: her stated goal is always to write a story that is "steadily visible from its outside, presenting a continuous, shapely, pleasing and finished surface to the eye" (*Eye* 120). She concedes that her stories neglect plot and that "the *shaping* idea . . . can't be mapped and plotted" (109; Welty's emphasis); in fact, the surface appearance of her fiction more closely resembles a spatially relative puzzle than the background for causal plot continuity. Many stories are comparable to abstract tableaux with the spatial components of painting, drama, and dance. When Welty's collection *The Wide Net* was published, Diana Trilling criticized it, in a spatial analogy that is more appropriate than Trilling may have known, for being a "book of ballets" (57).[4] However, neither the lack of plotting nor the resemblance to ballet represents the faulty technique that Trilling implied; rather, Welty's concentration on the spatial dimension constitutes a unique source of meaning.[5]

To begin with, certain actions can be expected to happen in certain types of spaces; and certainly Welty's settings provide dramatic spaces. But in addition, she consciously shapes fictional space so that emotions and ideas are externalized on the printed page less in terms of semantic meaning than of sensuous imagery. Geometric lines of relationship and perspective as well as structural patterning subvert the progress of the narration in time while they enrich and advance the theme. A pervasive pattern throughout her fiction is that of convergence versus dispersion: centripetal, reversing to centrifugal, motions which represent, respectively, the equivalents of the threatening confinement inherent in ordered society and the opposite impetus toward chaotic dissolution of that order.[6] To experience the full potential of such a work, the reader must join with the writer in the romantic irony of deliberately destroying any illusion of the work as mimetic reality. (The term *romantic irony* indicates the necessity that the reader view units of meaning in a work of art *only* through relation to the whole, thereby deflating the work itself as an imitation of reality [see Daghistany and Johnson 54].) He or she must accept it as an artifact, a created product that exists in space as an entity that can be apprehended entire and whose meaning is achieved by an appeal to the abstract physics of spatial relationships. The characters do not need to speak of impinging forces or of the chaos that is freedom; the image patterns and the structure of the fiction reveal those themes.

In spite of the strong presence of nature and human life in her work,

Welty interests herself more in creation than in re-creation, and in essential states of being and underlying formal patterns than in representational reality. Her ability to speak to ontological essence with gravity and infinite suggestibility, through stylized characters and bold fictional brush strokes, is in line with Allen Tate's observation that complexity of feeling without complexity of character is essential to the American novel.[7] Similar effects are achieved by folk art and by the fine art of American visionary painters, both of which exhibit a personal instead of a historically received style and conceive of a work as a thing made as much as a culture expressed. Although the truth of folk art may be instinctive and that of fine art intellectual, both project an order based on formal structure and motif rather than mimetic realism—primitive totem poles no less than the cones and spheres that represent nature for Cézanne. A similar formal order in Welty's fiction, coupled with her unwillingness to be simply an illusionist, link her fiction with folk art and with Post-Impressionist painters, who, unlike their Impressionist predecessors, abstracted reality, desiring to create form rather than imitate nature.

The Post-Impressionists expressed an inner vision by manipulating color, line, and composition of space—the formal components of painting. This late nineteenth-century interest in the expressive rather than the imitative coincided in time with the symbolist poets' emphasis on inner vision. And, similarly, the inner world created by American visionary painters resembles the earlier literary visionary tradition of Poe and Hawthorne, which Welty follows in her own way by creating stories that approach the status of abstract visual artifacts. Indeed, the great mystery of Welty's art may reside in the paradox of her wide and sympathetic knowledge of human history and culture and her equal capacity to "forget knowing" in order to make each work a new beginning, as Jean Lescure said of Lapique's painting, and as Proust remarked that Elstir's roses were "a new variety with which this painter, like some clever horticulturist, had enriched the Rose family."[8]

With folk artist-crafters Welty shares the practice of the "sacrifice of relation"[9] to the outer world the better to reflect its vital inner forces. She also shares a trait that folklorist Bill Ferris acknowledges as common to both folk and literary artists: an extraordinary eye for the telling detail, the ability to recognize, for example, if a "dog's been a long way off and is headed home by the way it walks" (*Conversations* 181). The entire Welty canon is a compendium of such telling detail; and it is decorated with folk art, from the "hemstitched pillowcases" in "Lily Daw and the Three Ladies" to the finely crafted breadboard in *The Optimist's Daughter* in which Laurel sees "the whole solid past."

An early example of the abstract stylization and individual flair of American folk art is a three-foot-high pilothouse figure of a gold rooster,[10] whose sturdy form and brilliant color do not rely on inherited traditions but instead on practical, often self-taught, skills. If much subtlety of European artistic expression was lost in early American art, much also was gained: primarily the bold approach and the personal imprint of the artist-crafters on artifacts that were at once practical pieces for public use and unique expressions of their makers and of their places of origin.

Far from being something less than truly American, the colloquial style, as it is regionally and personally marked, may be the quintessential American expression in art. It is in this respect that the term *regional* is by no means reductivist when applied to that art, or to the fiction of Eudora Welty. Like the colonial sculptor, Welty is a particularly *American* artist not in spite of, but because of the regional character of her work and because of its place in what Hugh Kenner (205) calls the "homemade world" created by American writers (205).[11] Kenner uses this phrase to mean a nonliterary tradition of art; but, in addition, it connotes the ability to use whatever materials come to hand as the raw materials of one's craft, as the colonial artisan would use local pigments to make paint—never mind that no known rooster was such a shade of gold (or such a size). Welty is indeed as much a self-taught artist as were the New England limners of the seventeenth and eighteenth centuries, who created often monumental but always flat figures, and of the American primitivists of the nineteenth and twentieth centuries who, like Grandma Moses, created bright patterns of two-dimensional designs. As Welty has told us in *One Writer's Beginnings,* she taught herself to write largely by looking and listening.

Folk artifacts were not made to be enshrined as objets d'art but to be practical and decorative. Sculpted weather vanes, duck decoys, and tobacconist's Indians are examples, as are quilts, which are both warm and colorful, but which perhaps also tell the story of a family, a region, or a culture. One can only guess that the cheerful shape of the pilothouse rooster represented, to an isolated boat pilot, a visible link with the vigorous life of the land; and in addition, like a Welty story, it certainly presented "a shapely, pleasing and finished surface to the eye" (*Eye* 120). Pennsylvania Dutch painters created intricate abstract hex symbols without a trace of narrative significance. And yet these artists too resemble the storyteller of the oral tradition and its modern practitioners such as Eudora Welty, because both types of art can be described in terms of Constance Rourke's category of "applied art" (12). Welty's stories naturally differ from static visual art in their temporal component and from all applied art in that they do not illustrate a recipe that can be reproduced. Yet they can be seen as applied art in the sense that they not only entertain but also *serve* as skilled transmitters of a unique part of America's cultural heritage.

It is not, however, that her prose continues a literary local-color tradition; rather, her literary equivalents of historically received visual art forms contribute to her unique fictional form. In spite of her delightful ability to reproduce the colloquial southern idiom and manner and to decorate her stories so that they double as repositories of cultural history, they are also, paradoxically, avatars of the modernist idea of art for art's sake. Although Welty, like Faulkner, says she simply wants to tell a good story the best way she can, her stories are finely crafted verbal artifacts; she has consciously made the visual arts as much a part of her own sophisticated vision as Carol Manning has shown the storytelling art to be (*With Ears*).

A recognition of aesthetic similarities between Welty's fiction and the visual arts is not an attempt to draw lines of direct influence, but merely to say that hers is a poetics as much of dynamic patterns, of space and motion, of shape and color, as of language. The stylization of her visual grotesques, for example, makes a primarily visual, not psychological or social statement. The tonglike legs of Clytie, drowning in the rain barrel, and the cone of light Virgie Rainey perceives connecting her to the moon in "The Wanderers" are as abstractly geometric figures as are those of other line- and color-conscious American writers. Two spatial images that Welty herself has admired come to mind. One is at the conclusion of Stephen Crane's "The Bride Comes to Yellow Sky." Welty describes Scratchy and Jack as

> two predicaments [who] meet . . . [and] are *magnetized* toward each other—and *collide*. One is vanquished with neatness and absurdity; as he goes away, Scratchy's "feet made *funnel-shaped* tracks in the heavy sand." Here are the plainest equivalents of comedy, two situations in a *construction* simple as a *seesaw* and not without a seesaw's kind of pleasure in reading. (*Eye* 87; emphasis added)

Not only Welty's attraction to the geometric image but also her critical terminology ("construction") and the dynamic motion implied in her reading of Crane indicate the physical sensuousness of her own vision.

Likewise, she is impressed by Willa Cather's spatial depiction of time in *My Ántonia*, which Welty describes in painterly terms as the work of "an artist with a pencil or a brush. . . . There is the foreground, with the living present," Welty argues, "and there is the horizon of infinite distance, where the departed, now invisible ancients have left only their faint track. . . . But there is no intervening ground. . . . no recent past. . . . no middle distance" (*Eye* 42). Cather's vision, juxtaposing that ancient past with Ántonia's present, Welty believes, is powerfully imaged forth when "the sword of Coronado and the plow against the sun are fused into one in *My Ántonia*." Such decorative shapes upstage the linear narrative by calling attention to themselves and yet perfectly signify the artist's intent: in Welty's words, "the past can be seen—[Cather] lets us see it—in physical form" (*Eye* 43). Welty, too, utilizes physically dramatic shapes, which she combines with equally decorative characters like those in "Lily Daw and the Three Ladies," who move and speak in stylized patterns.

Welty's two-dimensional figures result in virtual caricature; but the concept of abstract art they embody is as integral a part of her total vision as are the masses of light and shade in the art of Whistler, whose painting of his mother is significantly entitled *Arrangement in Grey and Black No. 1: The Artist's Mother* (1871): the pattern is more significant than the subject. The best of Welty's "flat" characters, to use E. M. Forster's term, which Welty knows well (*Conversations* 248), achieve the same complex effect as that of the flat surface of Grant Wood's double portrait *American Gothic,* which suggests by its title and confirms by its intricate design and by the haunting gazes of its ostensibly simple, wholesome subjects, the underlying negativity of American rural life, perhaps the dark underside of the American dream. And it is at least as much Wood's complexity of feeling and sophistication of technique as Thomas Hart Benton's "simple" celebrations of homespun ruggedness that Welty's work resembles.[12] For although Welty herself prefers criticism that simply celebrates art rather than analyzes it, and although much critical comment has justifiably emphasized Welty's celebration of human life and human mystery, there is much in the fiction itself that is not celebratory. Danger lurks behind the "curtain of green" in Welty's stories as does potential violence behind the Grant Wood pitchfork.

The art with which Welty's painterly methods have most in common is possibly that of Andrew Wyeth, whose work is strongly regional and whose unsettling silence and "strange suspension" in such works as *Christina's World* (1948) are marks of the Magic Realist tradition of American visionary painters (Davidson 101).[13] In *Christina's World,* a crippled girl in a faded pink dress drags herself up a hill of waving, yellow grass toward a small paintless frame cabin set starkly alone. The dramatic effect in the painting is largely achieved by the appropriateness of oblique perspective in conjunction with the realistic depiction of Christina's polio-twisted body and the stylized background. Similarly, the almost photographic realism in Welty's fiction is imbued, usually by unique perspective, with an element of fantasy or of the bizarre or the grotesque. Certainly the grotesque in Welty bears as much relation to unusual artistic perspectives such as Wyeth's as it does to the psychologically deformed characters of Flannery O'Connor and Carson McCullers.

In "Lily Daw and the Three Ladies" Welty creates a story that seems a virtual collage of the visual arts and the gestures of drama and of dance. Through the guidance of Welty's spatial imagination, we see the limited and distorted perspectives and prospects of her characters in a manner analogous to that by which we view those in Wyeth's paintings. Through the motion of three figures around Lily, we are drawn into the scene, to Lily, as by the line of perspective in a painting. The description of Lily as small, as compared with the larger figures who loom threateningly over her, contributes to our heightened sense throughout the story of her oblique perspective below the level of and from the midst of the circling ladies. By the central functioning of spatial imagery in this story, Welty suggests not only Lily's limited field of view but that as well of the ladies who focus all of their attention upon her. The bold strokes of the folk artist and also of the modern artist who mixes nonartistic materials on his canvasses are suggested by Welty's merging of the traits of static pictorial and sculptural art with those of choreography. The result is a collage of shifting limits, like a cubist superimposition of planes, which has the effect of variations on the theme of limitation. The narrative surface of "Lily Daw" is that of idiosyncratic regional speech, carefully selected and arranged by an omniscient authorial controller who is perhaps symbolic of the ladies' controlling force over Lily Daw. It is by the subtle shadings of their idiolects alone that they masquerade as traditional characters in mimetic fiction. It is not their words, however, so much as their hypnotic aural rhythms and their spatial disposition that convey the theme of confinement.

The three ladies speak and move in the manner of a chorus in a play. There is minimal description of character, for these figures, like Whistler's *Mother,* are more abstract items in arrangements—forms interacting with forms—than personalities. It is as if Welty had first imagined these characters as shadow and motion on a bare stage, in silhouette, behind a gauze curtain, a concept which, in fact, was used in the staging of a dramatic collage of Welty's work entitled *Sister and Miss Lexie.*[14] Perhaps it was Welty's fascination with the New York theater while she was a graduate student at Columbia University that led her to use the methods of almost classical dramatic movement, but her use of it is ironic; for she deflates her own stylistic suggestion of enlightened culture by the story's insistent comparison of people with poultry. Thus the Greek chorus of ladies amounts to parody, since they resemble nothing so much as chickens pecking purposefully at Lily as at a juicy tidbit on the ground at their feet.

The chorus meets at the center of communal life, the post office, where the news has arrived that Lily has been accepted at the Ellisville Institute for the Feeble-Minded of Mississippi:

> "What will Lily say," beamed Mrs. Carson. . . .
> "She'll be tickled to death," said Mrs. Watts. . . .
> "Don't you all dare go off . . . without me!" called Aimee Slocum. (*CS* 3)

The ladies confront Lily Daw in her home, a structure reflecting the incongruity and illogic that the ladies and Lily see in each other's actions and speeches—and which the reader sees in the ironic juxtaposition of characters who are all grotesquely limited and all equally ignorant of the fact. It also resembles the vaguely unreal, off-center house in *Christina's World,* which boasts a ladder to the roof but no porch or steps before its open door:

[Lily Daw's] paintless frame house with all the weather vanes was three stories high in places and had yellow and violet stained-glass windows in front and gingerbread around the porch. It leaned steeply to one side, toward the railroad, and the front steps were gone. (*CS* 5)

Inside, Lily sits in her petticoat on the floor by an old trunk lined with paper whose circular patterns suggest the confining, threatening motions of the three ladies. The three, alternately or in unison, stand and sit, converging upon Lily as they will soon "circle around the xylophone player" (*CS* 11), their chanting incantations in both instances suggesting the three witches of *Macbeth* conjuring around a vision in a kettle, while Mrs. Carson's "fingering [of] the tape measure which hung over her bosom" (*CS* 3) reveals them as three provincial Fates who would measure out Lily's life. First they sit and rock as they question her about her recent decision to marry a traveling musician whom she describes only as "a man last night" (*CS* 7). Then they begin to cast their spell, aimed at protecting Lily's virtue by committing her to the asylum:

"Why don't you go to Ellisville!" [said Mrs. Carson].
"Won't that be lovely?" said Mrs. Watts. . . .
"It's a lovely place," said Aimee Slocum. (*CS* 6)

When this does not convince Lily, they add choral movements to their performance.

They move in unison: "All the ladies *leaned down* toward her in impressive astonishment." Then they move in sequence: "Mrs. Watts *stood up*. . . . 'What?' demanded Aimee Slocum, *rising up*. . . . 'What?' 'Don't ask her what,' said Mrs. Carson, *coming up* behind" (*CS* 6; emphasis added). The three ladies' incantatory repetition of "what" and Welty's equally rhythmic stage directions—"stood up," "rising up," and "coming up"—reinforce the sequence of physical movements that they describe. Then the ladies try to bribe Lily, continuing the previously established pattern:

"I'll give you a pair of hemstitched pillowcases," said Mrs. Carson.
"I'll give you a big caramel cake," said Mrs. Watts.
"I'll give you a souvenir from Jackson, . . ." said Aimee Slocum. "Now will you go?"
"No," said Lily. (*CS* 8)

The up-down movement continues: "They sat sunken in despair." Then, as Lily weakens: "Silently they rose once more to their feet" (*CS* 8). And as she finally agrees, they nod, smile, and back away together. The rhythmic elements create what Edwin Muir calls a "widening present,"[15] due to the time delay that results from the text's calling attention to its own spatial patterning. Thus, in spite of the cliffhanger plot with its last-minute escape, in this story space is more important than time, the narrative's traditional medium.[16]

Welty's extraordinary critical attention to the spatial dimensions of her fiction points the way to our understanding of its spatial form. She is concerned, for example, with "seeing that [a story's] inner and outer *surfaces* . . . lie . . . close together" and with giving fiction "a *surface* that is continuous and unbroken, never too thin to trust, always in touch with the senses." She quotes Flaubert's statement that "poetry is as precise as *geometry*," and notes that "place, to the writer at work, is seen in a *frame*." "When the good novel is finished," she asserts, "its cooled outside *shape*" has the illusion of reality (*Eye* 120–25; emphasis added). The essence of her characters' confining situations is conveyed not so much through a plot that unfolds in time as through scenes constructed from the shapes and patterns of enclosure. The crucial mimetic illusion, then, is that of spatiality.

Countering the syncopated movements of the three ladies, and reversing the centripetal motion of their convergence upon Lily to a dispersion such as that caused by a centrifugal force, is the frenzied comic activity that erupts at the train station as Lily Daw is put on board for Ellisville. The town has turned out and the band arrives, without orders and with Ed Newton giving "false signals" to play (*CS* 9). Baby chicks run loose, Aimee screams, bells ring, the brass horn sounds, and the train steams. The commotion is like that in the crowded murals of Thomas Hart Benton[17] or the bright splashes of color in a Grandma Moses canvas. Welty's story throughout is a collage not only of motion but of colors, from the muted earthtones of the earlier choric scene, in which the ladies look "mutely" at each other, with brown, green, and Lily's "milky-yellow hair" (*CS* 6), to the brash reds, blacks and whites in the frenzied depot scene, the latter more vibrant palette suggesting Van Gogh's theory of arbitrary color choice "to suggest any emotion of ardent temperament" (Gardner 704). The catalyst of Lily's ardor himself has red hair, a red coat, and a red notebook. When this live prospect shows up, the ladies quickly pull Lily off the train; and now they "circle around the xylophone player" (*CS* 11) to arrange a hasty wedding.

The circle is one of Welty's favorite images of the power to contain, to include or exclude; and it functions in "Lily Daw" as part of a larger symbolic network of images of mental and physical limitation, of the small-town society that sees fit to confine Lily, as they see it, for her own good. In the process, the ladies themselves are shown as limited and confined in many ways. Their obsession with restraint and big-sister watchfulness perhaps betrays an ulterior wish to see that others are likewise restrained, as Jinny Love Stark in *The Golden Apples* wants to "drive everybody . . . into the state of marriage along with her" (*CS* 445). The ladies leave sentences unfinished, censoring their own verbalization about what they fear is Lily's scandalous predicament: " 'Last night at the tent show—' said [one], and then popped her hand over her mouth" (*CS* 3).

Mrs. Carson carries a tape measure on her bosom. Mrs. Watts knows how to "pin people down" (*CS* 6). Aimee Slocum makes her living stamping and bundling mail, and she even observes the ten-word limit in her telegram to Ellisville. Mrs. Watts is confined in a tight corset from which she plans to free herself as soon as the train pulls out, while she attempts to restrict even Lily's view from the train. Lily's stranger is limited too and confesses that he doesn't hear well. And in the crowd of representatively limited folk are those described as small, as one-eyed, and finally as cheering without knowing why.

More serious implications of limitation result from the grotesque comparisons of humans with animals and inanimate objects. Aimee wonders which is more terrible, "the man [or] the hissing train"; and the narrator implies a connection as "the bell began to ring hollowly, and the man was talking" (*CS* 10). The ladies cluck their tongues and make noises "sad as the soft noises in the henhouse at twilight" (*CS* 5); people and chicks run wild on the station platform; and Lily, named for a jackdaw and sucking on a zinnia between her teeth, makes a sound "exactly like a jaybird" (*CS* 6). Pictures of redbirds on a school tablet adorn wires inside the store, while Estelle perches outside on a rail fence. The story reads like the script for an absurdist comedy in which the silent and controlled pantomime of modern dance alternates with the apparent randomness of what was called in the 1960s a theatrical happening.

In "Lily Daw," Welty has utilized the rhetorical patterning of a folk or fairy tale, in which things often happen in threes. She combines mnemonic qualities of the oral folk tradition with the rhythms and shapes of the drama and of the plastic and painterly folk and fine arts. Her story depicts a lyric and individual impulse toward freedom in Lily's carefree bestowal of favor and unconventional behavior. And it portrays the culture's limitation of such freedom because of its threat to safe conventions and its attempt to hide the other than normal (that which cannot be neatly stamped and bundled) behind institutional walls. And, not least, it reveals the ironic situation of women who, blessed and limited by fertility, must therefore be controlled when they are "mature for [their] age" (*CS* 4). It portrays a community tangle of women who close in around a little innocent wild life to see it safely entrusted to one institution or another—to the asylum or to marriage. The flat (unrealistic), yet hauntingly real, characters are effective metaphors for the flat, unreal roles that Ruth Vande Kieft has noted are not only assumed by men but that are often forced by men on women in Welty's South ([1962], 114–15); but in "Lily Daw," as in other Welty stories, these stereotypical roles are forced on women by other women who have become so rigid in their assigned roles that they do not realize they are performing. In their own way, like Fay in *The Optimist's Daughter,* Welty's three ladies are "making a scene" (*OD* 131).

While such human concerns are important in the story, the piece itself is less a social treatise than an abstract design that evokes a sense of grotesque human limitation. Its treatment in spatial, more than temporal, terms underscores its metaphoric confining lines and spaces. Even the language itself functions as a metaphor for limitation. For, as Welty has said, "We start from scratch, and words don't" (*Eye* 134), her own critical vocabulary suggesting a linguistic dimension of the concept of limitation. Language is loaded with accumulated meanings; it is a grotesquely limited and delimiting automatism that Welty extends by creating the illusion of spatiality. "Lily Daw and the Three Ladies" is Welty's earliest portrait of the virtual confinement of women in society by their inscription in its linguistic and cultural codes. Lily herself symbolizes the victim of such limitation as well as the hope of escape; and the circling, threatening, talking ladies reveal woman's own complicity in what Michel Foucault has called a "carceral society," one that not only supervises criminal incarceration but also incorporates a series of enclosing devices, a network of forces, including "walls, space, institution, rules, discourse," all intended to normalize human beings in accord with the prevailing cultural mythos (*Discipline,* esp. 307–08). The few props in the setting for "Lily Daw" contribute to the sense of a "bare stage" on which Lily is cruelly exposed to the elements in her world that threaten her freedom, investing her small figure, however deflated, with dramatic monumentality.

At the story's end, Lily understandably hangs her head, for her hope chest is gone on the train to Ellisville, while she herself is as trapped as the hat thrown into the electric wires. Welty leaves us with an image as graphic and functional as the fused sword and plow that she admires in Cather's *My Ántonia.* For, in the final scene, those electric lines, like the lines of perspective in a painting, now draw our attention past Lily to the focal point that represents her: the hat itself, an object caught.

"June Recital"

Virgie Rainey Saved

"They were the two of them
still linked together."

"June Recital's" action constructs the relations between the townspeople of Morgana, Mississippi; the music teacher, Miss Eckhart, who arrives without explanation to live and work there; and Virgie Rainey, the talented and free-spirited daughter of the town's "poor" family. Morgana holds itself apart from these "different" people—the German woman whose manners are alien and the Morgana girl who refuses to acknowledge the social supremacy the leading families assign themselves. Basically, the townspeople ostracize Miss Eckhart, and they express their jealousy of Virgie Rainey's talent by linking her with Miss Eckhart. Cassie Morrison, another of Miss Eckhart's pupils, is the insider through whose memory and reflections we learn the history of these social relationships. She informs us that the old relationship the town has constructed to deal with the woman and the girl who do not follow their rules is still—even two or three years after Virgie has quit taking piano lessons and Miss Eckhart has lost her studio and home—both unfinished and influential:

> Perhaps nobody wanted Virgie Rainey to be anything in Morgana any more than they had wanted Miss Eckhart to be, and they were the two of them still linked together by people's saying that. How much might depend on people's being linked together? Even Miss Snowdie [Miss Eckhart's landlady] had a little harder time than she had had already with Ran and Scooter, her bad boys, by being linked with roomers and music lessons and Germans. (CS 306)

This linkage the Morgana people have constructed is the central pressure point in the story's present action.

Welty's narrative technique in this story is to wrap the past in the present. Loch Morrison, Cassie's young brother, watches activity in and around the empty MacLain house next door, where Miss Eckhart used to teach her piano pupils, while Cassie, after hearing the initial phrase of Virgie's signature piece, falls into a revery of memory evoking the years of the piano lessons. What Cassie remembers explains what Loch sees.

Without recognizing her, Loch watches poor old Miss Eckhart come back to the house where she taught Virgie and Cassie and the other, untalented daughters of the town. There she has tried to persuade Virgie to pursue a musical career such as the one she seems to have trained for in her youth. But Virgie has turned to using her musical knowledge to accompany the silent movies at the Bijou. To achieve some exorcism of her disappointed efforts and affections—for Miss Eckhart has given all her love to her most talented pupil—the old woman tries to burn the house down. Not only Loch, but the adults as well, abet her, letting her set the fire. After putting out the fire, however, Morgana, in the representative figures of the town marshal and a helper, leads Miss Eckhart off to be incarcerated in a mental institution. This present action ends the old relationship between Miss Eckhart and the town.

This ending seems to be characterized by further Morgana meanness and Virgie's ingratitude. Toward the end of the story, with Morgana adults watching and not intervening, Miss Eckhart and Virgie cross paths on the sidewalk in front of the house without speaking to one another. Virgie is on the scene because she is in the house when the old woman tries to burn it. Virgie has taken to coming to the empty house to sport with her sailor boy; and while Miss Eckhart, now mad, is making her incendiary efforts downstairs, Virgie is, unknown to Miss Eckhart, over her head in an upstairs bedroom, making love and romping with her juicy young lover. When Miss Eckhart has been brought out of the house by the town marshal, Virgie has been driven out by the smoke and her need to get to work. Cassie Morrison watches them pass one another without speaking and is appalled, frightened that a relationship once, and only recently, so intense, can be gone. She sees the world dissolving before her. She understands that the actions are not Miss Eckhart's and Virgie's alone, but the town's. She accuses her mother: "You knew it would be this way, you were with them!" (CS 326). Loch, on the other hand, has been fascinated by the metronome he images as dynamite. He is attracted to its energy and retrieves the intriguing thing that somehow condenses the day's action for him.

Those critics who have formulated the social cruelty in "June Recital"—Danièle Pitavy-Souques, Marilyn Arnold, and Neil Corcoran—have primarily adopted Cassie's view despite a difficulty the story poses for doing that. Cassie has sensitivity and insight but little daring. Daring in meeting and embracing life is Virgie's forte. That quality makes Cassie both hate and love Virgie; Cassie's secret hate and love authenticate Virgie and her *joie de vivre*. That quality indicates a closeness to living unobtainable by mere adherence to the best of society's rules: those that prescribe, for instance, gratitude. Cassie's reluctance to be touched, noted by many critics, is an indication of her limitations not only for living but for understanding what is happening among the people she is watching.

Critics presumably adopt Cassie's view despite the difficulty Welty plants in the way because Cassie's view is a familiar one—the normative view, the way human beings *ought* to behave. American literary criticism as a whole (and French, in the case of Pitavy-Souques), except where this orientation is disrupted by currently authoritative deconstructionist theories, emerges from a construction that allies literary value to normative prescriptions. Mid-twentieth-century literary criticism derives this orientation from Victorian authors' and critics' belief that literature should educate. Welty's fiction, however, does not lend itself thoroughly to normative readings. It makes them fine so far as they go, but limited to one side of double realities.

Welty herself clearly takes a non-Victorian perspective. She ends the preface to her *Collected Stories* by eschewing judgments and absolutes:

> I have been told, both in approval and in accusation, that I seem to love all my characters. What I do in writing of any character is to try to enter into the mind, heart, and skin of a human being who is not myself. Whether this happens to be a man or a woman, old or young, with skin black or white, the primary challenge lies in making the jump itself. It is the act of a writer's imagination that I set most high. (xi)

By her orientation, quite like that of anthropologists Victor Turner and Clifford Geertz, then, Welty seeks to explicate behavior rather than judge it. She is looking not for what her characters have done wrong but rather for what they think they are doing and why they are doing it.

Welty allows the assumption, the axiom, upon which her fiction rests to become explicit in two places, especially. These are Clement Musgrove's speech to his daughter about the doubleness of everything in *The Robber Bridegroom* (126) and Virgie Rainey's contemplation of the closeness of opposites in "The Wanderers" (*CS* 452–53). In "June Recital" we get hints of doubleness, of another action going on besides the ostensible, familiar, social jostling, in two of Cassie Morrison's observations. One is about the now-empty MacLain house: "Yet in the shade of the vacant house, though all looked still, there was agitation. Some life stirred through. It may have been *old* life" (*CS* 286). The other passage is about activity obscured by namelessness and willful disbelief. Cassie learns this from her father's refusal to believe that Mr. Voight, a socially respectable salesman who rooms at the MacLain house, exhibits himself to Miss Eckhart's pupils during the piano lessons: "Some performances of people stayed partly untold for lack of a name, Cassie believed, as well as for lack of believers" (*CS* 296).

". . . all the opposites on earth were
close together, love close to hate,
living to dying. . . ."

Doubleness in social action is explicated in the theories of anthropologist Victor Turner. Turner argues that people interrelate with one another in two modalities: social structure, which he shortens to "structure," and "liminality." *Structure* is all that divides people hierarchically in a society. It is the operative mode in which the ordinary work of the mundane world gets done. It is sustainable and authentic insofar as it reflects the axiomatic first principles that sustain life, usually hidden from the mind by everyday, superficial social consciousness. *Communitas* is the state of recognizing shared humanity; it is a society's people come together. When it does occur, it occurs in *liminality,* a state and time that occur when people set social structure temporarily aside. People set aside social structure to get back to the underlying axioms and to reexamine their social structure and its practices in light of those life-maintaining axioms.

Liminality, serving the need to respond to change, to realign social practice with authorizing definitions of reality and current facts which have outmoded old constructions, is characterized by imaginative, speculative and irreverent behavior. Turner says "it is the analysis of culture into factors and their free recombination in any and every possible pattern, however weird, that is most characteristic of liminality" (*Dramas* 255). Such liminal activity is frequently partly spontaneous, but there are also ritual types, observed cross-culturally, that both ancient and contemporary people use on liminal occasions. The ritual types carry their own organizing and symbolizing procedures and thus serve as formats for the materials of the new occasion.

These ritual types seem to be our inheritance from the distant human past. They belong to a nonrational, symbolic vein of modern people's thought that Richard Shweder argues is in fact stronger than rationality in most twentieth-century people. Welty may well have found them central in all the mythology she read as a child. They are well known to Welty's Morgana townspeople.

One of the ritual types works by means of reversal to turn the "world upside down." This ritual is explicated with many examples, factual as well as artistic, in Barbara Babcock's *Reversible World: Symbolic Inversion in Art and Society,* a volume influenced by Turner's theories. This collection of essays identifies characteristics that place the Morganans' activity *with* Miss Eckhart and Virgie, in the old MacLain house on the present day of "June Recital," as a world-upside-down ritual. That activity Cassie identifies without being able to name it, the *"old* life," is liminal activity. It is a world-upside-down fumigation of Morgana social laws that have put the town into partly wrong relations with Miss Eckhart and largely wrong relations with Virgie Rainey.

It makes a great deal of difference whether one sees the Morganans conducting the action Loch Morrison obliquely reports to us as belonging to structure or to liminality. If it is structure, then the Morganans are provincial, narrow, ignorant, death-dealing. If, however, these are the events of liminality, then the Morganans are using their "deep knowledge" (*Dramas* 239, 258) to keep the two modalities of their interrelationships in balance.

Danièle Pitavy-Souques, most thoroughly, and Marilyn Arnold and Neil Corcoran along with her, have constructed the story's action with the underlying assumption that it all belongs to social structure. From this perspective, the Morganans reveal themselves as both very limited in their humanity and destructive. I paraphrase Pitavy-Souques's primary argument from her 1983 *Southern Review* essay: Prejudiced people who unjustly ostracize Miss Eckhart, the Morganans are tragic people. They give in to their prejudice, and in doing so they fail to encourage life. Rather, they discourage it. In shriveling Miss Eckhart's life (Pitavy-Souques implies or assumes what Turner states [just below] about people's need to experience communitas, shared humanity), they shrivel their own as well. Not very persuasively (because there is no solid evidence that Virgie is destroyed), Pitavy-Souques sees Virgie as merely one more of the mean Morgana people, denying Miss Eckhart's love for her and thereby destroying herself.

Marilyn Arnold makes roughly the same case. From the normative perspective, the law demanding that people meet one another's needs for recognition and fellow feeling is a social structural law, and an absolute, as Arnold clearly articulates it:

> When the [individual's] quest counts for all, human relationship counts for nought; gratitude is obliterated and human beings are destroyed. The tragedy is that one human being who loved another is broken by the ingratitude of the beloved. And even one instance of destruction by ingratitude cracks the facade of the whole system of social order, undermines the premises we think we live by. (71)

Arnold's statement is useful in that it demonstrates social structure taking too much to itself, usurping territory that is not its own. It is incredible that one crack destroys the whole fabric of the social system.

As for the events in and around the MacLain house that Loch observes, Pitavy-Souques and Neil Corcoran alike see nothing but waste and shamefulness in them. To both, they are a soulless farce.

Turner's explanations of liminality and communitas, however, put the present events of "June Recital" in a quite different light, a positive one. Communitas is alive in the unconscious of societies. Both social legitimacy and personal comfort in relations with others depend on periodically renewed recognition of and participation in communitas. Wrong social relations bring pressure on the people who perpetrate them. In a sense, all relations among people in social structure are wrong relations in that they divide people; communitas, as the mode of sharing both humanity and the construction of reality, is the source of both legitimacy and solace. Part of Turner's argument about communitas is that it is both frequently repressed and crucially necessary:

> The basic and perennial human social problem is to discover what is the right relation between these modalities at a specific time and place. Since communitas has a strong affectual component, it appeals more directly to men; but since structure is the arena in which they pursue their material interests, communitas perhaps even more importantly than sex tends to get repressed into the unconscious. . . . People can go crazy because of communitas repression. (*Dramas* 266)

Note that Turner speaks of repression here rather than deprivation. Communitas deprivation may certainly contribute to Miss Eckhart's going mad; communitas repression, however, pressures the Morganans.

The need for communitas puts pressure on those who have ostracized others to reverse that behavior and join with the people whom they have shut out. Social division has to be balanced with communitas. The Morganans are responding to this pressure with the action in and near the MacLain house. The apparently farcical action is ritual reversal. The Morganans are carrying out a collective action that they cannot know with the kind of superficial awareness we commonly call consciousness. The ritual knowledge is available to them through the collective of communitas. They are operating on intelligent knowledge of this type of ritual for constructing change.

Turner's account of liminality and communitas, then, puts a different construction on the Morganans' ending their relationship with Miss Eckhart. From a Turnerian perspective, the Morganans are beneficently unlinking Virgie Rainey from Miss Eckhart.

Structure and liminality can operate simultaneously in the same situation or scene, Turner reports. Furthermore, in liminality people are close to the matrix life-stuff, to the place where destruction and creation meet, close to Welty's closeness of opposites. The way the Morganans end their relationship with Miss Eckhart has the duality Welty attributes to all phases of living. The Morganans unlink Virgie by denying Miss Eckhart's identity, but as they do that, they give her a new identity. Seen structurally, this is cruel—for they make her a madwoman; seen liminally, their changing her identity allows them, after a fashion, at last, to take her into the community. And although they are further removing her with that identity by sending her to Jackson, before they send her off, they enter communitas with her once again. These aspects of doubleness in the action reveal intelligence and life in the Morganans. They reveal the Morganans coping well with *life's* doubleness, *its* kindness and cruelty.

Turner's anthropology serves Welty criticism by retrieving parts of human experience that twentieth-century modernist thought, with its heavily dominant rationalism, and the literary criticism that is part of it, have tended to lose sight of. Turner's analysis of social behavior in its double modalities retrieves society's unconscious much as Freud and Jung retrieved the personal, psychological unconscious. As in those psychologists' theories, the unconscious holds evil but also creative good.

"Let the story arise of itself.
Let it speak for itself. Let it
reveal itself as it goes along."
Conversations

"June Recital," working out its full logic, turns up the Morganans' knowledge of and capacity for enacting communitas; it turns up as well the double of people's right to communitas. This is the right to get rid, kindly rid, of the spoiled. The Morgana people get rid of Miss Eckhart by keeping her at a distance during the years she is teaching. In the present action of the story they get permanently rid of her by denying her old identity and assigning her a new one. Their action is not merely cruel because the Morganans are faced with a real problem that normative prescription ignores as they live with and beside and at a careful remove from Miss Eckhart.

Miss Eckhart comes to Morgana with a clear background of trouble elsewhere. This small town is quite unlikely either to support concert performances by her or to produce numbers of music pupils worthy of her professional training. She must have come here primarily to detach herself from whatever places she has been in that once seemed promising but in which she has had no success: Pitavy-Souques makes this point. When Miss Eckhart arrives in Morgana, with her old mother, the Morganans send their daughters to her for piano lessons so that she can make a living and, in doing so, contribute to townswoman Snowdie MacLain's fiscal solvency by renting the downstairs of her house. Apart from this accommodation to Miss Eckhart's needs and Miss Snowdie's, the Morgana adults keep away from the German woman.

They cite these differences as reasons for staying away from Miss Eckhart: she is unmarried, she belongs to a religion no one has heard of—the Lutheran, she does not allow herself to be called by her first name, she is German and cooks food in strange ways—cabbage with wine. But these stated reasons are not to be taken at face value; they are, rather, the usual sorts of acceptable, speakable covers for other, unspeakable reasons. The stated reasons are to be taken as the type of relatively polite excuses for people's declining. In fact, "June Recital" pretty much validates the Morganans' only apparent ignorance. Below it, and unspoken, at least publicly, is a quite legitimate recognition of disorder in Miss Eckhart and an associated desire for self-preservation through distance.

Miss Eckhart is certainly to be pitied, as Cassie pities her, for being a suffering outcast whose one love, Virgie, does not return the passion. But that truth does not present the whole story. Another truth is that something is deeply wrong with Miss Eckhart. Welty's suggestive comment on Miss Eckhart, in one of her interviews, is this:

> But Miss Eckhart was a very mysterious character. Julia Mortimer was much more straightforward and dedicated and thinking of the people as somebody she wanted to help. Miss Eckhart was a very strange person. . . . She herself was trapped, you know, with her terrible old mother. And then no telling what kind of strange Germanic background, which I didn't know anything about and could only indicate. I mean we don't know—they had tantrums in that house, and flaming quarrels. (*Conversations* 339–40)

The Morganans have some present evidence of disorder in Miss Eckhart. The rumors they circulate about her late in her career as a piano teacher may be cruel, but they may also have some basis in fact. Cassie and Virgie witness Miss Eckhart slapping her mother, and Cassie also reports that one day the old mother deliberately broke the Biliken doll that Mr. Sissum, whom Miss Eckhart was sweet on, had given her. We do not know what derailed the concert career Miss Eckhart seems to have trained for. The causes must be multiple; among them, her relationship with her mother may have been a major one.

21

We do know that the result of Miss Eckhart's history is her living in Morgana unable to establish clear relations with other people. She does not know "how to do" about Mr. Sissum when he is alive (*CS* 296). She cries (they have to decide that that is what she was doing) very oddly at his funeral, moving herself like her metronome. She wars with her mother. She gives all her love to Virgie Rainey, which is not a good thing for a troubled adult to do to a child. (Perhaps this is at least part of what Cassie is looking at when she says Miss Eckhart's love never did anybody any good.) Kind Cassie Morrison realizes in the course of her meditation about Miss Eckhart that if there had been some small opening in Morgana for the piano teacher, she herself might have closed it. That she is sympathetic to the teacher and yet realizes she too would have excluded the woman if she had been close to getting into Morgana society tells us she is sensing something deeply amiss in the woman.

There is such a thing as too much relationship with one's community; we do not want Virgie, for instance, to accept the town's prescriptions. Yet there is also too little relationship, which can result in further emotional twisting, imbalance, distortion—what Welty gives us in Miss Eckhart. This, I think, is what the community shies away from.

The Morganans compensate themselves and Miss Eckhart for keeping at a distance, in the years when she is teaching in Snowdie MacLain's house, by participating in the annual June recitals she produces. In the recital preparations, performance, and party, the Morganans have had an annual exercise in shifting from social structure into communitas. They have thereby annually made right, balanced, their relations with Miss Eckhart. Pitavy-Souques argues that the mothers of Miss Eckhart's pupils comply with her recital orders only to celebrate themselves. No doubt social structure holds sway in the recitals as elsewhere, and the Morgana ladies do celebrate themselves. Nevertheless, they simultaneously acknowledge their communitas with Miss Eckhart.

Having kept away from the social person for eleven months, for the preparatory month of May and the day of the recital, the Morgana adults recognize that Miss Eckhart's greatest need, like their own, is for communitas. They also need to know themselves as gracious people. They accede to her recital directives to fulfill the joint need for communitas. Cassie knows that her mother made her keep taking piano lessons after Virgie had quit and the other mothers had withdrawn their daughters because Mrs. Morrison despised herself for despising Miss Eckhart. All the parents have that other dimension of feeling, as indicated by their participation in the recital. The mothers prepare the dresses, or get them prepared, and attend the performance and party. Only one father, Virgie's, attends the recital, but the other fathers are participants in the role of suppliers—of a second piano, programs, and flowers. With the parents' participation, Miss Eckhart is transformed again each year from outcast to member of the community—so much an insider that it is she who produces the hospitality, glowingly.

While social structure (excluding) and communitas (including) have thus both been served in those years, the situation at present is different. Having lost her pupils and home, Miss Eckhart has dropped out of sight and is presumed to be living at the county home. But, as Miss Eckhart's return to the MacLain house on the present day amply demonstrates, her losing her job does not put an end to her activity in or awareness of Morgana. Passionate dramas such as Miss Eckhart's attempt to compensate herself for her own lost career in music by setting aflame the passion that was once her own do not just drift away, whatever the superficial circumstances. They have to be ended. Both parties to the relationship between the Morganans and Miss Eckhart know that: she comes to construct one ending; and they, when they discover her doing that, construct another ending by denying any knowledge of her.

King MacLain appears, on one of his forays back into Morgana to take a peek at the family he has abandoned. Marshal Moody asks King if he can identify the old woman he has taken into custody. Cassie has remembered Miss Eckhart's and King's passing one another in the house in the old days, and Miss Eckhart speaks MacLain's name. But MacLain denies all knowledge of this old woman. The women coming back from the Rook party, crossing paths with the marshal and the old woman now, follow the same procedure. Mrs. Morrison simply comes on to her own home, while the marshal and his helper go in the other direction with the unidentified old woman.

Unidentified, Miss Eckhart becomes no longer that person but rather just a little old mad lady who belongs in Jackson. She is no longer a stranger, different, but now a type with whom the community is familiar. As a person of this type, she can be taken in peaceably, without outrage and hostility. The men who take her into custody rather enjoy her and treat her fairly nicely.

It is licentious creation, this act by which the Morganans alter Miss Eckhart's identity. The act takes account of combined losses and gains, inseparable from one another in Miss Eckhart's removal from social recognition in Morgana. First, in altering Miss Eckhart's identity, the Morganans subvert and prevent potential disaster. That disaster lies waiting, ticking with time, in Miss Eckhart, whose trouble has more depths than I have yet mentioned.

Perhaps she really did drug her mother, as town rumor says she did, first to keep her quiet and then to kill her. She may have done that out of animosity or out of desperation or with euthanasia as motive. The pupils, the money, and the food have been dwindling. Then there is Miss Eckhart's response to being attacked by the black man. That she does not evade the event by leaving, as her pupils' mothers wish she would, is all very well. To the extent that the Morganans consider her an accomplice with her attacker, as Pitavy-Souques charges, they are acting cruelly. But that is not the end of the matter. Miss Eckhart's treating the event as relatively negligible may reveal a tolerance, however come by, for violence, somewhere along a continuum with swatting flies when they alight on her students' playing hands. To borrow Cassie's phraseology, what may be implied, after all, in one's not perceiving one thing to be so much more terrifying than another? Miss Eckhart has come to do violence on this day.

Further, when Miss Eckhart once plays for her pupils during a storm, "Coming from Miss Eckhart, the music made all the pupils uneasy, almost alarmed; something had burst out, unwanted, exciting, from the wrong person's life" (CS 301). Patricia Yaeger finds this passage proof of Miss Eckhart's capacity for passion; she argues that "having given the daughters of Morgana's community a forbidden vision of passion, the genderless ecstasy available to the woman artist, Miss Eckhart is ostracized and incarcerated—punished more severely for her iconoclasm than are the men of Morgana" (574). (But isn't Miss Eckhart incarcerated on the same grounds Darl Bundren is, in Faulkner's As I Lay Dying, for setting fire to other people's property?) From my perspective, Welty's passage suggests that more than great music, power, and the capacity for fine passion break out of Miss Eckhart. In her passionate but rough playing there is denial as well as embrace of the music; there is trouble as well as transcendence. The little girls, finely attuned to the unspoken as children frequently are, react in a way that shows they are perceiving incongruity between Miss Eckhart and the music she plays. This is incongruity not of the sort that bridges the distance between human beings and gods, as we say, but the incongruity of which monsters are made—monsters indicating chaos. Neil Corcoran, getting into the doubling in the story, says, "The suggestions of sadism in her relationship with her mother confirm our sense of an inner hollowness that *uses* music, but will not be led into sympathy or generosity by it" (31).

A victim indeed, Miss Eckhart is also an aggressor. She, Virgie, all and each of the story's characters, are people inalienably in charge of their own lives, willingly or unwillingly, like George Fairchild in *Delta Wedding* standing in the path of the train, taking living's risks.

Second, the Morganans' altering of Miss Eckhart's identity is licentious creation because this act allows them to set right their relationship to Virgie Rainey, which has long been out of balance. By removing Miss Eckhart's old identity, they make her a stranger. They make her, therefore, a person Virgie Rainey *can* pass without speaking on the sidewalk. They thus unlink Virgie from the woman they have for years used the girl to control for them. For this is yet another aspect of the relationship the town has created—and is thus responsible for ending—between the teacher and the pupil.

Clever, intelligent Virgie has attracted the social job she has been assigned by her more timid elders: controlling dangerous Miss Eckhart. She has attracted the job by meeting the town's instructions in social humility with gay mockery. Virgie has even pushed the town's reigning lady's daughter—Jinny Love Stark, a brat—into her own lily pond. With such cool bravery and defense of her own position, Virgie can be trusted to put up a defense against Miss Eckhart. Virgie reliably does just that. In the studio she turns Miss Eckhart into something other than an absolute authority, a teacher; at the public speakings, where Miss Eckhart has sat in fragile companionship with the adults who largely ignore her, Virgie has mocked the unpopular, unwooed woman (who has a crush on a townsman, Mr. Sissum), with the clover-flower chains of popularity.

Morgana has never acknowledged Virgie's services. At the recitals, even while giving Miss Eckhart her due, they have given greatest applause not to Virgie's fine talent but to the daughters of socially prominent mothers, to Cassie Morrison and Jinny Love Stark. Just recently, one of the churches has given its music scholarship to Miss Eckhart's former second-best pupil, Cassie. Furthermore, as Cassie notes, the town maintains the old link between Virgie and Miss Eckhart. When she arrives in the Bijou to play to the silent films, Virgie is still mockingly saluted by her piano-pupil name, "Virgie Rainey *Danke-schoen*." Despite her services, that is, or perhaps because they have somewhat shamefully assigned this talented and excluded child the role of social guardian, adult Morgana has never forgiven her for mocking their social proprieties. Perhaps they have felt that in mocking them, she was creating her own payment. But Virgie has never done the other Morganans any real harm. There remains, then, the pressure of their communitas with her to be acknowledged, in action. On the present summer day, with much the same indulgence Loch awards the invaders of "his" house next door, the Morganans indulge Virgie at last. They express their communitas with her by unlinking her from Miss Eckhart.

"June Recital" is about community and communitas. Readers who are thinking that Virgie simply frees herself from Miss Eckhart are ignoring the story's portrayal of the complexity of relationships in Morgana (or anywhere). There is no such thing as a simple, one-to-one relationship between Virgie and Miss Eckhart here. There is, rather, a web of relationships to which the community is a full party. Virgie cannot and does not free herself alone.

". . . the opposites . . . unrecognizable
one from the other sometimes, making moments

double upon themselves and in the doubling,
double again, amending but never taking back."

The unlinking achieved by denying Miss Eckhart's old piano-teacher
identity is partly cruel to Miss Eckhart. Yet it is more dominantly creative
and beneficent since the Morganans come to this result by means of deeper
communitas with Miss Eckhart—and with Virgie—than they have ever
given themselves over to before. Before they deal Miss Eckhart out, into
the mental asylum, that is, they conduct one last recital with her. For the
activity in the MacLain house on the present day is also a recital, the
culminating, odd and transformative, June recital.

Seeing this activity as not a humanity-denying farce but rather a life-
maintaining ritual calls for a difficult reversal of vision. Welty knows well
that reversal is hard to accept, hard even to believe when proven. In this
story Cassie sees Miss Eckhart slap her mother and then immediately
distrusts the evidence of her own eyes. She thinks it must have been the
mother who slapped the daughter. Even having made that point, Welty
herself falls into Cassie's mistrust of reversal. In an interview, she "remembers" the mother slapping the daughter (*Conversations* 340).

Nonetheless, it is possible to fix on the idea of reversal; Turner and
The Reversible World assist greatly in that endeavor. Furthermore, Welty
demands the effort. She gives Cassie the capacity to hold on to her sense
of reversal as well as the inability, at times, to countenance it. She discovers
while reliving past years so intensely on this afternoon that while she cannot
remember Mr. Voight very clearly, she could *be* Mr. Voight (*CS* 296). She
does that "without thinking," but by making the desperate face he used to
make while the piano lessons were going on. It is communitas that Cassie
is experiencing here: sharing, experiencing one's alikeness with other people who otherwise seem very different. It abrogates distances among
people.

On this June day when the Morganans are used to participating in
recitals, they could be Miss Eckhart or they could be Virgie. Accordingly,
they are attracted to bridge the distance that is only one of the double
relationships between themselves and Miss Eckhart and Virgie. After all,
the deviance from social rules they associate with these two is something
they share with them. In performing the odd recital with them, they also
take cognizance of the usually hidden side of their own humanity.

Turning the world upside down is *old* human activity, the *old* life Cassie
perceives in the empty house. We know this hidden ritual with our "deep
knowledge." World-upside-down activity is apparent mayhem with the
most serious of goals, keeping life going. Turner points out that societies

require skepticism from their members as well as adherence to the rules that seem to work to maintain life-giving relations among people (*Dramas* 256). Expressing skepticism is exactly what the Morganans are doing in and away from that "vacant" house. The family home, with the symbol's capacity for condensation, stands for family life as the center of social life, for all of society's order, security, morality, sanctity, and the rest. At the same time, standing for all the normative rules, it stands for a network of constraints against all the lawlessness normative social life refuses to recognize.

The family home begets skepticism as well as loyalty because it has double effects: it protects, nurturing a young woman like Cassie, and at the same time, it excludes and lies. It speaks for the social structure that refuses to give Virgie Rainey the pianist her due, and as well for the patent willful blindness demonstrated by Cassie Morrison's father. Cassie's father is the town's newspaper publisher (the man who determines what can be made public): "If there was anything that unsettled him it was for people not be on the inside what their outward semblances led you to suppose" (*CS* 327). Therefore, in the Morrison house, aberrant things, from tales of Mr. Voight's exhibitionism to Mrs. Morrison's apparent alcoholism (indicated in the vague manner in which she addresses her son every afternoon) and/or the amours some critics suspect her of conducting, to the hayrides on which Cassie is going despite her father's prohibition, are simply repressed, denied.

The story's doubling of the family home announces that normatively aberrant behavior holds a fair amount of sway in ordinary life and cannot always be controlled to the extent that Mr. Morrison controls it in his domain. The empty MacLain house is the Morrison house's double. Here more of the antinormative has long leaked into view. Here the ordinary social dictates have not been able to keep a regular cover on life's erratic or rebellious impulses. The husband has been long gone, off on his wanderings; there have been—right along with the normative piano lessons and the teacher's making a decent living thereby for herself and her mother— Germans with tantrums and strange cooking smells (strange and enticing but forbidden); there has been Virgie Rainey bringing her teacher magnolia blossoms but also turning the teacher into something inscrutably or ambiguously more complex than a mere teacher with authority over pupils; and there has been the exhibitionist, regularly flapping his bathrobe skirts while wearing nothing underneath, frantically opposing the piano lessons that are apparently as horrible to him as the ostracizing Morganans are to Pitavy-Souques and Arnold.

Morgana and the world cannot live by norms, kindness, and the social graces alone. If social ostracism can destroy, so can the normative rules. Thus breaking the rules is sometimes a necessity. The old MacLain house—

its deviant history and its emptiness suggesting that the antinormative impulses have in that place vanquished the family home's constrictions and lies—becomes on the present June day, when the Morganans are accustomed to conducting the summer communal celebrations, not just an available stage but a magnet. Here the liminal impulse—the call to ostensible mayhem and to collective rites—takes over. Once someone begins the action, the others all fall readily into their corresponding roles.

Through the "turning" (*CS* 360) of life Welty explicitly notes in "Moon Lake," Miss Eckhart becomes an insider very much a part of the town's action. She tries to burn down the family home; for it is the place that excludes the demands of Beethoven for yet finer, subtler order and for wilder, deeper passion. While Loch Morrison literalizes the symbolic action by hanging upside down out of the tree, the other Morganans do the following. Instead of keeping the home safe from the incendiary likes of the disappointed piano teacher, Mr. Holifield sleeps as if he were Rip Van Winkle in the Kaatskills, giving us family-abandoning King MacLain via a stand-in. Insofar as this family home stands in direct opposition to free love of the sort King MacLain is famous for, with its utter disregard of the primacy of family, Virgie and her sailor mock this citadel with their playful lovemaking. They do not even take their free love seriously; they eat pickles out of a bag for rest periods.

When adults come to the house—males, thus authorities, and one of them even the marshal—they let the old mad lady set her fire, twice. They run and romp with their lady downstairs much as Virgie is romping with her sailor upstairs, having a wonderful game. They demonstrate male solidarity with MacLain and Holifield in doing so; skepticism, along with the influence of the silent movies comics (manifesting the same skepticism) surely contributes to their delight at Miss Eckhart's torching the family home. When King MacLain shows up in person, he does not even know where his family is currently located, that they do not live here any more.

And what about the women: the sacred flames of the family home, the stable heart of society, trained to give their all for morality, order, family, children, the light of goodness, the prestige of husband? They have gone off duty. Cassie's mother and the other ladies have flightily abandoned their stations, gone off to play Rook and eat food fit for the fairies of *A Midsummer Night's Dream*. Gone off, and so left what will happen if they go away to happen: the ladies have allowed all this, permitted these depredations.

In thus reversing their procedures, from sanctifying the home to mocking it, the Morganans are both joining with those who regularly hold out against its constrictions and giving themselves the deep satisfaction of acknowledging what they normally, in the modality of social structure, hide. Even a socially prominent and humorous woman, Mrs. Morrison, has something to share with the piano teacher she thinks of as a witch; Mrs. Morrison would like the MacLain house to burn down. Is Loch mistaken, perhaps, in thinking that the old woman is lucky in not having been seen by the ladies going off to their party? Have they seen her and in tacit agreement pretended not to? In any case, at whatever moment in the afternoon's events they come into the action, the Morganans once again follow Miss Eckhart's lead in creating a recital. That this is the last one in its series does not authorize our finding more sorrow in it than recovery and release. When things are ready, they do not, cannot, stay (Welty makes that point explicit in "Moon Lake" [*CS* 356]); and in sending Virgie and Miss Eckhart off in different directions, this odd recital creates what Turner calls "the openness to the future" (*Dramas* 14).

When Cassie envisions the two "roaming, like lost beasts" (*CS* 330) she is phrasing a double reality: cut off from mere social structure, they are at the same time more intense and more mysterious, living deeper and farther, than the mere social personages she has known before this afternoon's revery and activity. Cassie does not merely remember on this afternoon; her awareness, like Josie's in Welty's "The Winds," grows suddenly, within hours. She sees a vortex in which Morgana is swept up together with Miss Eckhart and Virgie. They stretch her knowledge of humanity beyond the familiar and allowed, even as they frighten her. Her sudden growth in vision comes from her communitas with them.

If the afternoon's action is beneficent as much as it is cruel, why, then, does Cassie Morrison work in apparent opposition to everyone else's denial of Miss Eckhart's identity and lament the woman's injuries? Once again, because things double, because here the right to remove and alter someone's identity comes accompanied by the obligation to preserve that identity, to recognize it fully by meditating on it, as Cassie does, going over Miss Eckhart's whole history in the town. Furthermore, moments of knowing just what to do, just how to preserve oneself and one's group, intersect with contrasting doubt about one's rights, one's kindness and cruelty, with moral anxiety emerging at once out of both the social separation of people and human communitas with other people. While her townspeople and family members get to cavort to produce this day's transformation, Cassie (though collaboratively dotted with unpatterned spots suitable to participation in the day's carnival) gets assigned the role of memory and contemplation that will knit sensitive appreciation of Miss Eckhart into the complex strands of the day's action on relationships.

In other words, Miss Eckhart is *both* a woman with a past in this town *and* a little old mad lady. While it is important to the town to remove her, it is also important that the woman she was be remembered. Perhaps acknowledging the woman is possible because the potential disaster is averted. The story keeps pointing to disaster unfulfilled, averted: Loch is sick but his life is not threatened; the ticking is not that of a bomb, it is only a metronome; Mrs. Morrison's disappointment is only in the food she has been served, not in something so great as whatever it is later that instigates her suicide. In this context, Miss Eckhart goes mad sanely, her explosive impulses no different in kind from all the overturning impulses of all the people around her in the group action. Further, because the Morganans take this preventive action, there is no Eckhart-holocaust to supplant the story of her earlier days here. For Cassie it is still possible to imagine the mother and daughter in a happier vein: "sometimes you could imagine them back far away from Morgana, before they had troubles and before they had come to you—plump, bright, and sweet somewhere" (*CS* 304). Thinking so, Cassie constructs continuity in time, and in the time of the present odd recital there is redirection and ease for the passage of power from one generation to the next.

For the action is caught up in that regular temporal movement as well. Cassie must be the one to do the remembering, to acknowledge the life of the woman called Lotte Elisabeth Eckhart, because Cassie is her inheritor. Cassie's feeling for Miss Eckhart may itself be double, too—one part genuine generosity, as Pitavy-Souques declares, and another part self-concerned, in Cassie's anticipation of her own life. She has been granted the music scholarship and already knows she will have a life as a piano teacher here in Morgana; she already sees her life as a long row of yellow Schirmer music books. Unlike Miss Eckhart, she will have success here and pupils as long as she wants them. She is an insider, with familiar and cautious ways. Without Virgie's higher talent or great need to mock, Cassie will know how to make classical music genteel and acceptable within the social structural life of Morgana. Cassie is specially concerned about Miss Eckhart because she knows what she owes Miss Eckhart, what she has taken from Miss Eckhart personally—life. Cassie, in inheriting, has stolen Miss Eckhart's job and livelihood; she has found that growing up means in some fashion displacing the people who came before you—the inevitable way of denying people's old identities, we might recognize.

In the events of "June Recital," past and present, ordinary events of social prejudice and hijinks, accepting and rejecting relationships, the many interwoven strands of destruction and creation bound together validate that term, "mystery," that Welty often offers her readers. Relations among the Morganans, Miss Eckhart and Virgie Rainey are not reducible to any single reality we can anathematize or approve. Welty entered her profession just after the "great moderns," whose work is weighted towards a vision of destruction. She wrote in response to them, I think, implicitly arguing that life is quite as powerful as death. She shows vibrant life greater than any individual's life or any group's life, in which all individual and group lives participate. That triumphant life is everywhere implied in "June Recital"—in the beginning-of-summer day with all the generosity of life summer implies, in Loch's figs, in the hummingbird Cassie would not try to catch, in Miss Eckhart's Beethoven and that other, outside world that is the double of this world here in Morgana—the world King MacLain goes to and comes from, which somehow overlaps with the place in which a respectable Mr. Voight covers seven states promoting a respectable product in business, the backbone of America, and the place where World War I is fought and Victor Rainey killed, and also the place where Miss Eckhart had crippling troubles before she ever came to Morgana.

Welty works against reduction, towards the multivocality Turner sees as the primary property and function of symbols. Miss Eckhart's aloneness (which Loch observes) is matched by communitas. Ignorance comes paired with knowledge, and cruelty with kindness. Morgana, however cut off from the larger world outside, is also in that world, continuous with it. Virgie has had to hate Miss Eckhart as well as love the teacher because the Morganans have linked the two; she has had to hold off the woman's neuroses. But there was also good in the link during the piano lesson days: it led Virgie deep into great music; and until Virgie gave up her lessons, it must have kept Miss Eckhart sane. All of this life is what compensates in Welty for the damages that come with the risks, what allows us to love life rather than lament over it.

SUSAN V.

D O N A L D S O N

"Contradictors, Interferers, and Prevaricators"

Opposing Modes
of Discourse
in Eudora Welty's
Losing Battles

"They're all living on stories," Eudora Welty once observed of the garrulous characters in her 1970 novel *Losing Battles* (*Conversations* 307). Taking her at her word, a good many critics have read *Losing Battles* as a novel about making stories and about language itself.[1] Critical opinion remains divided, though, on the perspective to be taken by the reader of the rambling stories told by Welty's collection of Mississippi farm folk in the 1930s. Do those tales told by members of the Beecham and Renfro clan represent an imaginative triumph over adversity and poverty—a triumph celebrating kinship, community, and the oral tradition of storytelling? Or are those tales swapped on the front porch oppressive and confining, apt symbols of the provinciality and narrow-mindedness fought so fiercely by the much maligned schoolteacher named Miss Julia Mortimer?[2]

This debate suggests that *Losing Battles* is one of those elusive and difficult texts that thematize interpretive operations and anticipate quarrels among critics and readers. As Barbara Johnson, Shoshana Felman, and Jonathan Culler have pointed out, critical arguments of this kind might be described as a "displaced re-enactment of the story," repetitions of structures and battles already inscribed in the text.[3] For *Losing Battles* is a text not just about two different worldviews but two opposing modes of discourse, that is, two different structures of representation and ways of speaking, listening, and seeing that are socially constituted and constituting, determined and determining.

By far the loudest mode of discourse in the text, of course, is the storytelling of the Renfro and Beecham reunion, gathered together to celebrate Grandmother Vaughn's birthday and to await the return of favorite son Jack Renfro from the state penitentiary. The stories they tell suggest something of the workings of discourse long honored in white southern culture—discourse that is defined by devotion to kinship, tradition, community, and oral storytelling. In opposition to this endless round of storytelling, seemingly natural and unassuming, is the much more muted and fragmentary discourse of Miss Julia and her former pupils, Judge Moody and Gloria Short Renfro, married to Jack Renfro, all figures associated with writing, solitude, and change rather than oral speech, community, and tradition.

As different as these two modes of discourse are, though, they have in common a rather brutal disregard of alternatives, contradictions, and anomalies, all of which threaten the coherence of the world created by each mode of discourse. From the perspective of Michel Foucault, we might say that the discourse of the reunion and the discourse of Miss Julia and her former students are each defined by peculiarly distinct "dividing practices" delineating the boundaries between orderly self and community and all potentially disruptive forces (Foucault, "The Subject" 208). Such practices, Foucault argues, make "centering" and coherence possible by expelling to the margin all those who appear different or threatening. The Renfros and the Beechams are able to define themselves as a unified, tradition-loving family in part because they perceive Miss Julia, Judge Moody, and Gloria as everything they are not—book-loving, solitary, ambitious, disruptive— just as the latter three define their sense of individuality, open-mindedness, and appreciation of learning in opposition to the clannish, benighted Beechams and Renfros. Each opponent in the battle uses the other as precisely that—an "other" to define the self, to be expelled, resisted, and ignored, but never heeded or regarded as a genuine subject to whom one listens and responds. Speakers abound in *Losing Battles,* but *genuine* listeners appear to be all too rare.

This abundance of speakers, accompanied by a paucity of listeners, is responsible for a good deal of the book's comedy, as I think Welty would be the first to point out. In a 1972 interview she observed that Chekhov's work seems to have in common with southern literature a penchant for characters who are self-absorbed talkers: "You know, in *Uncle Vanya* and *The Cherry Orchard,* how people are always gathered together and talking and talking, no one's really listening" (*Conversations* 75). But *Losing Battles* is not just a comedy of speakers stranded without listeners; it is a text about power, its struggles, impositions, and inequalities. In this respect, Welty, who has always noted that her fiction focuses on "private relations," seems to have a good deal in common with Foucault and with feminist critics who argue that the personal is always political, always a question of unequal power.[4] Foucault, after all, reminds us that the term *subject* has two meanings: one refers to the notion of individual identity and the other to the idea of being "subject to someone else by control and dependence" (Foucault, "The Subject," 212). Welty herself is just as sensitive to the ambiguous and often treacherous nuances of human relationships, which, as she has noted of *Losing Battles* in particular, "run the whole gamut of love and oppression" (*Conversations* 221).

Welty might also agree with Foucault's suggestion that any form of discourse, any form of seeing, talking, acting, and representation, inevitably involves a certain degree of "violence," an imposition on "things" and "events" in order to achieve coherence and unity (*Archaeology* 229). It is this sort of violence, along with the problem of power in personal relationships, that seems to shape *Losing Battles* and a good deal of Welty's fiction—rather than the wielding of power in the public world of politics. Indeed, in a 1978 interview with Reynolds Price, Welty observed:

> There's plenty of violence in life, and I would be the last to deny it—none of my fiction does deny it—but it comes from within human beings. *That's* its source, and you can write about that source with any set of tools you wish. The novel has got to reflect life—life is violent and it has to show violence, but the novel doesn't have to show it in a self-defeating way. (*Conversations* 233)

In the case of *Losing Battles* violence emerges in a surprising range of forms—from Jack Renfro's enthusiastic scuffles with his rival Curly Stovall to the watermelon fight that serves as Gloria Short Renfro's baptism into the world of the Renfros and Beechams. Less explicit, though, is the violence underlying the nonstop round of stories told by the reunion, a term suggesting not just a family gathering but, as Welty herself observes, "everybody remembering together" (*Conversations* 78). For underlying those amusing family tales is the collective determination of the reunion to impose unity and reassuring familiarity on everything that suggests change, contingency, and the passing of time itself. As fragmented and as episodic as all the stories seem, they ultimately form, as Miss Beulah says with satisfaction, "all the one sad story" (219), a narrative that traces the boundaries of the world recognized by the Renfros and the Beechams and thereby rejects the possibility of alternative stories and perspectives.

The "one sad story," of course, is mostly about Jack Renfro and the scrape that sent him to the state penitentiary—a fight with Curly Stovall to "protect" Jack's sister Elly Fay and to retrieve a family ring—but the story is also about the family itself because Jack is perceived as the clan's exemplar, the most perfect representative of devotion to kinship, duty, continuity, and tradition. Told and retold, the stories about Jack and the rest of the family become in a sense stories about the importance of family stories. The act of storytelling itself, confirming and reconfirming the history of the family, serves as a means of fortifying the clan against potential threat and change. They are, as Miss Beulah belligerently tells newcomer Aunt Cleo, "ready here for all comers" (13); and that readiness requires the constant telling of stories to close a protective circle around the family. For the Renfro-Beecham clan, then, little that is worthwhile can exist outside the boundaries of the stories they tell; and not surprisingly, they are astonished to learn that Aunt Cleo, newly wed to Uncle Noah Webster Beecham, hasn't heard the story of Jack's imprisonment. "What's Noah Webster been doing all this time," Aunt Birdie asks incredulously, "if he hasn't told you all the sad story?" (14).

That the Renfro-Beecham clan is warranted to a certain extent in barricading itself off from the world through tried-and-true stories is compassionately acknowledged throughout *Losing Battles*. Besieged by poverty, death, and change in the midst of the Great Depression, the family surveys a landscape of ever-rising dust that obscures vision and very probably their future as well. Family members, like the revered Grandpa Vaughn and the adored Sam Dale Beecham, have died; others, like the parents of Miss Beulah and her brothers, have disappeared; and the latest generation seems to have "scattered," as Uncle Curtis Beecham says plaintively of his far-flung children (66). Beyond the weekend of the much-enjoyed reunion little seems certain. What little is left to the Renfros and the Beechams is the occasional gesture of defiance, like the new tin roof that Mr. Renfro has put up in honor of Jack's return and that "speaks just a world, speaks volumes," in Miss Beulah's words. It is a gesture, Miss Beulah tells us, designed "to show the reunion single-handed the world don't have to go flying to pieces when the oldest son gives trouble" (66). If anything, the shiny new roof signals the family's determination to maintain solidarity and clarity of purpose against dust, drought, and the strangeness of the outside world.

Also left to the clan, of course, are their stories and the oral tradition they represent, and these are far from insignificant weapons against time and change. As both Jacques Derrida and Walter Benjamin have shown, oral speech and storytelling frequently serve in Western culture as emblems of continuity and community. In an analysis of Claude Levi-Strauss's work, Derrida observes that portraits of societies defined by oral speech rather than by writing suggest an "image of a community immediately present to itself, without difference, a community of speech where all the members are within earshot" (136). In such a community, tales exchanged face-to-face and sanctified through repetition take on special significance precisely because such stories exist in what Benjamin calls "the realm of living speech" (87). They suggest an unbroken chain of experience linking all of those who have passed along the tales. In the very act of storytelling, Benjamin maintains, lies the creation of a special sort of community, one defined by the "companionship" between the storyteller and the listener (100).

We know from Derrida and Foucault, though, that unity and certainty of this kind can be achieved and defended only, as Derrida writes in *Of Grammatology,* "through expelling the other, and especially *its own* other, throwing it *outside* and *below*" (39). This sort of rejection of alternatives, ambiguity, and multiplicity of meaning underlies the amusing family stories told and retold by the Renfros and the Beechams. They are determined to maintain a celebratory sense of community, something akin to Belshazzar's Feast, the preacher Brother Bethune declares, but "without no Handwriting on the Wall to mar it" (177). As confirmed oral storytellers, the clan implicitly rejects the possibility of alternative forms of discourse, in particular the reading and writing that Miss Julia Mortimer so relentlessly champions. Such solitary acts suggest an openness to multiple impressions and interpretations—possibilities all too threatening to the oral chain of experience defining the family and its sense of community.

Accordingly, the Renfros and the Beechams make every effort to denigrate alternatives to tales swapped back and forth on the front porch. They are all full of stories of Miss Julia's peculiar proclivity for books and the doubtful honor of winning books in recognition of schoolroom achievements. "I dreaded to win," Aunt Birdie remembers (240). Even listening to Judge Moody read Miss Julia's letter aloud to the assemblage seems something of a trial. "I can't understand it when he reads it to us," Aunt Birdie complains, and she adds, not incidentally, "Can't he just tell it?" (298). Telling it seems to be far preferable to reading, and consequently, the family is not all disturbed by the courthouse fire that has destroyed all the county's legal (and written) records. For them the truth of their collective experience lies in the stories they exchange, not in the written record.

They also have no qualms about reducing anyone associated with difference and with alternative forms of discourse to the status of *other,* a mere object of representation, to define their own sense of communal selfhood. For them Miss Julia is simply an abstract figure in the stories they tell, a "cross to bear," as Uncle Dolphus observes (240). She is also something of a disturbing anomaly, a spinster in a community where people marry early, a voracious reader among farm folk who consider reading in the middle of the day "surpassing strange for a well woman" (294), and above all, an instigator of ambition and change in a region where deviation is viewed with suspicion. Hence the family feels that Miss Lexie Renfro, charged with "nursing" Miss Julia, is perfectly justified in destroying the dying schoolteacher's letters and thereby robbing her patient of the ability to speak. Lexie's own name, after all, seems to equate a particular lexicon with legality (if we remember that *lex* is the Latin word for law), and from the family's perspective, Miss Julia *is* something of an outlaw. Miss Beulah notes ominously that Miss Julia overstepped herself, to which Aunt Beck adds: "I don't suppose for a minute that Miss Julia saw the danger ahead. I think she had all the blindness of a born schoolteacher" (316).

Equally blind, as far as the clan is concerned, is Judge Moody, the man responsible for sending Jack to the state pen for fighting with Curly Stovall. The real issue, for Miss Beulah and her kin, is Jack's gallant willingness to fight Curly in order to retrieve a family ring, not their brawling in the street; and Judge Moody's failure to "see" that issue suggests just how much of an outsider the Judge really is. "Born and bred in Ludlow, most likely in the very shadow of the courthouse!" rules Miss Beulah, herself something of a judge. "A man never spent a day of his life in Banner, never heard of a one of us!" (66).

The most disturbing anomaly of all for the Renfro-Beecham clan, though, is Gloria Short Renfro, an orphan groomed to follow in Miss Julia's footsteps who nonetheless puts aside teaching for marriage to Jack. Taking a good deal of pride in her status as orphan, Gloria holds herself apart from the rest of the family, and her solitude strikes the Beechams and the Renfros as unsettling and even disturbing. She is, as the Beecham aunts keep informing her, "a little question mark" (197), someone who can't be "read" (69). Is she in Miss Julia's camp or their own, a deviant to be expelled and objectified like Miss Julia herself, or a member of a family constantly recreating itself through the telling of stories?

Hence the family is delighted when a few words from Granny, a forgotten postcard, and fragmented recollections from several family members make it possible to construct yet another reassuring family narrative, one that brings Gloria within the family fold. She is, they decide, a true Beecham, the illegitimate daughter of long-lost Uncle Sam Dale Beecham and yet another forlorn orphan, and hence she is Jack's first cousin as well as his wife. For the Beechams and the Renfros, the best part of this discovery is Gloria's changed status; she is no longer that puzzling question mark uncomfortably associated with Miss Julia but a genuine family member enfolded by the clan's stories. As such, she no longer suggests all those disturbing alternatives the family rejects.

A good deal of comedy resides in these efforts to turn anything and everything into a family story, but the clan's appropriation of Gloria is also quite possibly the most violent scene in *Losing Battles*. Delighted with the stories they have woven of Gloria's background, the Beecham aunts and "girl cousins" throw Gloria to the ground and force pieces of watermelon "down her little red lane"—an image that suggests nothing so much as sexual violation. "Say Beecham and we'll stop," they tell her laughing. "Let's hear you say who's a Beecham" (269). Stubborn to the last, Gloria never really yields, but the Beechams do succeed in reducing her at least temporarily to tears and silence. From their perspective, of course, the watermelon fight serves as a particularly boisterous but good-natured induction into the family. For Gloria herself, though, the scene is one of violation. Underlying it is the drive for power and dominance shaping so many of the tales of the noisy Beechams and Renfros. It is a scene that signifies the refusal of the clan—and even its inability—to consider other possibilities, other forms of meaning, other modes of discourse. Despite Gloria's pleas, the aunts and cousins do their best to make Gloria say what they want to hear—the name *Beecham*. Their determination and the force they exert suggest that the name and the values underlying it—unity, continuity, tradition, oral storytelling—are neither natural nor inevitable, but rather the imposition of dominant discourse.

After this scene, in fact, we cannot quite take for granted the naturalness or even the appeal of the values associated with Beecham storytelling. Indeed, we would do well to remember that those values—associated with kinship, tradition, community, unity, continuity, and a sense of place—have long characterized the work of white southern polemicists who have defended the region since the early nineteenth century. In the knee-slapping stories of the Beechams and Renfros, we can hear echoes of George Fitzhugh, Thomas Roderick Dew, and James Henry Hammond, men who helped define and were defined by discourse evolving in opposition to that of the fast-changing, industrialized, atomized North. If we read their works, we discover a picture of the white South espousing much the same worldview as that of the Renfros and the Beechams, one of a traditional, organic, hierarchical society bound by memory and history.[5]

Hence the few figures in *Losing Battles* whose language and views constitute a broken and muted "counter-discourse," if I may use Richard Terdiman's term here, are all the more important precisely because they served, like Gloria, as question marks (13). Their presence and their perspective, rooted in solitude, writing, and change, serve notice that possibilities do exist outside the all-encompassing stories endlessly recited by the Renfros and the Beechams. Relegated to the margin by the "center" defining the Beecham family and reduced to the status of other, Gloria, Judge Moody, and Miss Julia Mortimer herself have, as Terdiman would say, "the capacity to *situate*" (Terdiman's emphasis). By their very marginal position they are able to "relativize the authority and stability of utterances which cannot even countenance their existence" (15–16).

Indeed, these three "outsiders" seem to prize the very solitude that marks them as marginal in the communal world of Renfros and Beechams. Jack Renfro might welcome the support of kith and kin who adore him, but as far as Gloria is concerned, Jack's primary problem *is* his family. To Judge Moody she declares, "I'm here to tell you Jack Renfro's case in two words—home ties. Jack Renfro has got family piled all over him" (163). Gloria herself takes considerable pleasure in her self-described identity as orphan, and she is as upset by the notion of being a true Beecham as she is by the roughhousing of the watermelon fight. "If it wasn't for all the other people around us," she tells Jack repeatedly, "our life would be different this minute" (112).

Hence Gloria and her fellow outsiders turn decidedly deaf ears to the constant round of stories largely defining the clan's sense of communal well-being. "The way your family loves to tell stories," she complains to Jack, "they wouldn't hear the Crack of Doom by this time." From her perspective, the family stories simply "embroider" (129). Just as critical of Beecham storytelling is Judge Moody, who quite simply asks, "Can't conversation ever cease? Can't anybody offer just a single idea?" (390). Even harsher is the assessment of Miss Julia, who in her last days has been subjected to the callous "nursing" of Miss Lexie Renfro, Jack's aunt. "They prattle around me of the nearness of Heaven," Miss Julia writes in her last letter to Judge Moody. "Is this Heaven, where you lie wide open to the mercies of others who think they know better than you do what's best— what's true and what isn't? Contradictors, interferers, and prevaricators— are those angels?" (299).

Much to be preferred, from the perspective of Gloria, Judge Moody, and Miss Mortimer, is the opposing authority of the written word, to be written and read in solitary silence away from the clamor of boisterous family folklore. Hence when all three feel the need to make a momentous statement, they do so through the medium of the letter, addressed by one individual to another. Gloria, as she loftily informs the assembled family, is not one to be "afraid of pencil and paper," and accordingly, she has already written Jack at the state penitentiary about the birth of their daughter (91). Much more adamant than Gloria about the worth of the written word is Miss Julia, who supposedly once threw herself on the school dictionary to protect it during a wild cyclone. In fact, the only times that she makes an appearance of sorts, outside the stories told about her by the Renfros and Beechams and by neighbor Willy Trimble, are in the letters she writes to her former protégés—to Gloria, whom she chastises for wanting to marry a pupil, and to Judge Moody, to whom she appeals for help during her last, bedridden days. And when Judge Moody feels the need to rebuke the Renfros and the Beechams for their narrowness and callous treatment of Miss Julia, he turns to the letter smuggled out to him by his former teacher. As he tells his wife, "this bunch had it coming" (304).

In fact, writing in general seems to serve all three of these "marginal" characters as an all-purpose rebuke to the ceaseless and confining chatter of the family. For them the written word opens the door upon a wider world than the one enclosed by the never-ending round of family stories— a world defined by the future rather than the past and propelled by ambition and change rather than the need for continuity and permanence. It is, after all, through the written word that Miss Julia in her heyday manages to fire the minds of her most promising students and to send the very best away to all parts of the country to pursue professional occupations. Her most prized pupils are "scattered," a word and state that the Renfros and Beechams consider deplorable, and what community remains among them is through the tenuous and fragile tie of written correspondence that Miss Julia maintains. As Judge Moody curtly observes, there are "other ties" than those of kin and hometown (301). The Judge and his fellow pupils may not be "blood kin" to Miss Julia, as Miss Beulah darkly suspects; but they are bound to her by virtue of the far-ranging vision the teacher bestows upon them, in particular, the ability to see beyond the expectations and boundaries of family and community and even to negate those familiar ties. As Uncle Noah Webster wittily observes, "She thought if she mortified you long enough, you might have hope of turning into something you wasn't" (236).

Aware that the written word undermines the bulwarks constructed by the family stories, Judge Moody, Gloria, and Miss Julia also understand implicitly that writing seems to subvert the solidity of the spoken word as well. By the lights of the Renfros and the Beechams, for instance, the question of Gloria's background is finally settled once a suitable "story" can be constructed for her; but from the perspective of written law, Judge Moody tells the clan, the question is far from resolved. "I don't think much of your proof," the Judge declares. "In fact, there's not a particle of it I'd accept as evidence. Fishing back in old memories. Postcard from the dead. Wise sayings." As far as he is concerned, Gloria's family history is still an unwritten cipher. "The fact is," he tells Gloria, "you could be almost anybody and have sprung up almost anywhere" (315). The spoken word is apparently rendered suspect as soon as the standard of the written word is applied, and not surprisingly, the speech and stories of the Renfros and Beechams seem considerably less imposing whenever the family is forced to confront the written word. Listening to Miss Julia's will and her final letter to Judge Moody very nearly reduces them to the level of unruly schoolchildren, and even the redoubtable Miss Beulah seems somewhat intimidated when she begins to read aloud from Sam Dale Beecham's long-lost postcard. "Her voice," the narrator observes, "suddenly lost all its authority as she began to read aloud from the written words" (266).

Indeed, the stories the family tells very nearly begin to unravel once they are examined by the standards of written law represented by the Judge. For the "latest" story to emerge from the family's narrative efforts—the "discovery" that Jack and Gloria may be first cousins as well as husband and wife—is one that directly violates state law. As Judge Moody coolly informs the family, first cousins are not permitted to marry under Mississippi law. Such unions are considered "null and void," in Gloria's horrified phrase (321). Nor can such a marriage be described as "the only safe thing in the world," as Miss Beulah wistfully suggests (314–15). "Not safe," responds the Judge, "if that's what *has* happened, and supposing the State has any way to prove it" (315; emphasis added). But the fact remains, he adds, that by the standard of written law the clan has simply "told a patched-together family story and succeeded in bringing out no more evidence than if their declared intention had been to conceal it" (322).

But if the written word with which Judge, Gloria, and Miss Julia associate themselves manages to subvert the seemingly self-evident and natural veneer of the Beecham stories, these three marginal characters nonetheless resort to the same demeaning tactics that rule out the possibility of dialogue and acknowledgment of their opponents' subjectivity. Like the family, they use their loud and boisterous opponents as others to define their sense of self as absolute. The Beechams—Gloria, Judge Moody, and Miss Julia declare time and time again—are everything that those associated with the written word are not: close-minded, wishful-thinking, ignorant, chained to the past and to the demands of family. Miss Julia, for one, is able to think of herself as Saint George precisely because the Beechams and their ilk seem to represent a ready-made dragon of ignorance primed for slaying, just as Judge Moody finds a good deal of personal satisfaction in denouncing Banner as "the very pocket of ignorance" (304). Gloria herself is even more rigid in drawing the lines. Determined to maintain her status as orphan in a household valuing family above all else, Gloria tells Jack that she simply has no "room" for anything and anyone but Jack and her baby daughter (362). She may have forsaken Miss Julia for Jack, but she has no intention of allying herself with her husband's family.

In the end, both sides do indeed, as Miss Julia wryly admits in her letter to Moody, stoop to "using the same tactics" (298); and the ever-present dust constantly rising from the barren landscape, and in a manner of speaking, from these unceasing battles, suggests just how confined and blinded both sides are by the discourse that defines them. To a great extent, they are all "contradictors, interferers, and prevaricators," self-serving liars whose mode of discourse, whether oral or written, establishes hierarchies by ruling out alternatives, anomalies, and even the possibility of acknowledging responses. Determined to keep their ranks closed, both sides refuse even to recognize their own contradictions and suspect motives; and the battlefield, as a result, is strewn with the casualties which that determination has cost—like Gloria's estrangement from Miss Julia, who once represented every ideal the younger woman cherished.

Most poignant of all, though, is Uncle Nathan Beecham, the oldest of the Beecham brothers, who holds himself strangely apart from the rest of the family and who roams the countryside leaving crudely painted signs warning of God's power and impending judgment. It is a lonely existence that serves as penance, as Uncle Nathan confesses toward the end of the reunion despite Miss Beulah's best efforts to stop him. Years before he killed a man who represented a threat to the family and let a black man hang for the murder—all in the interest, it is implied, of the family from which Uncle Nathan carefully kept his secret. Such is the price to be paid, Welty suggests, for the closed ranks maintained so desperately by the Beechams and the Renfros. And even after the confession is made, the family is left strangely untouched. Uncle Nathan's moving confession is gently buried under the ever-mounting layers of family talk. To the end Welty's compulsive talkers refuse to listen. They are propelled by the endless and thoughtless momentum of their own words, words that scarcely give them time to consider, evaluate, or even pity at times.

In this respect, then, M. M. Bakhtin would readily label both sides and both modes of discourse, whether oral or written, as monologic.[6] Each mode imposes rigid restrictions on the natural diversity, possibility, and range of language. The letters that Miss Julia's side write and the stories that the family tells wield words "that expect no answer" (*Problems* 63). And so enamored are all Welty's embattled foes of their own words that they scarcely have time to listen to themselves, much less others.

The most prominent exception is, of course, Jack, who soberly listens to tales of Miss Julia's life and announces, "I heard her story" (361). When Gloria tells him that Miss Julia represents everything that she has forsaken for Jack, her husband replies quite simply, "Me and you both left her out today, and I'm ashamed for us" (362). His is a response that *appears* to offer an alternative to the everlasting battles of Miss Julia and the Beechams and Renfros. Having heard Miss Julia, Jack implicitly acknowledges his bond with her, a bond suggesting the interdependence of self and other and the possibility of genuine exchange binding speaker and listener. It is a remark, finally, that offers, from Bakhtin's perspective, the prospect of dialogic discourse, a mode of language and representation based not on rigid unity and the refusal to listen but on multiplicity and the readiness to acknowledge and respond to a chorus of differing voices.[7]

Whether Jack actually rises to the occasion, though, remains to be seen. To the end he remains the favorite of his garrulous family, still their most cherished representative of family duty and loyalty and still all too susceptible to the lure of their love and enfolding stories. When he raises his voice in song at the close of *Losing Battles,* the narrator remarks, simply but significantly: "All Banner could hear him and know who he was" (436). He is, after all, largely defined by the community and family that so happily "brags on" him; and like Banner and the Renfro-Beecham clan, he is not likely to change—even if Gloria is determined to wean him from his family.

It is left to his younger brother, Vaughn Renfro, hovering on the edge of the family storytelling and of the narrative itself, to offer a more substantial alternative—that is, his ability to stand aside and question, made possible in part by his curious alliance with both sides. If he is the offspring of talkative Renfros and Beechams, he is also a devoted student who cherishes books and his talent for spelling down the rest of the school. Above all, he is, not insignificantly, the only character who has a few introspective moments apart from the endless round of stories and talking in the whole of *Losing Battles,* as Welty herself has pointed out.[8] His mind is the only one that we as readers enter. Once there we learn of his instinctive knowledge that a larger world exists outside the cocoon of charming and seductive family tales and that those stories have their own powerful and dangerous momentum. The narrator tells us:

> [The sound of the night] was all-present enough to spill over into voices, as everything, he was ready to believe now, threatened to do, the closer he might come to where something might happen. The night might turn into more and more voices, all telling it—bragging, lying, singing, pretending, protesting, swearing everything into being, swearing everything away—but telling it. Even after people gave up each other's company, said good-bye and went home, if there was only one left, Vaughn Renfro, the world around him was still one huge, soul-defying reunion. (363)

It is this sort of distanced perspective, of course, that Welty's work has always advocated—in particular, a skepticism about tidy categorizations and systems. "Questioning our old acceptances pleases me," Welty once remarked in an interview; "that's healthy and promising" (*Conversations* 38). For those old acceptances, Welty suggests time and again, have the capacity to distance, diminish, and even erase those around us. Much to be preferred is Vaughn Renfro's acute awareness of "people's getting tangled up with each other" (363). He is, like Welty herself, an accomplished listener but like Welty again, a skeptic and a questioner, one who resists resolutions and easy answers. He and Welty herself know that "all things are double, and this should keep us from taking liberties with the outside world, and acting too quickly to finish things off," as Clement Musgrove in *The Robber Bridegroom* would remind us (126).

That sense of doubleness, of course, largely eludes the opposing sides of *Losing Battles,* who are nothing if not true believers in singleness, but Welty surveys their failures and their defeats with equal measures of compassion and tough-minded wariness. Her strategy is not so much one of censure as it is of exposure—of unacknowledged prohibitions, restraints, violence, and exertions of power. She says it best herself in "One Time, One Place": " . . . my wish, indeed my continuing passion, would be not to point the finger in judgment but to part a curtain, that invisible shadow that falls between people, the veil of indifference to each other's wonders, each other's human plight" (355).

SUZANNE
FERGUSON

THE "ASSAULT OF HOPE"

Style's Substance in Welty's "The Demonstrators"

The prose of any great author, like the music of a great composer or the painting of a great artist, is always identifiable by the traces of a distinctive style.[1] Arguably, when we speak or think about an author, we are referring to a style, to a complex of typical sentence structures and the rhythms these structures produce, a characteristic vocabulary, habitual use of certain kinds of figures of speech or even parts of speech, patterns of modification, as much as to a complex of themes and subjects or (more rarely) structural patterns. Although we rarely pause in our reading to analyze these microfeatures of a literary text, they determine not only how we interpret its meanings but how we feel about it, how we identify with or stand apart from its implicit creator. Even if not consciously, we remember them "the whole enduring time." We can tell them "from all the others in creation" (CS 148).

My project is for a brief space to raise into readerly consciousness some features of Eudora Welty's style, features that not only identify her with a distinctive signature, but that produce what seems to me to be the central characteristic of her identity as a writer, of her vision of life-in-fiction: her insistence on representing side by side the beauty and the terror, the tenderness and violence of everyday life, the "hideous and delectable face" (CS 461) of experience, without ever yielding one to the other. The syntax of her sentences, the schemes that are structural as well as ornamental, the varied registers of her diction and imagery, have certainly been noted and admired by many commentators.[2] What I hope to provide in undertaking a detailed tracing of the stylistic features of one short story is both a summary of Welty's stylistic strategies and a demonstration of how, through these strategies, she manipulates and modulates tone so as to transform a theme of desolation into an affirmation of faith in the resilience of the human heart.

Her late story, "The Demonstrators,"[3] with its interwoven plot elements and political subtext, powerfully represents Welty's characteristic strategies for suiting her style to subjects about which both writer and reader must feel some ambivalence: subjects in which pain and joy, despair and hope, alienation and community, sublimity and ludicrousness keep house together, tempering each other through the controlled play of cognitive dissonances manifest in the several aspects of her style.[4] In "The Demonstrators," the continual alternation of positive and negative images, the opposition of highly figured and bare passages, the arresting juxtapositions of vigorous dialectal speech, fanciful impressionism, and exhausted, near parodic journalese constitute the chief stylistic features. Bitterness and despair pervade the story's substance, and these emotions are given full value in the diction and imagery; but love and hope are also present. Welty confronts death but welcomes birth and survival, too. Imagery of natural death and natural renewal, images of community, order, and affection, of the joys of children in toys and celebrations, of color and light, determination and restfulness break through the darkness and sickness of a community, lifting the spirit from conflict and contempt into equilibrium and acceptance.

In her early work, the stories of the thirties and early forties, Welty focuses upon single, unified incidents so that clashes between style and substance, as in "Keela, the Outcast Indian Maiden," "Lily Daw and the Three Ladies," or "Death of a Traveling Salesman," produce complication: levels of meaning in the works. As early as some of the stories in *The Wide Net,* notably, "A Still Moment," she also began to experiment with joining diverse plot elements by means of a unifying style, a practice that culminates brilliantly in "June Recital" in *The Golden Apples.*

In "The Demonstrators," first published in the *New Yorker* in November 1966, the tonality—established through various stylistic strategies—ranges from playful to despairing, mundane to fantastic, while the multiple strands of the narrative substance are almost unrelievedly grim. In 1966, the title of the story referred to something quite specific and immediately pressing the real world; and demonstrators against the war in Vietnam and for civil rights make brief but significant appearances in the story. The work is not about these demonstrators, however, nor their causes. Its real demonstrators mutely act out their messages of love and despair, rather than shouting or singing or carrying signs.[5]

The story's main character, a Mississippi Delta small-town doctor called Richard Strickland (one of Welty's allegorical names), tries on a November

Saturday night to come to terms with his own grief over the death of his handicapped child and departure of his wife as he treats patients: an old woman, Marcia Pope, who suffers "attacks"; a young woman, Ruby Gaddy, dying of a stab wound. Then he witnesses the death of a third patient, Ruby's lover and killer, Dove Collins, himself fatally wounded by Ruby. In a brief coda to this narrative, he reads a few days later a newspaper account of the two deaths in which prominent white citizens worry over possible racial implications in the killings. Auxiliary narrative motifs are correspondingly bleak: another patient, his neighbor and the town's mayor and mill owner, is dying of a painful disease; a young man is killed in a motorcycle accident; Ruby leaves a baby motherless. In speaking of the story, Welty has said that it was an attempt to capture that time of troubles.[6] The style of "The Demonstrators" is multivalent, conveying both the bitterness of its substance and the exhilaration of its true subject, "the assault of hope" (CS 618) that rescues Dr. Strickland from despair.

Although the third-person narration enters the consciousness of the protagonist only, the actual language is not always plausibly his thought or speech, but rather that of an authorial narrator. Cutting into this supple, skillfully modulated narration, the style and perspective of the thousand-odd-word newspaper report Dr. Strickland reads are clearly at odds with those of the other parts of the story. The clash between the authorial and journalistic styles brings about a clarification of meaning similar to that of the newspaper article in the early Welty story, "A Piece of News," or its model, the newspaper report of Mrs. Sinico's death which initiates Mr. Duffy's epiphany in Joyce's "A Painful Case."

One odd stylistic device of the authorial narrative voice of "The Demonstrators" is the unconventional use of the past perfect verb form for events that happened "tonight." The imperfect, the normal narrative tense, indicating events happening in the present of the narrative, doesn't begin until several paragraphs into the story, when the doctor has returned to his office after treating old Miss Pope. The shift subtly introduces a movement between the remotely contemplated and the immediately sensed that characterizes the different types of experience presented in the story. Thoughts of the near and the far past, recalled later in the story (also in the past perfect), are equally remote from the powerful demonstrations of the fictional present.

From the beginning of the story, an easy colloquialism characterizes the doctor's thought: he had "got into playing" bridge; Miss Pope is known for "giving out great wads" of Shakespeare and Virgil; he "could not be sure [an] answer got by her" (CS 608). In the gap between the character's voice and the authorial voice, we find as well elaborately formal rhythmic patterns of syntax and elegant diction: "Now bedridden, scorning all medication and in particular tranquilizers, she had a seizure every morning before breakfast and often on Saturday night for some reason, but had retained her memory. . . . The more forcefully Miss Marcia Pope declaimed, the more innocent grew her old face" (*CS* 608). Such syntactic schemes are the only ornament of the opening passage, and their juxtaposition to the colloquial phrases foreshadows the dissonances that will typify both style and substance throughout the story.

As the doctor moves out of the refined world of the retired schoolteacher, Miss Pope, in which his broken marriage is a solecism punishable by a whipping, the syntax loosens, the imagery becomes more sensuous, and metaphors and similes begin to appear: driving past "the vast shrouded cavern" of the cotton gin, his car lights make the dead goldenrod beside the road look "heavier than the bridge across the creek." Arriving at the as yet unidentified destination, he has difficulty seeing: "at first his eyes could make out little but an assembly of white forms spaced in the air near a low roof—chickens roosting in a tree. Then he saw the reds of cigarettes. A dooryard was as packed with a standing crowd as if it were funeral time" (*CS* 609).

Suggestions of a magical night journey are implicit not only in the apparition of the doctor's guide (a young girl), his ignorance of his goal, and the strangeness of his arrival, but in the meandering syntax and the intrusions of figurative language. Similes, in particular, proliferate, evoking mixed sensations. The dying girl's forehead "looked thick as a battering ram," "a necklace like sharp and pearly teeth was fastened around her throat," "the nipples of her breast cast shadows that looked like figs," "sweat . . . rose and seemed to weaken and unstick the newspapered walls like steam from a kettle already boiling," women's sighs "travel around the room, domestic sounds like a broom being flirted about, women getting ready for company." These impressionistic figures increase immediacy at the same time as they begin to establish the dominant notes of the tone: mystery in the "shrouded cavern" and the "assembly of white forms spaced in the air," and the conflict of light against darkness, life against death in the heavy goldenrod, the funereal waiting, the white of chickens, the glow of the kerosene lamp, the red banner and white, "shiny, clinging stuff" of Ruby's dress, the glittering of a tambourine on the bedpost. There is violence in the "battering ram" of her forehead, her hand which "clawed at his . . . with her sticky nails," the necklace like "sharp" teeth, the wound that "quickened spasmodically as if it responded to light" (*CS* 609–10).

Intensifying the sense of disorientation set up in the conflicting images is the ritualistic dialogue established between the doctor and the onlookers:

> "How long ago?" He looked at the path of newspapers spread on the floor. "Where? Where did it happen? How did she get here?"
> He had an odd feeling that somewhere in the room somebody was sending out beckoning smiles in his direction. He lifted, half turned his head. The elevated

coal that glowed at regular intervals was the pipe of an old woman in a boiled white apron standing near the door.

He persisted. "Has she coughed up anything yet?"

"Don't you know her?" they cried, as if he never was going to hit on the right question.

He let go the girl's arm, and her hand started its way back again to her wound. Sending one glowing look at him, she covered it again. As if she had spoken, he recognized her.

"Why, it's Ruby," he said. (CS 610–11)

The "beckoning smiles," the "glow" of the pipe (and earlier, of the "radiants" of the gas stove), prepare for the "glowing look" which brings about the doctor's recognition of his cleaning woman, Ruby. But indecent laughter from outside, "a regular guffaw, not much different from the one that followed the telling of a dirty story or a race story by one of the clowns in the Elks' Club" (CS 611), brings him up short.

Another bizarre and incongruously humorous interruption, guinea pigs running freely through the house, leads to another revelation, as colloquial dialect in brief exchanges gives birth to a ritual naming:

"Catch those things!" he exclaimed.

The baby laughed; the rest copied the baby.

"They lightning. Get away from you so fast!" said a voice.

"Them guinea pigs ain't been caught since they was born. Let you try."

"Know why? 'Cause they's Dove's. Dove left 'em here when he move out, just to be in the way."

The doctor felt the weight recede from Ruby's fingers and saw it flatten her arm where it lay on the bed. Her eyes had closed. A little boy with a sanctimonious face had taken the bit of celery and knelt down on the floor; there was scrambling about and increasing laughter until Dr. Strickland made himself heard in the room.

"All right. I heard you. Is Dove who did it? Go on. Say." He heard somebody spit on the stove. Then:

"It's Dove."

"Dove."

"Dove."

"Dove." (CS 611–12)

The dialect is used not only for authenticity but for vividness and urgency: "They lightning." The sevenfold repetition of Dove's name within a hundred words—the last four times consecutively—is peculiarly effective in establishing an ambivalence about Dove, the lover and murderer. The midcentral vowel and soft alveolar and labial stops impart a gentleness congruent with the conventional peaceful associations of Dove's name. Repeated, they sound a soothing music, like cooing, rather than the accusation of a killer. By this strategy Welty throws our conventional expectations into suspension. Act and meaning seem parted as the repeated name cleaves the imaginary air of the room.

New dissonant pairings of radiant and threatening images ease and increase tension. Now a lamp is lifted about "the dipping shadows of [the women's] heads," to allow a valentine to "radiate" its color before descending "closer to the girl like something that would devour her" (*CS* 612). Ruby's baby's hand is "gray as the claw of a squirrel," hers has a "horny palm, blood-caked fingers," as the lamplight comes and goes, "striking" and withdrawing, and the old woman's pipe continues to "glow with regularity" (*CS* 613). In a hush, all Strickland can hear is "guinea pigs racing." The odd incongruities of the scene and the figures in which it is described prepare for another night journey experience.

> When he stepped outside onto the porch he saw that there was moonlight everywhere. Uninterrupted by any lights from Holden, it filled the whole country lying out there in the haze of the long rainless fall. . . . Just one house and one church farther, the Delta began, and the cotton fields ran into the scattered paleness of a dimmed-out Milky Way.
>
> Nobody called him back, yet he turned his head and got a sideways glimpse all at once of a row of dresses hung up across the front of the house, starched until they could have stood alone (as his mother complained), and in an instant had recognized his mother's gardening dress, his sister Annie's gold dress, his wife's favorite duster that she liked to wear to the breakfast table, and more dresses, less substantial. Elevated across the front of the porch, they were hung again between him and the road. With sleeves spread wide, trying to scratch his forehead with the tails of their skirts, they were flying around this house in the moonlight. (*CS* 615)

The moonlight is Hawthornesque, creating an experience of fantasy out of the mundane: Lucille, Ruby's mother, is a laundress and has received these dresses as castoffs, perquisites of her work. Like several women in the story, the dresses seem hostile to the doctor. Grotesque and slightly sinister, the moment of vertigo or vision is an impressionist prelude to the moment of reflection and analysis the doctor is about to experience.

As he drives back to town, the flexible syntax and easy flow of metaphor and simile associated earlier with the doctor's stream of thought reemerge. Descriptive details reveal visual ugliness, the division and perhaps despair of the economically drained community, and the seasonal dregs of the year; but the figures are often whimsical, even humorous. The Negro church is "flat-roofed as a warehouse" but has "its shades pulled down like a bed-room," implying a secret life carried on inside. Discarded paregoric bottles, ironically labelled "Mother's Helper," "glitter" along the creek bank, "the size of harmonicas," and "the telephone wires along the road were hung with shreds of cotton, the sides of the road were strewn with them too, as if the doctor were out on a paper chase." The smell of the mill is "a cooking smell, like a dish ordered by a man with an endless appetite." The scene is festive: "Pipes hung with streamers of lint fed into the moonlit gin, and wagons and trucks heaped up round as the gypsy caravans or circus wagons of his father's or even his grandfather's stories, stood . . . waiting . . . outside" (*CS* 615).

His journey becomes the biblical Exodus when a grass fire sends up a "pillow-shaped glow"; "pillow" aurally summons up *pillar,* for the next phrase is "a *cloud* with the November flush of the sedge grass *by day*" (emphasis added) that leads the doctor to his conclusion. A closing simile, however, cuts short any anticipation of deliverance from this waste land. The glow is "not to be confused with a burning church, but like anesthetic made visible" (*CS* 616).

Stopped at a grade crossing, Strickland at first hears a creaking sleeper as "complaining," but then as "an old-fashioned porch swing holding lovers in the dark." The coziness of this image prefaces a series of positive images. The "thin, porcelain cup" in which he had been given water, "his lips and his fingers had recognized. In that house of murder, comfort had been brought to him at his request. . . . He had . . . reeled into a flock of dresses stretched wide-sleeved . . . like a child's drawing of angels. . . . The feeling of well-being persisted. It increased, until he had come to the point of tears" (*CS* 616).

At this point in the story comes a more or less straightforward summary of the doctor's life: he has followed his father as town doctor; his parents are dead and his sister married and gone; his wife, who was " 'the prettiest girl in the Delta,' " has left him after the death of their brain-damaged, thirteen-year-old daughter, to whom she had "dedicated her life . . . giving all [her] devotion to something that cannot be helped" (*CS* 616–17). Strickland recalls a visit of a civil rights worker to their house, one whose cynicism about untruths in a polemical newspaper article left a bad taste, though the doctor's wife reproached him with similar hypocrisy for his lies to dying patients. Later, anti–civil rights demonstrators had put glass in his driveway; and when he ruined his tires, not having "seen what it wouldn't have occurred to him to look for," his wife "had suddenly broken into laughter . . ." (*CS* 617). This laughter, capable of several interpretations, is left unmodified and suspended in the text by ellipses. After her departure, in a separation that seems permanent, "he was so increasingly tired, so sick and even bored with the bitterness, intractability that divided everybody and everything." In this entire passage, some thousand words long, not a single simile or metaphor occurs, in contrast to the previous section of description, in which they cluster, sometimes several to a sentence. Partly, of course, the reflective passage *is* only summary, an account of the past, while figures are used to give sense impressions in the narrative present. Still, the absence of figures and emphasis on abstraction underscores the barrenness of the life reported. When Strickland gives himself back to feeling once more, it is again in similes:

> He had felt as though someone had stopped him on the street and offered to carry his load for a while—had insisted on it—some old, trusted, half-forgotten family friend that he had lost sight of since youth. Was it the sensation, now returning, that there was still allowed to everybody on earth a *self*—savage, death-defying, private? The pounding of his heart was like the assault of hope, throwing itself against him without a stop, merciless. (*CS* 618)

The image, "to carry his load," is traditional. Although the emergence of a savage, death-defying, private "self" is hardly Christian, the terms *hope* and *mercy* reach back to earlier religious references in the story. Ruby was in the church choir, but her vengeance was purely individual and familial. The church, throughout the story, seems more a social institution, with music and dancing "on many another night besides Sunday," than a religious one. Thus, while the "assault of hope" is not necessarily Christian Grace, its power to heal and reconcile the individual with the community *is* something supernatural, like the attack of the dresses on the porch. Hope is positive, but when it "assaults" one without "mercy" (*CS* 615), and against all logic and memory, its effect may be ambivalently received. The feeling "ebbed away, like nausea put down" (*CS* 618), for the struggle between hope and despair is to be rejoined in a stronger test.

The festive imagery of the earlier description of the gin is reinvoked in Strickland's impression of the moonlit "drygoods store with its ornamental top that looped like opened paper fans held by acrobats," the town water tank "pale as a balloon that might only be tethered there" (*CS* 618). When the lights of his car fall upon a man "lying prone and colorless in the arena of moonlight," Strickland sees his clothing as turning "golden yellow. The man looked as if he had been sleeping all day in a bed of flowers and rolled in their pollen and were sleeping there still, with his face buried. He was covered his length in cottonseed meal" (*CS* 619). This culmination of the imagery of light in the story, with its magically beautiful simile, transforms the dying murderer, Dove, into a figure of myth or dream: a sleeping flower-god absorbing life from pollen. Dressed for death and natural resurrection, he is metamorphosed into an animal; pushing himself up on his hands, Dove looks at the doctor "like a seal. Blood laced his head like a net through which he had broken" (*CS* 619). Again the simile is visually accurate, but its connotations are mythic; Dove seems to be the seal-lover of ballad and folktale, killed by the faithlessness of his human mistress.

In a line of descent from some of the male characters of earlier Welty stories, Dove is associated with elemental vitality. Like Cash McCord of "Livvie," he keeps guinea pigs; like Billy Floyd of "At the Landing," he resists being caught in social bonds. Ruby, with her ties to home and church, loved but couldn't keep him. The exact nature of their quarrel cannot be known. Two selves, "savage, death-defying, private" (*CS* 618), loved and destroyed each other. The imagery connected with their death agony is mainly but not wholly heroic. In the end Dove's plea is not to be helped but to be hidden, preserving the privacy of the self at the moment of death: "Then he hemorrhaged through the mouth" (*CS* 619).

In strong contrast to the rhapsodic, mysterious description of the events as seen by Strickland is the newspaper account of the deaths of "an employee of the Fairbrothers Cotton Seed Oil Mill and a Holden maid, both Negroes." About a thousand words long, the report is dense with ironies and written in the chatty, cliché-ridden style of such papers. The pair were "stabbed with a sharp instrument" and "later expired." "The mishap boosted Holden's weekend death toll to 3." (The other victim, Billy Lee Warrum, Jr., "was pronounced dead on arrival" at the hospital in Jackson after a motorcycle accident in which he hit a truck "loaded to capacity" with holiday turkeys.) Although witnesses thought Collins was stabbed in "his ear or his eye, either of which is in close approximation to the brain," Dr. Strickland "alleg[ed] his death to chest wounds." Repeatedly, the racial theme is struck: "the incident was not believed by Mayor Herman Fairbrothers to carry racial significance," and the authorities are "satisfied no outside agitators were involved and no arrests were made." The county sheriff, off on a fishing vacation, comments, "That's one they can't pin the blame on us for. . . . Please take note our conscience is clear" (*CS* 619–21).

The syntax of the article is heavily modified, with embedded clauses and phrases loading in often apparently irrelevant facts: the ice pick, "reportedly the property of the Holy Gospel Tabernacle, was later found by Deacon Gaddy, 8, brother of Ruby Gaddy, covered with blood and carried it to Marshal Stubblefield."[7] The reader may retrieve from this ungainly (even grammatically incorrect) sentence the boy with the "sanctimonious" face who lured guinea pigs with wilted celery and brought fresh water in a "thin porcelain cup." Two styles, two realities.

Although the syntax of the earlier portions of the story is quite intricate and varied, ranging from strongly patterned sentences in the opening section and the summary account of Dr. Strickland's past to very loose, often densely modified cumulative sentences in the sections dealing with Ruby and Dove, the density of the journalistic sentences is of a different sort: they are lumpish, lifeless, ponderous things which avoid perception through precast phrases and constructions. The so-called inverted pyramid of newspaper form fragments the account of the deaths by shifting among different aspects of the incident and comments by leading public figures: the mayor, the Baptist preacher, the sheriff, the marshal. But errors of fact (including the spelling of Dove's name as *Dave*) are obvious. This is a style that has no way of knowing a private, death-defying self: it concludes, "No cause was cited for the fracas" (*CS* 621).

The stylistic authenticity of the newspaper account, like the authenticity Welty establishes for Holden's topography, social structures, and speech patterns, is completely persuasive. No metaphors are allowed, but absurd details, like the truckload of turkeys and the bottle caps flipped down at the wounded Dove when he fell into a ditch, let us know we are in a story by Welty. The eagerness of the white official population to disown any responsibility for the black community and its individual members is the dominant theme here, but the ineluctable mystery of Dove and Ruby's passion remains impervious to cheapening.

As when he witnessed the two deaths, Dr. Strickland reads this travesty without apparent emotion. He simply goes out into his screened back porch, his view cataloguing the scene:

> The roses were done for, the perennials too. But the surrounding crape-myrtle tree, the redbud, the dogwood, the chinese tallow tree, and the pomegranate bush were bright as toys. The ailing pear tree had shed its leaves ahead of the rest. Past a falling wall of Michaelmas daisies that had not been tied up, a pair of flickers were rifling the grass, the cock in one part of the garden, the hen in another, picking at the devastation right through the bright leaves that appeared to have been left lying there just for them, probing and feeding. (*CS* 621)

The festive and the vital converge in a moment that gives the doctor just barely enough strength to endure. Some plants are "done for," but more are "bright as toys." A pear tree is "ailing," Michaelmas daisies are "a falling wall," but the birds "pick . . . at the devastation . . . through the bright leaves" in one of the supple, cumulative sentences that characterize Welty's own authorial style. The male flicker's wing is exotic, "showing as a zebra's hide," and its "red seal" gives the sign that the "assault of hope" has not finally been repelled.

On a first reading, "The Demonstrators" may appear to be fragmented, too ambitious in its conflation of contrasting themes and styles. But the protagonist's perception of the story's events in contrast to the official perception of the newspaper account; the interrelated verbal patterns of symbolic proper names and imagery of light and dark, life and death, festival and natural; the alternation of a highly figured, concrete, vigorously natural diction with one that is bare, abstract, and exaggeratedly conventional; and the deliberate juxtapositioning of grammatically different types of sentences, from the formally balanced through loosely cumulative and awkwardly embedded, contribute to a complex structure not only complete and shapely but resonant. Similarly, the discrepancy between the uniformly painful substance and the alternately jocular and self-consciously beautiful style may seem to call up a muddle of responses. The conflict has a resolution, however, in the second-last paragraph (quoted above), where com-bined imagery of desolation and survival, even affirmation, underlines the thematic resolution that is going on behind the verbal surface of the doctor's quiet observation of the two birds. In the final paragraph he is preparing to resume his burden—life, his profession, his social obligations, his moral witnessing—and to carry on, though he sees anew just how difficult that will be. As in her earlier stories that bring together love and violence, such as "At the Landing" or "A Still Moment," Welty is incapable of leaving a scene dominated wholly by death and destruction, for her own vision is incorrigibly, mercilessly hopeful.

2

WOMEN

"who had felt
the wildness of the world
behind the ladies' view"

ELIZABETH

E V A N S

Eudora Welty and the Dutiful Daughter

The literature on the relations of mothers and daughters, ranging as it does from the story of Cinderella to Nancy Friday's *My Mother, My Self,* to Sue Miller's novel, *The Good Mother,* is forbidding by its sheer abundance. And whether mothers are like Adele Ratignolle in Kate Chopin's *The Awakening* or the stereotypic wicked stepmother, the relation of mother and daughter is a central one to women's existence. In her 1986 study, *Stealing the Language: The Emergency of Women's Poetry in America,* Alicia Ostriker suggests that "we can expect the subject of the mother-daughter relation to be central in women's writing and to reflect the ambivalence of the daughter who must both identify with and reject the mother" (167). The topic of the dutiful daughter is a rich one in Eudora Welty's fiction, one that touches nearly every title. In looking at three pairs of Welty's mothers and daughters, one sees that daughters may choose to be dutiful, though they often must pay a heavy price in so doing.

When I first read *The Optimist's Daughter,* one passage deeply shocked me. I have never gotten it out of my mind, nor have I been fully able to consider it simply an episode within the lives of the characters. It comes near the end of part 3, that long retelling of the past. Laurel, recently widowed, is as powerless as her father to save her mother, Becky, from the ravages of illness and the advance of death. Neither family, friends, nor clergy can give solace; and Becky McKelva dies, Welty writes, "without speaking a word, keeping everything to herself, in exile and humiliation" (151). A hard passage, but the stunning words come next: "To Laurel while she still knew her, she had made a last remark: 'You could have saved your mother's life. But you stood by and wouldn't intervene. I despair for you' " (151). We react seriously to the last words of a dying person. To the intelligent, sensitive Laurel, Becky's dying words must have wounded, wounded to the quick.

This passage suggests the price many a woman has paid for being a dutiful daughter, particularly one like Laurel McKelva. In fiction as in life, it is difficult to generalize about mothers and daughters and about the process of passing a strong female tradition on from one generation to the next. However, expectations make the accepting of that female tradition especially difficult for many daughters in Welty's fiction. Certainly happy mother-daughter relations exist—one only has to look at *Delta Wedding* and a day in Ellen Fairchild's life to see that real and even surrogate children find strength in Ellen's strength, comfort in her nurturing. Such is not the case with Becky and Laurel. Admittedly, we are denied Becky's point of view. Dead ten years before the novel opens, Becky is presented through the perceptions of her Mt. Salus neighbors and friends as well as from the memories her husband and daughter hold. Early in the novel, Judge McKelva mentions Becky when he describes his eye disorder to Dr. Courtland. He had, the Judge says, been pruning the famous rose (Becky's Climber), but pruning at the wrong season. "Becky," he adds, "would say it served me right" (5). That is, he deserved the injury that followed pruning at the wrong time. The Judge's supposition may reflect a reasonable memory of typical responses that Becky made.

One may expect a father to spoil his only daughter and so be unsurprised at the extravagance Judge McKelva has lavished on his daughter's wedding. There was pink champagne and a five-piece Negro band from New Orleans in spite of World War II restrictions and difficulties. And, judging from those ever-present bridesmaids, Laurel had a big church wedding. If we can trust Tish Buloch's memory, we know that the Judge's actions were, in his wife's eyes, "utter extravagance. Childfoolishness" (124). In the present time of this retelling, as perhaps a dutiful daughter would, Laurel rises to her mother's defense. However, her two statements are intriguing. One is an outright declaration—"Mother had a superstitious streak"—and its completing thought is expressed in a conditional sentence: "She might have had a notion it was unlucky to make too much of your happiness" (124).

If so, Becky had a singularly unfortunate superstition, one which would render all great moments of happiness suspect. The gods, if you will, may punish those who appear too happy; indulgence in joy may cause luck to go sour. If Laurel's might-have-been statement about Becky is accurate, then surely her demeanor at the time of Laurel's wedding would have cast an unspoken pall on the joyous celebration, foreshadowing the event that proves the superstition: Laurel and Philip Hand's marriage is one "of magical ease" (121); but then Philip Hand is dead, killed by a Japanese fighter plane, and the extreme happiness is gone.

If one explores the mother-daughter relationship throughout the novel, the pleasant memories of Laurel's childhood (epitomized in hearing her mother and father reading aloud to each other as she herself drifted off to sleep) pale before the memories of Becky as a young woman. She was independent, more courageous than her brothers. And as the stories of her youth are told and retold, it is clear that any daughter would be hard pressed to measure up.

Who else could ride a horse miles to the schoolhouse and there teach strapping boys hardly younger than herself? Ride reciting reams of poetry because she could memorize so well, so easily? Who else could have taken the raft through the icy river, much less *made* the fire burn when Becky bore her dying father toward the train and the operating room at Johns Hopkins? And who else could have so impressed those doctors with her courage, her independence? For that matter, who could even have taken Becky's place in that tough bridge foursome in Mt. Salus?

In her 1978 journal, *Recovering,* May Sarton observes that "mothers are very good at tenderness, and it is, no doubt, the mothering part of us that can give it, and the child part of us that longs to feel it in the atmosphere" (15). Carol Gilligan in her book, *In A Different Voice,* suggests that "sensitivity to the needs of others and the assumption of responsibility for taking care lead women to attend to voices other than their own and to include in their judgment other points of view" (16). Sarton and Gilligan voice views of women, of mothers, that many today find reasonable, sensibly judgmental, and acceptable. But if the criteria are applied to Becky McKelva—whose personality is best described as resilient, independent, courageous—the tenderness, sensitivity, nurturing seem almost absent, secondary at best.

Laurel is a dutiful daughter to a mother who was insensitive, who did not come easily to tenderness, who literally cursed her daughter as she died—despairing of Laurel because this dutiful daughter could not do the impossible. Laurel's experience forces her to sort through the remaining possessions of her dead parents; and as she relives the memories, she is forced to reassess not only her parents, their marriage, and their shortcomings but also to reassess her own role as the dutiful daughter.

Welty allows Laurel insight, and through the epiphany she experiences with the discovered breadboard, she can distill from the past what is necessary to survive the memories, to abandon all physical possessions associated with it, and to give up the unrealistic expectations arising from her life with her mother. (Helen Hurt Tiegreen points out the deletion from the *New Yorker* version of *The Optimist's Daughter:* Laurel's first emotion had been anger after something happened. In the book version, the anger has been altogether internalized, save for the verbal outburst to Mr. Cheek. Laurel's kitchen confrontation with Fay shows only the beginnings of anger, which she checks.)

It is true that throughout the novel Laurel declares that her parents loved each other. But in the end, Becky dismisses husband as well as daughter. She dismisses Clinton with a gesture of pity; she simply dismisses Laurel. Clinton, in the despair known only to optimists, had promised the dying woman he would take her back home to her mountain. To these futile words she hurls back, "Lucifer! Liar!" For a moment there is communion for all three as they hold hands, holding, the text says, "long after there was nothing more to be said" (150). Then come those final and awful words—Becky's last lucid ones—the curse to this daughter whose short-coming was (like her father's) the inability to fully and completely identify with and participate in the desperate singleness of the dying.

Most of the daughters in Welty's fiction identify with their mothers and are dutiful at least until their parents die. And some parents expect far too much. Miss Tennyson Bulloch, a powerful mother figure, blames Laurel for the Judge's marrying Wanda Fay. Daughters, Miss Tennyson declares, ought to stay at home and look after the old folks, not go kiting off to careers in Chicago.

In *The Golden Apples,* particularly in "June Recital" and in "The Wanderers," we witness dutiful daughters in Virgie Rainey and Cassie Morrison. From the outset, the similarities between *The Optimist's Daughter* and "The Wanderers" are striking. Both works focus on the death of a parent. Both feature a funeral where the gathered neighbors speak of the dead in exaggerated terms that bewilder the dutiful daughter who cannot contradict by speaking the truth. Both have relatives who come from afar and whose behavior is not up to the standards of the natives. The Chisoms arrive in a pick-up truck from Madrid, Texas, for Judge McKelva's funeral— Bubba wearing his windbreaker, Sis pregnant and declaring she'll never take Wendel anywhere again, and Mama suggesting to Wanda Fay that the McKelva place would make a fine boardinghouse.

In "The Wanderers" the Mayhew family appears for Katie Rainey's funeral, alighting from their pick-up truck and asking at once for water and iced tea. They seek the ordinary courtesies of southern homes. Like the Chisoms, the Mayhews head for home immediately after the funeral. Wanda Fay rides on her mama's lap in the cab; the Mayhew children ride in the back of their truck, at rest on Katie's bed.

In both works, an old man from the family appears. Wanda Fay's grandfather comes on the bus from Bigbee, having shelled pecans the whole way to stay awake and to have as a gift to present at the funeral. His gesture is that of a southern fulfilling the obligations of manners. Fate Rainey's old brother appears to help bury Katie, a man nobody around Morgana has seen since they buried Fate years ago.

Finally, both works have dutiful daughters with demanding mothers.

"June Recital" was first published in 1947 (under the title "Golden Apples"); *The Optimist's Daughter* appeared in 1969 in the *New Yorker* version and in 1972 as the revised novel. Becky McKelva and Katie Rainey have obvious differences. Becky has a college education, marries a professional man, lives in town. Katie lives in the outskirts of Morgana and makes her living by selling flowering plants and ice cream. Her husband, Fate, is the traveling vegetable man, and they live an altogether rural existence. Although twenty-two years separate these two works, they share the theme that strong mothers take for granted that their daughters will be what the mothers need and what they expect.

In *The Golden Apples* Virgie starts out as anything but a dutiful daughter. She is Miss Eckhart's prize pupil who challenges and finally cuts her teacher. She carries on a flagrant teenage love affair with Kewpie Moffitt. She becomes the pianist at the Bijou theater, where she plays "You've Got to See Mama Every Night" while the audience watches advertisements. She has long ago quit playing such recital pieces as *Fantasia on Beethoven's Ruins of Athens*. And then Virgie has even up and left Morgana, ran off to Memphis. We are not told how long she stayed, what she did, whom she slept with. We are simply told that at 17 she came back, stepped off the Y. & M. V. train and walked home. And here, from "The Wanderers," is her mother's greeting: " 'You're back at the right time to milk for me' . . . and untied her bonnet and dashed it to the floor between them, looking up at her daughter" (*CS* 452). (Is it too much to suggest the irony here? Is the bonnet a female version of the gauntlet? Only here, one picks up the bonnet to acquiese, not to accept a challenge from which one might emerge victorious.)

If Virgie has a story of hurt and sorrow and disappointment and shame to confess or tell or share, she never gets a chance to do so. If she has expected to weep on her mother's shoulder, she does not get to. If she is the prodigal returned, nobody rejoices, much less offers to kill the fatted calf. Indeed, we are told at this point in the story that weeping is the mother's prerogative; and the mother weeps not for the daughter, but for son and husband. "Nobody," the narrative voice says, "was allowed weeping over hurts in her house, unless it was Mrs. Rainey herself first, for son and husband, both her men, were gone" (*CS* 452).

The tension between Katie and Virgie continues, centering in "The Wanderers" upon the night Katie dies and the day she is buried. Katie, who once perched gloriously in that swivel chair King MacLain himself had provided, can no longer grow her flowers and fruits to sell at the roadside. Old, maimed by a stroke, she simply watches all day for Virgie to return from work in Nesbitt's Hardware Store. Finally, when she gets home, we read these lines:

[KATIE]: "Look where the sun is. . . ."

[VIRGIE]: "I see it, Mama." (*CS* 430)

Virgie is late; and before she can change out of her high heels and flowered voile dress, Katie has recited the duties Virgie faces: "You have to milk before dark, after driving them in, and there's four little quails full of shot for you to dress, lying on my kitchen table." Virgie says nothing and coaxes her mother into the house while Katie murmurs, "I been by myself all day" (*CS* 430).

Katie dies on a Sunday. That day, Virgie has cut out a hard plaid, and Katie takes satisfaction in thinking, "It's a wonder, though. . . . A blessed wonder to see the child mind" (*CS* 430). It is perhaps more of a blessed wonder to have a forty-odd-year-old dutiful daughter. Later, Virgie heeds Katie's call, comes, fans her with the *Market Bulletin,*[1] and watches her die. But the death of the mother does not end Virgie's role. Next day, the Morgana women insist that she view the body; when she refuses, Miss Perdita Mayo pronounces in praise of the mother: "Your Mama was too fine for you Virgie, too fine" (*CS* 435). Here Miss Perdita echoes the community response and underscores again the expectations placed on daughters. Because Virgie refuses to view her mother's body, Miss Perdita judges swiftly: Katie Rainey was "too fine"—that is, too good to deserve the slight Virgie has just delivered.

That night Virgie milks the cows as usual; and the next morning she drives them to pasture, chops wood, and, so that the place look respectable for the funeral, she begins on the high grass with her sewing scissors—an absurd and futile task. She momentarily thinks, too, she has to obey Miss Lizzie Stark, who sent her orders through Juba, her servant: "Tell her I can pack up better without you. Do I have to pack everything?" Juba assures her that indeed she must (*CS* 455).

And Virgie almost does. This dutiful daughter again disobeys mothers and surrogate mothers. Virgie takes one look at the household effects and tells Juba she and Minerva can share them all, can take it all away—what they have not already stolen. And she presses those ever-to-be-milked cows on Old Man Rainey since he has a truck to take them home in.

Like Laurel, Virgie does come to her own self, does in a real sense cease to be the dutiful daughter. Her decision comes naturally, without preparation, without forethought. Someone asks, "You staying on in Morgana, Virgie?" And she answers, "Going away. In the morning." The narrative voice adds that "Virgie said nothing more; she had decided to leave when she heard herself say so—decided by ear" (*CS* 450). Thelma J.

Shinn, in *Radiant Daughters: Fictional American Daughters,* emphasizes Welty's powerful line about mothers and daughters: " 'Should daughters *forgive* Mothers (with Mothers under their heels)?' Welty writes of Miss Eckhart [Welty's emphasis]. And Miss Eckhart, that mysterious artist living in Morgana, is cut off from the culture that produced her and is now burdened with an ill and thoroughly unpleasant Mother for whom she must care" (40). Shinn suggests that southern women (native or transplanted) are, far more than men, obliged to attend to family duties. In portraying dutiful daughters in Virgie and Laurel, Welty acknowledges that daughters are literally or figuratively bound by their mothers' presence and demands. Daughters probably cannot *forgive* their mothers while the mothers live and are under their heels. But when the mothers die, the daughters can at last literally leave home, if they choose to do so.

Cassie Morrison, dutiful daughter who will remain one all the days of her life, assumes that Virgie will go way off—perhaps to New York like Loch Morrison—and have "a life of your own" (*CS* 457). But at least within the bounds of the story, Virgie only gets seven miles away and stops beneath the big tree in front of the courthouse in MacLain. Nevertheless, she has left her mother's house, she has had that famous swim in the Black River, and now in this place and in the strangest of company—"an old wrapped-up Negro woman with a red hen under her arm" (*CS* 460)— Virgie makes that mysterious connection between the present moment and the picture in Miss Eckhart's studio. There she had always seen Perseus slaying the Medusa, knowing finally that to have or to be a hero one must have a victim. And for a woman to cease being a dutiful daughter—at least on the primary level—her mother must die. And if the daughters have, in a sense, been the victims of their mothers' incessant demands, their mothers, Becky and Katie, become the victims when they die. In that act, the mothers release the daughters from the literal daily relationship.

Virgie may be only seven miles away, but it could just as well be 7,000. She is now, Welty writes at the close of "The Wanderers," part of a wider world and hearing "the magical procession." There is the real sound of rain, but there is also that spring catalogue of magic sounds: "the running of the horse and bear, the stroke of the leopard, the dragon's crusty slither, the glimmer and the trumpet of the swan" (*CS* 461). Welty has conceded that these sounds quite defy literal representation and explanation. What, for example, *is* the "stroke of the leopard"? She has also said she loves the sounds of this catalogue. The point, perhaps, is not to analyze the visual and auditory context of the magic procession but to willingly accept the catalogue as magical, as suggesting a world beyond the routine, the banal, the everyday. We don't know Virgie's fate, her future. But because the mother is dead, Virgie is now free to go and, perhaps, to follow that magical procession.

In *The Golden Apples* Cassie Morrison nearly dominates "June Recital" and then appears briefly in "The Wanderers" when, at age 40 or so, she comes to pay condolences and to report on her limited life. It is not until this latter appearance that we learn her mother's first name is Catherine and not until this latter appearance that we learn Catherine Morrison committed suicide. Mrs. Morrison, mother of two, is an elusive character, known to the reader almost exclusively through her relationship with Cassie and her brother, Loch.

Throughout "June Recital" Loch Morrison is sweating out malaria, and her careful attentions show that of the two children he was Catherine's favorite. They were, the text says, almost allies. When Cassie goes through her phase of playing the ukulele, Loch wants to imitate and does so by beating a pencil on his christening cup and asking: "Mama, do you think I can ever play music too?" (*CS* 315). Indeed he will, she promises, because "You're *my* child" (*CS* 315). For all the apparent closeness, there is a distance between this mother and her children, often seen in Catherine's avoiding physical contact. On one visit to Loch's sickroom, they talk briefly; and when Catherine goes off to take her nap, she merely pats his hair, the text says, "instead of kissing him" (*CS* 275). And on the day when the present action of "June Recital" occurs, Catherine Morrison goes to the Rook party at Miss Nell Carlisle's. First she stops by Cassie's room (locked because Cassie is tie-dying scarves) but does not want to confront her daughter. She goes out, leaving behind her the scent of rose geranium.

At this same moment in the story, Cassie Morrison (age 16) is preoccupied with her tie-dying enterprise and doesn't care whether her hair is curled for the hayride that night or not. It is that hayride from which she happily returns untouched. These facts suggest a teenager to whom courtship and sexual interest are unclear or undesired. However, Cassie's internal world is altogether different and probably a world her mother doesn't suspect, a world that includes passion and terror. Cassie associates terror with the MacLain house, calling it "dark and free," saying that "a restless current" flowed through it, thinking uneasily that within its walls a life exists that is "quicker than the Morrisons' life, more driven probably" (*CS* 286). Catherine Morrison simply refers to the MacLain house as "the vacant house" (*CS* 280).

Cassie occupies herself with the scarves, but her inner world is sharply affected as two forces present themselves. For the third time in the present time of "June Recital," the opening notes of *Für Elise* make their way from the MacLain house to Cassie's ears. At the same time, a Yeats poem comes into her mind for the second time, now not just with one line, as on the first occasion, but with three lines ending with the provocative, "*I will find out where she has gone. . .*" (*CS* 287).

The reader sees Cassie as she is, standing in her bedroom: "small, solemn, unprotected" (*CS* 287), and in her petticoat. Characteristically, she tried hard to keep the petticoat perfectly clean, but dye spots every color of the rainbow mar the whiteness. Thanks to Louella, the Morrisons' cook, her pale hair is covered and burdened with paper twists. Louella hoped to make her pretty for the hayride, but the twists at this stage simply look as if she wears a too-big hat. The text now adds three more adjectives: Cassie is "pathetic—homeless-looking—horrible" (CS 287), surely an ugly duckling. But the mysterious sound of the music, Für Elise (always signaling the presence or memory of Virgie Rainey), and the Yeats lines (described now as "pellucid") reveal another person altogether. With the Yeats lines "in her head," Cassie, the text says, senses the poetry "lifting from side to side. . . . until the wave moved up, towered, and came drowning down over her stuck-up head" (CS 287).

This brief sexual hint is followed immediately in Cassie's mind by a far more explicit episode in her memory—Mr. Voight flapping his old bathrobe to expose himself to Miss Eckhart's young girl piano pupils. That occasion brought three responses. Miss Eckhart said if any of the girls told, she would beat their hands until they screamed. Cassie goes right home and tells. Her father does not believe her (Mr. Voight represents a large concern and covers seven stages) and says that if Cassie tells this story, he will stop her picture-show money. Catherine Morrison simply laughs—a laugh that is "soft and playful"—and issues neither a threat nor comfort. Instead, she gives advice: "Live and let live, Cassie"; and she provides words since there were no "ready words" to describe what Cassie had reported. Just call it, Mrs. Morrison explains, "spontaneous combustion" (CS 295). This curious euphemism links fire and destruction, but Mr. Voight appears incapable of committing an act of violence. His sexual pursuits are the crude gestures of an exhibitionist. As far as we know, he has made no tactile sexual advances. Rather than ravage or destroy, he probably can do little more than self-destruct—"spontaneous combustion."

At least one other moment in the story juxtaposes Cassie's responses to music and her sexual awakening, or at least her sexual awareness. On that sudden stormy day when Miss Eckhart plays the piano so powerfully, Cassie is one of three pupils to listen. As she listens, her memory flits to that 9:00 P.M. scene when, out walking alone, Miss Eckhart passed the school hedge, and "the crazy nigger" jumped out and dragged her down.

Even though Catherine and Cassie Morrison are not confidants—especially about matters pertaining to sex—there is a constant effort on Cassie's part for close proximity. In "June Recital" we are told that at those political speakings that most of Morgana attended in the Starks' backyard, "Cassie would try to stay in sight of her mother" (CS 298).[2] However, Cassie cannot resist following Virgie Rainey off—down the hill or away for a cone from Mrs. Ice Cream Rainey. And when Cassie "got back to their place her mother would be gone," always claiming that she had simply "been through yonder to speak to my candidate." Then Catherine gently turns the tables: "It's you that vanishes, Lady Bug, you that gets away" (CS 298).

Part of the agony of Cassie's life is her mother's failure to appear when she should, especially at June recital time. Catherine Morrison would always delay getting Cassie's dress made; and on the recital night she arrived so late that Cassie never knew if she were really going to appear or not. Of course, Catherine gets there "dressed beautifully in a becoming flowery dress just right for a mother on recital night" (CS 312). But she is unable to "walk across two [front] yards on time to save her life" (CS 312). At the end of the recital, "she creased the program into a little hat," a gesture apparently charming to Cassie who, the text says, "could have fallen at her feet" (CS 313).

Finally, there is a significant moment toward the end of the story when, in time present, Cassie watches Miss Eckhart being led out of the smoking MacLain house. In her anxiety, Cassie runs from the house crying, "You can't take her! Miss Eckhart!" (CS 324). Loch comes from around the house and then Cassie cries softly, "Oh, Mother!" At this line, the brother and sister look at each other; and then Loch says, "Crazy," and Cassie says back, "Crazy yourself" (CS 324). Cassie's "Oh, Mother!" is in fact not crazy, but it is urgent. She could be calling her real mother, who is at Miss Nell's and out of earshot—calling her softly to come and perhaps to intervene. Cassie also identifies briefly with Miss Eckhart, both dutiful daughters.

The procession from the Rook party now comes near, Miss Billy Texas Spights loudly identifies the scurrying lovers, and again Cassie calls out: "Mother!" There is not yet an answer. The brother and sister scuffle, this time over the metronome Loch is hiding in his shirt. In exasperation, since Loch won't even beat away the mosquitoes, Cassie calls a third time: "Mother!" And now the lovely answer finally comes—"Well, here I am" (CS 326)—and the children are led into the house, the sidewalk drama put behind.

The last time the reader sees Catherine Morrison alive, she visits Loch in his room to say good night. She recites every detail of Miss Nell's refreshment table and then she sighs. Loch asks abruptly, "Were you hungry, Mama?" (CS 328). The narrative voice observes it is always at this hour—just at dark—that Mrs. Morrison uses this particular voice. She is not talking to anybody, not even to the evening itself—just to the blank wall, sensing, perhaps, her secret and silent self. Now, leaving the room, she does kiss her son, kisses him hard and bends over him seriously. And then she sways out of the room. We sway, I suppose, for many reasons.

Then one day—we do not know how much later—this charming woman "went out of the room one morning and killed herself" (CS 449). And as the years pass, Cassie increasingly becomes the dutiful daughter, tending with great care the 232 bulbs that, every spring, spell out CATHERINE in the yard of the Morrison's house. As Virgie prepares to leave Morgana and a distant life, Cassie is busy reporting that she had that morning before it rained "divided all the bulbs again" (*CS* 456) and that the flower shrine ought to be prettier than ever in another year. She will go on and on through the years, tending the flowers, dividing those bulbs.

Louise Westling has provided one of the best feminist readings of Welty, centering her study on *Delta Wedding, The Golden Apples,* and *The Optimist's Daughter.* One concern in her book, *Sacred Groves and Ravaged Gardens: The Fiction of Eudora Welty, Carson McCullers, and Flannery O'Connor,* is "an attitude toward the mother" (4). Westling explores "the situation of daughters seeking independent lives distinct from the example set by their mothers"—a literal gesture Westling sees in Welty's own example as she left home and the South to complete her education. Of Welty, McCullers, and O'Connor, Westling argues that they themselves "did not want to become what their mothers were, and by going away to the North for advanced education, they had already distinguished themselves as different" (54–55). Indeed, *One Writer's Beginning* documents the quiet trauma that must characterize much of the relationship between Eudora Welty and her own mother. In 1931, Welty returned to Jackson from New York, her return prompted by her father's early death and by the insecure financial conditions everywhere. But the return was decisive and meant that in the years that followed when her mother fell ill, Welty was the dutiful daughter at home.

When Mrs. Welty died in 1966, Eudora Welty apparently never gave a thought to leaving home. The mother's death does reposition the daughter's role. Her life is now her own, her role is no longer defined as that of the dutiful daughter who carries out the daily routine of her mother's house. A daughter's dutiful role with the mother is inevitable; the relationship assumes it, and the reality of defying the mother, as Ostriker suggests daughters must, is not always so obvious. Virgie and Laurel do physically remove themselves from the houses and towns of their mothers. Cassie is incapable of doing so and apparently cannot—like her brother—go off to New York. Cassie's preoccupation with the flower memorial on the lawn shows her as a middle-aged woman who finds her identity in the mother who died long ago.

Cassie's inability to defy the mother by leaving indicates that her woman's life is thwarted and stunted. To defy the mother is a necessary step for the dutiful daughter, if she is to be fully her *self.* Yet that act of defiance may not require the daughter literally to leave. Welty did not leave, and her publications flourished after 1966, perhaps because her time was more nearly her own.

There is in all this, I realize, the mothers' stories to tell; and there would be richness there. But the dutiful daughter story is one that sounds familiar to many women (real and fictional) who have willingly identified with their mothers but finally are driven to some stage of rejecting. In commenting in a taped interview on her poem, "My Father's Death," May Sarton says, "I think you only become yourself when both your parents are dead. It's a terrible thing to say, but it's true." That terrible thing may be especially true for daughters.

MARILYN

A R N O L D

THE STRATEGY
OF EDNA EARLE PONDER

Various commentators have remarked on the narrative role of Edna Earle Ponder in Eudora Welty's *The Ponder Heart*. Having cornered a stranger at the Beulah Hotel in Clay, Mississippi, someone stranded there because of car trouble, Edna Earle proceeds to tell her captive audience of Daniel Ponder's trial marriage with Bonnie Dee Peacock and his courtroom trial for her murder. Ruth Vande Kieft, who calls *The Ponder Heart* "a light-hearted 'murder-mystery' " (*Eudora Welty* [1962] 70), later suggests that ideally the reader enters the dramatization as Edna Earle's audience, her guest at the hotel ("The Question of Meaning" 30). Brenda G. Cornell, like reviewer Coleman Rosenberger, also assumes the reader's identification with the stranger, indicating that an important "narrator-reader intimacy" is established as the reader becomes a confidant of Edna Earle (210). Kurt Opitz is less than impressed with what he calls the novel's "artificial narrator" (88). In his view, Edna Earle displays a "loquaciousness [that] strikes us as hollow." Instead of developing scene or defining plot, her talk serves merely to "introduce the author's *ego*" by being calculatedly witty (87).

Critical assessments of Edna Earle Ponder, in acknowledging her function as an apologist for Daniel Ponder, her childlike uncle, say nothing of her role as a cunning strategist. Edna Earle and Daniel, who is a few years her chronological senior but many years her mental junior, constitute the last spunky remnants of a family in decline. In some sense, yes, the reader is drawn into unusually active participation in the story in response to Edna Earle's intimately chatty revelations to "you," her listener. In my view, however, the narrative ear is a character in her own right; her identity and Edna Earle's moderately subversive purposes in telling her about Daniel are important to our understanding of the novel. Furthermore, Edna Earle *is* intelligent, at least by Clay standards. We should not dismiss her matter-of-fact boast that she has always been hopelessly bright, having passed Daniel in the seventh grade though she hated to do it. She shamelessly confesses, "It's always taken a lot out of me, being smart" (10). Although her view of herself is not universally shared—*Harper's* reviewer Gilbert Highet, for example, regards the book as a satire on women of the Edna Earle type, "a tale told by an idiot"—it can be argued that Edna Earle is clever enough to entertain a hidden agenda as well as a shy young guest.

Surprisingly, at least two reviewers assume the guest to be a traveling salesman (Pritchett and the anonymous author of "The Human Comedy"). Their views notwithstanding, she is most certainly young and female, and probably shy and naive as well. In a manner appropriate only for addressing a younger woman, Edna Earle warns her guest in the novel's first paragraph that when Daniel "sees you sitting in the lobby of the Beulah, he'll take the other end of the sofa and then move closer up to see what you've got to say for yourself; and then he's liable to give you a little hug and start trying to give you something. Don't do you any good to be bashful" (7). Later, she says, "He's smart in a way that you aren't, child." Every indicator in the novel points to a listener whose gender, youth, innocence, and social status could make her a likely candidate—in Edna Earle's mind—to be Daniel's next bride.

Throughout the novel the adroit Edna Earle travels the course of her story selecting details meant to charm and impress a young woman, and at the same time she sets forth the expectations that would govern a liaison between her guest and Daniel. Edna Earle can be both strategically cryptic and frankly blunt: "I size people up," she warns. "I'm sizing you up right now" (11). And she is. Apparently, Edna Earle is at least preliminarily satisfied with what she sees—a young woman of an acceptable social class who is independent enough to be journeying on her own, yet reticent enough to allow Daniel full rein. Edna Earle indicates that she and her grandfather selected his first wife, Miss Teacake Magee, but "it was bad luck. The marriage didn't hold out" (27). Daniel himself picked his second wife, with uncanny appropriateness but without premeditation or consultation, in the ten cent store; and that marriage ended in comic disaster. The marriage also killed Grandpa Ponder, who could not handle the shock of his son's marrying a low-class Peacock. Even if he had survived the marriage, he would probably have died at the upshot of it. First, Bonnie Dee up and left Daniel, then returned and threw him out, then died of heart failure from being tickled during a thunderstorm. She was clearly inferior stock.

If Edna Earle has her way, any future brides will be first sized up, then courted, then forewarned and foreordained by Daniel's niece and protector.

It is obvious throughout the novel that Edna Earle's first concern is Daniel's happiness, for Daniel "loved happiness like I love tea" (14). He can give away the family fortune or marry white trash for all she cares, so long as he is happy. When Bonnie Dee leaves him forlorn and heartbroken, it is Edna Earle who places an ad—in verse, mind you—in the Memphis paper to tempt her back. Edna Earle will even endure the Peacocks if she can count on Daniel's happiness. And now, in an effort to secure that happiness, she informs her guest through an ingenious circumlocution that it is time for Daniel to fall in love again, at least it is if he holds true to his established pattern: "He went from giving away to falling in love, and from falling in love to talking, and from talking to losing what he had, and from losing what he had to being run off, and from being run off straight back to giving away again" (148–49). Logically, his next step is to fall in love again.

In Edna Earle's view, the current status quo is unacceptable. The trial is over, Daniel has moved back to the Beulah, and not a soul has entered the hotel for three days. Daniel, whose greatest pleasures are talking and giving away anything that can be owned, has no one to talk to and nothing left to give away. Small wonder he is not himself just now. When he turned his trial into a circus by waltzing through the courtroom pitching money in every direction, he won his acquittal but lost his audience. As Edna Earle explains, "You see, that money has come between the Ponders and everybody else in town. There it is, still on their hands. . . . Here Clay sits and don't know what to do with it" (155). The whole disappointing town is avoiding Daniel, and that is the one condition intolerable to him. "He comes down a little later every night" (155), Edna Earle sighs. She can put him up at the hotel and she can prepare his supper, "But he don't enjoy it any more. Empty house, empty hotel, might as well be an empty town. He don't know what's become of everybody" (154). At the very least, Edna Earle sees the newcomer as an audience for Daniel, and that alone should lift him out of the doldrums. On the other hand, with the right kind of encouragement this particular hotel guest might turn into a permanent audience for Daniel—a wife.

Daniel can always rely on Edna Earle and her unflagging loyalty; but she knows her devotion is not enough, and his dejection worries her. Slim as the pickings are in the way of brides in this town, a young, unattached stranger is practically heaven-sent. Edna Earle must be careful, however. Not only must she market Uncle Daniel's charms, but she must also prepare the young woman for a demanding new role and test her capacity to fill the expectations of that role. There is more at stake here than Edna Earle's penchant for talk, more than her finding someone with whom to pass the time of day. There is, in fact, a sense of urgency in her chatter. Uncle Daniel is losing ground and may soon require "a good course of calomel-and-quinine" (155). When the young guest attempts to escape with a book, Edna Earle intercepts and insists on telling her story. "And listen; if you read, you'll put your eyes out. Let's just talk" (11), meaning, don't read; listen to me. Daniel will be coming down to supper soon; and Edna Earle, his self-appointed guardian and general family caretaker, must lay the groundwork for a possibly auspicious meeting. Everything in her story is a preparation for Daniel's entrance, and it is no accident that the subject of her discourse is brides and marriage. In a dozen subtle and not so subtle ways, Edna Earle flatteringly gathers her young visitor into her confidence. Her opening sentence, for example, is broadly familiar and assuring: "My Uncle Daniel's just like your uncle." His only weakness, she confesses, is that "he loves society and he gets carried away" (7).

After extending a prefatory caution that Daniel might proffer a hug and a gift or two, Edna Earle launches into her campaign. Borrowing method from John Alden, she exclaims over Daniel's sweet disposition, his large-size hat (implying that he is blessed with a goodly share of the legendary Ponder brains in spite of his childlike nature), his generosity, his popularity, and his father's money. Then she shifts to a physical description of Daniel, painting a romantic portrait for one she deems to be an impressionable and not overly discriminating young woman. Edna Earle is especially careful to stress Daniel's youthfulness in spite of his fifty-plus years ("Don't believe it if you don't want to" [11]), and she takes every opportunity to mention that Bonnie Dee was only seventeen when Daniel married her and still looked only seventeen in her coffin. Age difference, Edna Earle implies, is inconsequential with Uncle Daniel. What's more, he has stature in a crowd, and style: "He's unmistakable. He's big and well known." His "short white hair" is "thick and curly, growing down his forehead round like a little bib." As a bonus, "He has Grandma's complexion. And big, forget-me-not blue eyes like mine, and puts on a sweet red bow tie every morning," and a "large-size Stetson" that he has always "just swept . . . off to somebody." Daniel "dresses fit to kill . . . in a snow-white suit"; but more important, he is "the sweetest, most unspoiled thing in the world. He has the nicest, politest manners—he's good as gold." No one can "hold a candle to Uncle Daniel for looks or manners" (11).

Edna Earle strengthens her case by emphasizing the prominence, wealth, and superior social standing of the Ponders and by suggesting that Daniel's marital failures can be traced to his marrying beneath him, even though the practice is common. The young bridal candidate apparently passes muster on this point because Edna Earle addresses her as one of "us" and refers frequently to the inferior Baptists and Peacocks. The ingenuous

Daniel is too naive to be discriminating and therefore must be protected from himself. He "didn't mind old dirty people the way you and I do" (91), she confides. Moreover, he finds nearly all young women fascinating, from Intrepid Elsie Fleming and her motorcycle to the burlesque dancers at the fair. In spite of his sweetness, "he's a man, same as they all are" (16), she admits.

Impressing her guest with the Ponders in general and Daniel in particular is only one part of Edna Earle's design, however. Assuming that the young woman is interested, and knowing how quickly Daniel acts if the inclination strikes him, it is possible Edna Earle sees this as her sole opportunity to influence the course of Daniel's next marriage. She must accomplish a great deal in this conversation. Since Edna Earle is the only person living or dead who understands Daniel and knows how to handle him, it is her example any future bride must follow. Even Daniel's father, Edna Earle's grandpa, though he "worshiped Uncle Daniel" (12), did not know that an attempt to teach Daniel a lesson by sending him to an asylum would end in calamity. Daniel quite innocently turned the tables on Grandpa and came home, leaving Grandpa in custody instead of himself. Furthermore, Edna Earle assures her listener, "they couldn't find anything the matter with [Daniel]" (15).

From the time he was very small, Daniel had lived virtually without restraint. "They had him late—mighty late," she says. "They used to let him skate on the dining room table" (9). And this is no time, as Grandpa discovered, to try a different mode of operation. "He's as good as gold," Edna Earle cautions, "but you have to know the way to treat him" (16). Her narrative becomes in part a lesson on how to treat Daniel: that is, how to protect him and let him do whatever makes him happy, even if it means perjuring oneself in court for his sake and letting him indiscriminately dispense the family fortune to the Peacocks and half the town of Clay. "It *was*," after all, "cheering him up" (148), she says. Edna Earle virtuously reminds her listener that if anyone had a stake in shutting off Daniel's spontaneous philanthropy, she did: "Now I'll tell you something: anything Daniel has left after some future day is supposed to be mine. I'm the inheritor. I'm the last one, isn't that a scream? The last Ponder. But with one fling of the hand I showed the mayor *my* stand: I'd never stop Uncle Daniel for the world." Sensing some disapprobation in her guest, Edna Earle exclaims parenthetically, "(And I don't give a whoop for your approval!)" (146). She instantly remembers herself, however, and seeks the young woman's sympathy for her benevolent perjury and her efforts to keep Daniel from revealing how Bonnie Dee really died. "(You don't think I betrayed him by not letting him betray himself, do you?)" (148), she asks. Whatever Edna Earle does, she convinces herself that her motive is Uncle Daniel's happiness. Her last instruction to her guest before calling to supper is in fact a plea to humor him should he try to give her something: "Make out like you accept it. Tell him thank you" (156).

Essentially, Edna Earle's advice to her guest, to anyone who might marry Daniel, is to please him at all costs, to allow him to do whatever he likes, to accept his loving nature, and to forget about changing him. A very large order. She even drops hints about things he likes, such as divinity candy. Again, Edna Earle suggests that her own example is the one to follow: "I don't even try, myself, to make people happy the way they should be: they're so stubborn. I just try to give them what they think they want" (57). She does, that is, if "they" happen to be Daniel.

Perhaps the most important skill to be acquired by Edna Earle's apprentice is the art of listening. It is probably Welty's little joke that the one who preaches listening does nothing but talk, but anyone who marries Daniel has to know that he loves an audience. Moreover, Edna Earle's lengthy monologue makes it quite clear that love of an audience is a Ponder trait that afflicts niece as well as uncle. The irony is that Edna Earle sees the trait in Daniel but not in herself. Welty, however, knows that Ponder heaven is a new face with ready ears. Edna Earle may be summing up the measure of her own happiness as well as Daniel's when she says, "if he wasn't in the thick of things, and couldn't tell you about them when they did happen, I think he'd just pine and languish" (67). It would be humanly impossible for Daniel to remain silent at his own trial with an eager audience already assembled. And with him, talking and giving are two manifestations of the same impulse; they function alternately, not simultaneously. As chance would have it, just as he is about to tell the court how Bonnie Dee died from his tickling her (to distract her from her fright at the storm), he remembers the greenbacks stuffed in his pockets, money he had earlier withdrawn from the bank. He abruptly stops talking and begins to hand it out. In the bedlam that follows, the court never learns the precipitative cause of Bonnie Dee's death, though Edna Earle wants the prospective bride to know that Bonnie Dee was killed by love, not hate.

Edna Earle's lesson is this: if you want to keep Daniel from giving, let him talk. And listen without interrupting him. Grandpa, who did not handle Daniel wisely, was "the poorest listener in the world" (17). The "perfect listener" is someone like Mr. Ovid Springer, the traveling salesman whose chief entertainments when he comes to town are treating Edna Earle to the movies and listening to Daniel's stories. He came in "seldom enough to forget between times" and knew the Ponders "well enough not to try to interrupt." Moreover, he was "too tired to object to hearing something over" (17–18). In fact, he would beg Daniel to tell his favorite tales. But when Edna Earle realizes that Mr. Springer's ill-conceived efforts to help at the trial would have provided Uncle Daniel with a motive for murder, she questions his judgment and his loyalty. This episode predicts Mr.

Springer's scarcity in Clay and creates additional pressure on Edna Earle to cultivate a new listener.

It appears that Edna Earle is indeed cultivating a new listener, and testing one at the same time. If the young woman can listen attentively to Edna Earle, then she can listen attentively to Uncle Daniel. The guest apparently does set her book aside, interrupting Edna Earle at perhaps only the one point mentioned above, near the end of the narrative. Even a single interruption, it appears, draws a rather curt response. At times, too, Edna Earle pushes beyond impressing, instructing, and testing her young visitor. Her tone is never threatening, but occasionally it warns. A prospective bride must know what is required, must accept the ground rules in the Ponder league. Daniel could make another Peacock marriage, but Edna Earle will do all in her power to lead him into a different kind. Since he is likely to be as happy with one sweet young thing as another, he might as well have one that has been tutored by Edna Earle. The next bride, if there is one, must learn that the lovable but totally irresponsible Daniel requires someone to "mind out for him" (36).

For years, now, that someone has been Edna Earle; and a prospective bride should be apprised that Edna Earle is not likely to disappear regardless of Daniel's marital status. Edna Earle is proprietor of more than the Beulah Hotel, and she does not let her listener forget it. There is a double purpose to her strategy, to find Daniel a bride and to carve out a permanent place for herself in Daniel's life. She reasons, for instance, that "I don't really think Uncle Daniel missed Bonnie Dee as much as he thought he did. He had me" (54). And when "all the other children and grandchildren went away to the ends of the earth or died and left only me and Uncle Daniel— the two favorites," naturally "we couldn't leave each other" (55). Furthermore, the first time Edna Earle reports that Daniel was going to be accused of murder, she says, "they *charged* us" (80). Her emphasis is on the word "charged"; mine would be on the word *us*. Regretting Daniel's isolation from the town since the trial, she says that nevertheless, "*I'm* here, and just the same as I always was and will be, but then he never was afraid of losing me" (154). Lest there be misunderstanding about the matter, Edna Earle indoctrinates her listener to the view that a marriage with one of the two remaining Ponders is a threesome rather than a twosome. Her subject is purportedly her own contemplated marriage with Mr. Springer, but her point is clear: "I'm intended to look after Uncle Daniel and everybody knows it, but in plenty of marriages there's three—three all your life. Because nearly everybody's got somebody" (26). And in the end her intent is confirmed; Daniel and the young woman will not eat dinner alone. "Narciss!" she calls, "Put three on the table!" (155).

The visitor is served notice not only that a Ponder marriage is a package deal but also that a Ponder bride must take up residence in the groom's home a few miles from Clay. It is empty and waiting for Daniel's return, and Daniel is not the sort who can live among strangers unschooled in the ways of the Ponders. To the young woman's credit, she is at least "somebody from nearer home." Indirectly, Edna Earle also warns her guest against venturing too far from friendly faces (such as those she would find in Clay) herself. Walking the thin line between threat and persuasion, Edna Earle clarifies her position:

> The stranger don't have to open his mouth. Uncle Daniel is ready to do all the talking. That's understood. I used to dread he might get hold of one of these occasional travelers that wouldn't come in unless they had to—the kind that would break in on a story with a set of questions, and wind it up with a list of what Uncle Daniel's faults were: some Yankee. (17)

The listener has to see herself in the captious reference to "occasional travelers that wouldn't come in unless they had to," but Edna Earle diverts the insinuation by making a Yankee the suppositional culprit and by concluding with the reassurance that "he'd [Daniel] be crazy about you" (17).

There is just one more point Edna Earle wishes to make, one more strategic purpose for her narrative. She wishes to warn any future Mrs. Daniel Ponder that most of the Ponder money disappeared in the courtroom fiasco and that it would be unwise in any case to marry for whatever may be left. Her narrative suggests that the selfish prospect of social position and financial ease were what persuaded Bonnie Dee to accept Daniel's proposal. Moreover, she left Daniel and was brought back by the promise of "retroactive allowance." It was, in fact, the termination of that allowance that prompted her to summon him on the fateful day of the storm. As was mentioned earlier, too, the townspeople turned from Daniel because he showered money on them, converting their greed into shame. In the end, Edna Earle's warning is explicit: "The worst thing you can give away is money—I learned that if Uncle Daniel didn't. You and them are both done for then, somehow; you can't go on after it, and still be you and them. Don't ever give me a million dollars! It'll come between us" (149).

No doubt Edna Earle, like Eudora Welty, tells her story largely for the pure love of telling. She has experienced a few slow days at the Beulah and welcomes new blood herself. At the same time, there are enough indicators of a more strategic purpose in the back of Edna Earle's mind to suggest that she is already sizing up a possible candidate to be the next bride of Daniel Ponder, a candidate whom she both instructs and tests, both woos and warns.

Welty herself may also have minor strategic purposes she only hints at. Though her tone is light and her wit ready, an edge of ache encircles her tale. Less obvious than Sister's ache in "Why I Live at the P.O.," Edna

Earle's is defined by her loneliness, especially in her new relation to the town since the trial. Moreover, her relationship with Ovid Springer has been permanently altered, if not terminated, by his thoughtless betrayal. Edna Earle's narrative, like that of her counterpart in "Why I Live at the P.O.," reveals more about herself than about Daniel or anyone else. It may be, too, that Welty has purposefully obscured the identity of Edna Earle's guest—so much so that more than a few readers have assumed the guest to be male—because some part of Edna Earle wants the guest to be male, yearns for a new love interest to replace Mr. Springer. In a manner reminiscent of John Alden, she wishes she were doing the courting for herself. Nevertheless, she will seize whatever opportunity presents itself and make the best of it, in this instance, a potential bride for Daniel. Edna Earle, like Carson McCullers's Frankie, may not be the bride, but she is determined to be a member of the wedding.

PETER

S C H M I D T

Sibyls in Eudora Welty's Stories

> she carries a book but it is not
> the tome of ancient wisdom,
>
> the pages, I imagine, are the blank pages
> of the unwritten volume of the new;
>
> all you say, is implicit,
> all that and much more;
>
> but she is not shut up in a cave
> like a Sibyl . . .
> . . . .
> she is Psyche, the butterfly,
> out of the cocoon.
>
> H. D.

References to sibyls figure crucially in at least three of Welty's most import-ant stories, "Powerhouse," "Music from Spain," and "The Wanderers," though they may also be found in other stories, including "Petrified Man," "Clytie," "Moon Lake," "The Burning," and "Circe." They are also often twinned with references to Medusa. Here are the three most important passages:

> Then all quietly he [Powerhouse] lays his finger on a key with the promise and serenity of a sibyl touching the book.
> . . . He gets to his feet, turning vaguely, wearing the towel on his head.
> "Ha, ha!"
> "Sheik, sheik!"
> . . . He still looks like an East Indian queen, implacable, divine, and full of snakes. . . .
> "Come on!" roars Powerhouse. He is already at the back door, he has pulled it wide open, and with a wild, gathered-up face is smelling the terrible night. (CS 131, 135)

. . . .

Eugene felt untoward visions churning, the Spaniard with his great knees bent and his black slippers turning as if on a wheel's rim, dancing in a red smoky place with a lead-heavy alligator. The Spaniard turning his back, with his voluminous coat-tails sailing, and his feet off the ground, floating bird-like up into the pinpoint distance. The Spaniard with his finger on the page of a book, looking over his shoulder, as did the framed Sibyl on the wall in his father's study—no! then, it was old Miss Eckhart's "studio" . . . (*CS* 408)

. . . .

Miss Eckhart had had among the pictures from Europe on her walls a certain threatening one. It hung over the dictionary, dark as that book. It showed Perseus with the head of the Medusa. "The same thing as Siegfried and the Dragon," Miss Eckhart had occasionally said, as if explaining second-best. Around the picture—which sometimes blindly reflected the window by its darkness—was a frame enameled with flowers, which was always self-evident—Miss Eckhart's pride. In that moment Virgie had shorn it of its frame.

The vaunting was what she remembered, that lifted arm.

Cutting off the Medusa's head was the heroic act, perhaps, that made visible a horror in life, that was at once the horror in love, Virgie thought—the separateness.

Miss Eckhart, whom Virgie had not, after all, hated—had come near to loving, for she had taken Miss Eckhart's hate, and then her love, extracted them, the thorn and then the overflow—had hung the picture on the wall for herself. She had absorbed the hero and the victim and then, stoutly, could sit down to the piano with all Beethoven ahead of her. (*CS* 459–60)

The three quotations are points of descriptive excess or rupture in Welty's tales, points where the violence and strangeness of the tropes contrast strikingly with the language used before and after these passages. A black male musician is suddenly turned into a woman, his piano called a book, a towel a headdress. The pictures on the walls of Miss Eckhart's study are obviously invaluable evidence for how she sees herself, yet they are described not in the story we would expect, "June Recital," in which the music teacher Miss Eckhart is a central character, but in two other stories in Welty's 1949 volume *The Golden Apples*, "Music from Spain" and "The Wanderers," in which she is a peripheral presence haunting the action. Moreover, the pictures are described in a thoroughly contradictory way, as if Welty changed her conception of the pictures' meanings as she wrote *The Golden Apples*. We have no way of being sure how many pictures are being described, nor can we be sure we understand the link Welty is drawing between a picture of a sibyl that Eugene MacLain remembers in "Music from Spain" and a picture of Perseus slaying Medusa that Virgie Rainey recalls in "The Wanderers," the climactic story in *The Golden Apples*. Something is obviously going on here, but the symbolic meanings that sibyls have seem so volatile, so explosive, that Welty's narratives seem to approach them indirectly, with great caution, and then reveal them only briefly before covering them up again.

The sibyl references in these texts are thus truly sibylline: they are hidden rather than highlighted, cryptic rather than lucid. They do not merely ask for interpretation, or highlight moments in these stories when we see how characters' interpretations of the events are influenced by racial, gender, and class perspectives—though they do both these things and do them superbly. They also seem to ask us as readers to question the very grounds upon which any interpretation of Welty's text—including ours—will be offered. When thought through, the sibylline references in Welty's stories provide new keys to interpreting these narratives and allow us to link her with earlier women writers, European and American, who used sibylline prophecy as a complex metaphor for their own art and its relation to their culture.

What follows is a four-part meditation on the role references to sibyls play in Welty's stories. It begins with a reading of "Powerhouse," then considers the function of allusions to Medusa, the sibyl's dark alter ego, in "Petrified Man." Welty's references to sibyls in *The Golden Apples* are then briefly placed within the context of earlier art and literature, from Italian Renaissance painting to nineteenth- and early twentieth-century writing by women.

"Powerhouse" demonstrates that sibyls are important to Welty in at least three ways. The first contrasts the authority of oral language with that of written texts and suggests that a sibyl's prophetic power is subversive precisely to the degree that it undermines the authority traditionally given to writing over speech. Second, the sibyl is repeatedly linked with the Medusa figure, demonstrating that for Welty prophecy also carries a frightening price: women such as Miss Eckhart are inevitably seen as Gorgons— as monsters—by their society and even by themselves. Third, all references to sibyls give us a glimpse of a potential transfer of power from the sibyl to another person. Feminist criticism has given us a name for such a moment, calling it a *scene of instruction* (Gilbert and Gubar 93–104; Homans).

For the black musicians in "Powerhouse," the written word and the written musical sign are associated with the power of white culture: white music is written down, black music improvised without a score.[1] In "Powerhouse," each time a text is mentioned, it is a threatening text. Powerhouse's white audience always hands him written requests for songs, for example, making it clear that this act is symbolic of the power that his white audience feels it can exercise over him as its entertainer:

Powerhouse has as much as possible done by signals. Everybody, laughing as if to hide a weakness, will sooner or later hand him up a written request. Powerhouse reads each one, studying with a secret face: that is the face which looks like a mask—anybody's; there is a moment when he makes a decision. Then a light slides under his eyelids, and he says, "92!" or some combination of figures—never a name. (*CS* 132)

Note here how Powerhouse counters written requests with his own oral language, a system of signals and code words. Significantly, this system has the crucial function of disguising whether or not he has actually followed all of his audience's requests. Such a "mask" is important for maintaining a degree of freedom and dignity as an artist: he may very well have played what *he* wanted to play, not solely what the audience wanted.

The other piece of writing in the story, the telegram, of course threatens Powerhouse much more directly. But it too is transformed and partially evaded, as Powerhouse improvises different versions of what happened and, in the end, hints that the telegram may not exist: " 'No babe, it ain't the truth.' His eyebrows fly up . . . 'Truth is something worse, I ain't said what, yet. It's something hasn't come to me, but I ain't saying it won't' " (*CS* 139). The fact that the telegram may have been written by a black man (either Uranus or Powerhouse) does not diminish its link to white culture, for although all musicians have to confront fear, guilt, and loneliness on the road, racial segregation in the North and South in Powerhouse's time made the black musicians' plight more frustrating. The telegram symbolizes that truth. Powerhouse's improvising his blues choruses around the telegram's brutal four words, "your wife is dead," consequently stands as his protest against it. It is surely not a coincidence, moreover, that Powerhouse chooses the waltz number to begin that protest. He takes a form associated with his white audience ("Pagan Love Song," the only waltz he will ever "consent to play" [*CS* 133]) and then turns it into a *blues* number, overlaying 4:4 on 3:4 time and translating the original lyrics into a series of blues choruses. In the process, he forces his unexpecting white audience by the end of the story to see the pain as well as the power of his art. They are no longer able to see him as an exotic performing "monkey" (*CS* 131), the way they viewed him at the start.

If black men such as Powerhouse may revise the roles that white society writes for them, so may women. But with the exception of Ruby Fisher and Phoenix Jackson, the women in Welty's first volume of stories, *A Curtain of Green* (1941), do not really find a way to alter the cultural scripts that were given to them. The price that they pay is to become secret Medusa figures, full of rage that cannot express itself. The Medusa head that rears upward briefly in the midst of "Powerhouse" near the end of *A Curtain of Green* is the last in a series of portraits of grief-distorted, wild, and threatening women's faces in that volume. Significantly, these portraits are also associated with frustrated oral energy, the repressed voice of their inner feelings clamoring to get out. Mrs. Larkin's obsessive interior monologue in "A Curtain of Green" is complemented by Addie's shouting down her roommate's polite conversation in "A Visit of Charity," Mrs. Bird's screaming and Mrs. Marblehall's possessing "a voice that dizzies other ladies" in "Old Mr. Marblehall" (*CS* 95, 92), and Clytie's cursing in "Clytie." The end result of such a frustrated release of energy is silence: the face that greets Clytie in the water just before she drowns herself has a mouth "old and closed from any speech" (*CS* 90). With Powerhouse, however, Welty images a Medusa figure whose speech not only controls its audience but also carefully evades or rewrites the cultural texts she is "requested" to perform. In "Powerhouse" an image of emptiness and imprisonment that has tormented many of Welty's characters—the abandoned house that Lily Daw lives in, the "madhouses" of Addie, Sister, and Clytie—becomes a *power*house. Powerhouse not only shows his audience his Medusa-like grimace, emblem of the price his psyche pays for their treating him as a monster, but he presents himself as a sibyl, an interpreter and controller of texts. (In the passage quoted above Welty says "the" book, not "a" book, making the sibyl's power more inclusive.) Such a vision lasts only briefly. But Welty's image of Powerhouse as a sibyl altering his or her culture's texts is the single most powerful instance in *A Curtain of Green* of what she expects a heroine (and an artist) to be.

This vision of a sibyl's power is explored more fully in Welty's next three volumes of stories, *The Golden Apples* in particular. Before considering Welty's later references to sibyls and their proper context, though, it is worth making a brief detour to consider the sibyl's dark, twin image, the Medusa, and the story "Petrified Man," in which it is given its most provocative treatment. If a sibyl is associated for Welty with the power of rewriting cultural texts, the Medusa is the dark, reverse image of that power—its negative, so to speak, representing entrapment, anger, despair, and self-destruction.

Welty's critics have greatly praised "Petrified Man," but the readings they have given it seem somewhat odd, for they are unanimous in blaming the women in the story for the perversions of sexuality that it depicts. It is rather as if the story's Medusan gaze is so disturbing that its commentators—both male and female—have rushed to cast themselves in Perseus's role and wield righteous swords against the story's villains, arguing that the women have perverted "natural" sexuality, stripping men of their masculinity and, like modern Medusas, causing all they gaze at to turn to stone. Astonishingly, however, no commentator has fully confronted what it means to have a rapist be the central male character in the story or explored the connections that the story draws between representations of women in advertising and violence toward women in society.[2] The women may be Gorgons to their men, but the true Gorgon in the story is the world of mass culture, a Medusan world whose uncanny power consists in its ability to make women see themselves only through an essentially male point of view, both idealizing them and treating them as objects of rage and violence. Welty plays a better Perseus than her critics, for she knows how to spot the real villain and decode its dangerous gaze—and all this in 1941, years before the recent developments in feminist criticism that it anticipates. No doubt Welty's brief experience working in advertising in New York City in 1930–31 after graduation from the University of Wisconsin provided her with an inside view of how the mechanism of mass culture may work.[3]

"Petrified Man" is told entirely through two conversations that take place between Mrs. Fletcher and Leota while Mrs. Fletcher is getting her hair done on March 9 and again on March 16, 1941, in Leota's beauty parlor. The subplot of "Petrified Man" is concerned with lurid crimes and traveling freak-show exhibitions, whereas the main plot depicts the commonplace violence against women that occurs in a beauty parlor. In the subplot, a rapist joins a freak show and disguises himself as Mr. Petrie, the Petrified Man, realizing that a man whose body supposedly turns everything he eats into stone will be the perfect cover for his brutal appetites as a rapist. In the main plot, Mrs. Fletcher seeks to disguise the fact of her pregnancy—the fact that her body will change its shape and use its food to nourish another life—with a petrified disguise of her own, a "permanent" hair-do and "fixed" smile that conform to her conception of Beauty's eternal forms. A newcomer to town named Mrs. Pike is the only character in the story who figures in both plots. She first notices that Mrs. Fletcher is pregnant and that Mr. Petrie is the same man as the one pictured, with a $500 reward on his head for rape, in an old copy of *Startling G-Man Tales*.

Welty's story is less concerned with Mr. Petrie's private motives for rape than it is with unmasking the cultural connections between the marketing of ideal images of female beauty and the hidden rage and violence against women that underlie those supposedly pure images. For Leota and Mrs. Fletcher have been conditioned to see what is done to their bodies in the beauty parlor not as acts of violence but as acts of love—techniques that affirm their beauty, independence, and importance as women. Such thorough conditioning may be their culture's most disturbing act of violence against women, for unlike the crime of rape, the beauty parlor's ideal is universal and disguised as its opposite, as something indispensable to a woman's self-esteem, and it affects more women than all the rapists in the country.

Leota's beauty parlor is an elegantly appointed torture chamber with the female body as its victim. In order to achieve the physical standards that society sets for beauty, an array of tools and machines in Leota's shop remake nature. References to the technology of the beauty industry are frequent, from the "aluminum wave pinchers" used to make curls to the hair-drying machines that "cook" their occupants (CS 18). The natural shape of one's hair is given a new "body," and called a "permanent"; one's smile is no longer natural but "fixed" (CS 28) by face powder and lipstick. If the parlor's creations are not truly permanent—Welty notes ironically that Mrs. Fletcher speaks of her "last permanent"—nevertheless the body's new shapes aspire to the permanent and ideal standards that the beauty parlor's machinery represents. Even more important, Welty shows that the beauty parlor's standards of beauty are themselves created by a larger machine, the mass marketing apparatus of popular culture. Several times she mentions popular reading materials in the story, which vary from the purportedly high-class "rental library" (where Mrs. Fletcher primly says that she first met her husband) to the "drugstore rental" library supplying the cheap novels and some of the periodicals with names like *Life Is Like That* and *Screen Secrets* that entertain the parlor's customers while their hair is being dried. As the title *Screen Secrets* suggests, the standards of beauty that the parlor sells are created by the motion picture and advertising industries. Those mass cultural images of perfection themselves become molds that may create endless reproductions of their products in the women who are influenced by them. And although pop cultural icons purport to portray healthy images of women as wives and mothers, they in fact teach the women to treat their sexuality as threatening and scandalous—an affront to the image of proper beauty that the beauty parlor mass produces.

Welty first alerts us to this fact when she describes the women at the parlor as "customers" who are being "gratified in [their] booths" (CS 17)— a striking verb that suggests sexual pleasure perversely displaced, not merely onto consumer objects but on further, to the narcissistic contemplation of a constructed image that is sold with those products. When sexual relations do occur in the story, they threaten ideal standards of beauty by causing everything from dandruff to pregnancy. "I couldn't of caught a thing like that [dandruff] from Mr. Fletcher, could I," Mrs. Fletcher whines early in the story (CS 18), and Leota on the same page gingerly abbreviates and spells the word "pregnant" (as if it were something that must never be named aloud) and then asks, "how far gone are you?", implying that Mrs. Fletcher's pregnancy is a kind of dying. The women's belief that both sexuality and pregnancy are grotesque rather than beautiful is shown most clearly in their discussion of the traveling freak show that comes to town. Significantly, it occupies "the vacant store next door to the beauty parlor" (CS 20): businesses selling beauty and ugliness are adjacent, mirror images of each other. Indeed, as the women's conversations show, they need to have a sense of the grotesque in order to enforce a sense of their own normality; but the more they try to separate what is normal from what is monstrous, the more the two threaten to merge. Welty adroitly shows this largely unconscious connection in their minds by having Mrs. Fletcher's and Leota's conversation about the freak show continually stray from discussing the freaks to discussing their own lives. The show is first mentioned almost in the same breath as Mrs. Fletcher's newly revealed pregnancy; it's as if Mrs. Pike has as keen an eye for the spectacle that Mrs. Fletcher makes as she does for the freaks. As Leota says, "Well, honey, talkin' about bein' pregnant an' all, you ought to see those [Siamese] twins in a bottle, you really owe it to yourself" (CS 20). Part of the women's horror and fascination with this display is that it seems not only to be an example of the frightening disorder of nature (creating two babies instead of one) but also of what they take to be the sickening and unnatural union of mother and child:

". . . they had these two heads an' two faces an' four arms an' four legs, all kind of joined *here*. See, this face looked this-a-way, and the other face looked that-a-way, over their shoulder, see. Kinda pathetic."
"Glah!" said Mrs. Fletcher disapprovingly. (CS 21)

If the beauty parlor and the freak show next-door are the arbiters of the beautiful and the ugly, then, the lines that they draw are not nearly so sharp as the architectural lines dividing the two buildings imply. The mirrors on the wall of the beauty parlor (perhaps on the *very wall* that separates the parlor from the freak show) play a crucial role in "Petrified Man": they give us lucid glimpses of the many ways in which society defines beauty and ugliness as mirror opposites. More powerfully than any other piece of equipment in the parlor, the mirror presents a standard of beauty and measures the women against it. When they view themselves in the mirror, they view not only their own image but the ideal image of what they wish to be. The mirror (like a movie screen) holds the spectacle of infinite examples of Beauty itself, yet also cruelly presents an (also infinite) spectacle of monstrous failure: "[Mrs. Fletcher] stared in a discouraged way into the mirror. 'You can tell it when I'm sitting down, all right,' she said" (CS 23).[4] Beauty and the Medusa are twinned images, each the "negative" of the other.

The parlor's mirror does not hold an image, of course, so much as reflect one that is projected upon it. In Mrs. Fletcher's case, Welty shows, she projects that ideal image from her own imagination, which is in turn projected (much like a movie) by the powerful and subtle machinery of popular culture that has invented those beautiful images and then imprinted them in the women's minds. Here lies the subtlety of Welty's diagnosis of how commercial culture may corrupt. The women are dependent upon market images for their sense of beauty and normality, yet they do not realize this; rather, they take those very images as signs of their own independence and power, the irrefutable proof of respectability that they themselves have earned. The most powerful allure of mass culture in Welty's view is not that it sells the comforts of conformity, but that it promotes them as their opposite—as examples of an individual's independence and power. The function of the beauty parlor mirror is to show how this hidden process works. Looking into the mirror as she receives her shampoo and set, Mrs. Fletcher proudly boasts: "Women have to stand up for themselves, or there's just no telling. But now you take me—I ask Mr. Fletcher's advice now and then, and he appreciates it, especially on something important, like is it time for a permanent—not that I've told him about the baby. He says, 'Why, dear, go ahead!' Just ask their *advice*" (*CS* 25).

The beauty parlor is an all-female domain where women can mock men and assert their own power over them; this surely "gratifies" them (*CS* 17) as much as the beauty treatments. But like the beauty treatments, the sense of power that the parlor gives them—power over their husbands, over each other, and over their own bodies—is a dangerous illusion; it is not at all the kind of power it seems. The parlor's images of perfection dictate the terms by which Mrs. Fletcher must define her "independence," and all of those make her dependent upon mass cultural images of perfection that are marketed by men.[5] Welty subtly enforces this irony by having Mrs. Fletcher sitting down in one of the parlor's chairs staring at the mirror even as she speaks about women "standing up for themselves."

If there is a Medusa in "Petrified Man" who turns all who gaze on her to stone, it is the world of commercial culture, not the women who are its victims. And it has done its work not by merely petrifying its victims with a vision of ugliness, but also by hypnotizing them with a vision of false beauty. The presence of a rapist on the other side of the beauty parlor's mirror, moreover, exposes the connection between commercial culture's images of women as beautiful objects and its treatment of them as perverted monsters. The same advertising world that reproduces endless images of idealized women for women to copy also treats women as sex objects for men like Mr. Petrie to possess and desecrate: sexual relations are perverted into either utter passivity (as with Leota's and Mrs. Fletcher's husbands) or violent aggression (as with Mr. Petrie).

Who is Perseus in this retelling of the myth of Medusa? Welty, of course. Like Perseus, she uses her art to allow us to see how the Gorgon's gaze is directed at us without letting us succumb to its power. The story's meticulous commercial details of the parlor's decor and the women's slang may be thought of in traditionally mimetic terms, as a mirror. In Welty's hands, however, this mirror functions differently from the mirror in the beauty parlor or the screen in the movie house: it does not present these images under the guise of the natural but reveals them to be representations, a set of artifices and disguises. In doing so, Welty's story exposes the hidden, demonic *source* of the images that are projected onto its mimetic reflective surface and uncovers how those representations acquire authority until their naive consumers believe that "life is like that." Such an understanding of culture is the true "screen secret" of "Petrified Man," allowing us to decode the sexual politics involved in making some forms of representation become accepted as natural in mass culture, while others are excluded. These revelations are the reward Welty reserves for us if we read even more carefully than Mrs. Pike. But Welty's darkly comic analysis of mimesis as a paralyzing mirror is thoroughly disturbing. Ruth Vande Kieft is most eloquent on this point: "We can say of this story what a critic has said of the comic spirit of Jonathan Swift: it 'frightens us out of laughter into dismay' " (*Eudora Welty* [1962] 75; see also Sypher 235). The irony is that early in Welty's career, at the time of "Petrified Man" (and occasionally later), she was excoriated for her use of grotesquerie and cryptic metaphors, for not being "realistic" enough.[6] Another way to put this is to say that she was accused of being too sibylline. But the power of a story like "Petrified Man" comes precisely from its analysis of popular culture's production and consumption of dangerously naive notions of mimesis.

Sandra Gilbert and Susan Gubar have eloquently argued that the role played by the sibyl in women's fiction is essentially to initiate a feminist scene of instruction. Discussing Mary Shelley's account of a woman's exploration of the caves associated with the Cumaean sibyl in Italy, Gilbert and Gubar note that the narrative may be read as a parable about a

> woman artist who enters the cavern of her own mind and finds there the scattered [Cumaean] leaves not only of her own power but of the tradition which might have generated that power. The body of her precursor's art, and thus the body of her own art, lies in pieces around her, dismembered, dis-remembered, disintegrated. How can she remember it and become a member of it, join it and rejoin it, integrate it and in doing so achieve her own integrity, her own selfhood? Surrounded by the ruins of her own tradition, the leavings and unleavings of her spiritual mother's art, she feels . . . like someone suffering from amnesia. Not only did she fail to recognize—that is, to remember—the cavern itself, she no longer knows its languages, its messages, its form. . . . Bewildered by the incoherence of the fragments she confronts, she cannot help deciding that "I have forgotten everything / I used to know so long ago." (98)

These hidden sibylline powers are traditionally associated not only with the recovery of memory but with oral rather than written authority—song rather than text, inspiration and improvisation rather than imitation. In Domenichino's most famous painting of a sibyl, for example, a new, handwritten scroll is juxtaposed against an ancient printed text.[7] Translated, the scroll in the picture reads, "The Only and Almighty God His Great Unbornness [or, "Unborn Greatness"]." The sibyl appears to have just been inspired by these words before writing them down on a scroll. Although they have been received later than the printed scripture on which they rest, as a kind of supplement, the sibyl's words in fact overthrow, or at least challenge, the authority of the earlier text. Written in intentionally ambiguous syntax to reproduce the moment of *furor divinus* or divine inspiration, such a sibylline text overturns the traditional Western investing of greatest authority in written texts. It celebrates the potentially subversive and revisionary prowess of oral discourse, seeing it as a return to the original, oral authority of God's Word.

Three details are of particular interest in this juxtaposition of pointing hand, handwritten scroll, and printed book. First, the sibyl's scroll may be written, but its form is more provisional than the written text and thus is closer to their shared source of revelation. Paradoxically, the supplement supplants the earlier text, accruing priority and authority for itself. The content of the prophecy confirms this, for it stresses that the divine word has not yet revealed itself in its entirety: it is not fixed; it may be added to. Second, the sibyl is not shown holding a pen, even though she has presumably just finished writing down the text she points to. The absence of a writing tool suggests not only the author's gender but the link all her writing has to the original oral discourse that inspired it, and will inspire it again. The third detail may be most important of all. The sibyl points not to the printed text or to her recently written text but to the blank space following her writing. She indicates this space because her prophecies represent the power to open all texts, to make a space in them for revisions and supplementary revelations (the *unborn* referred to in Domenichino's painting). In H. D.'s eloquent words, the blank on the page represents "the blank pages / of the unwritten volume of the new" (103). Such a portrait of a sibyl's power is thus even more radically revisionary than that of Mary Shelley's parable as interpreted by Gilbert and Gubar; it argues that the true sibylline role is to write new texts, not only to recover and rearrange the fragments of old ones.[8]

When sibylline women appear in women's literature, they stage scenes of instruction that teach their initiates to identify, question, and alter the cultural texts—the stereotypes—that define what a woman's identity may be. Just as importantly, such authority is often associated with recovering the lost power of oral discourse—the ability to revise spontaneously what society has tried to make permanently fixed. Nineteenth- and twentieth-century women's fiction that appropriates Western images of sibyls thus gives them an even more subversive power than that bequeathed by Michelangelo and Domenichino. Now the sibyl's authority is applied to social roles, not necessarily God's Word; and it decrees that patriarchal society has not had the final word on what a woman's identity may be.

Acts of displacement, revision, and remembering thus characterize the comic heroines in Welty's stories, most notably Virgie Rainey in "The Wanderers," the climactic story in *The Golden Apples*. She appropriates the role of Perseus and slays Medusa, as Welty's tragic heroines (Miss Eckhart, Jenny, Old Addie, Clytie and others) cannot. With one stroke of the imagination, Virgie Rainey assaults Morgana's deadly, stereotypical image of a strong independent woman as a monster. To do this, like Perseus she reflects that dangerous image *back to itself,* identifying it *as* an image, a cultural fiction, thus taking the first step toward conquering its power to dominate her. And like the Cumaean sibyl in Mary Shelley's parable, Virgie meditates on how a new tradition may replace the old one, in which a woman may be Perseus, not merely Medusa. Her struggle, however, will be never-ending, always a part of the ongoing struggle of women's history. In Welty's words,

> She might be able to see it now prophetically, but she was never a prophet. Because Virgie saw things in their time, like hearing them—and perhaps because she must believe in the Medusa equally with Perseus—she saw the stroke of the sword in three moments, not one. In the three was the damnation—no, only the secret, unhurting because not caring in itself—beyond the beauty and the sword's stroke and the terror lay their existence in time—far out and endless, a constellation which the heart could read over many a night. . . . In Virgie's reach of memory a melody softly lifted, lifted of itself. Every time Perseus struck off the Medusa's head, there was the beat of time, and the melody. Endless the Medusa, and Perseus endless. (*CS* 460)

Domenichino's famous portraits of a sibyl may in fact be behind many of Welty's portraits of sibylline powers, especially those that inspire Miss Eckhart and, through her, Virgie Rainey. In "Music from Spain" we learn that Miss Eckhart has a picture of a sibyl on her wall who strikes the same pose as Domenichino's—she too has her finger on the page of a book, looking over her shoulder (*CS* 408). Why should a music teacher in Mississippi own a reproduction of a sibyl by Domenichino? One answer suggests itself: by Domenichino's time, this pose associated with sibyls was often transferred to St. Cecilia, the patron saint of music, as well. Apparently, the Cumaean sibyl's indelible association with "prophetic song" in Virgil's Fourth Eclogue caused her to become associated with other kinds of music, and eventually with St. Cecilia (Ferguson 197–98; Kaftal 250–58). But Miss Eckhart's sibyl, fittingly, represents not merely the teaching and performance of music so much as a sibylline scene of instruction—the creation and transmission of a new text for women's heroism, a dark and mysterious text that Virgie learns to read only later in life, as she realizes during the soaring epiphany that ends "The Wanderers" that she has loved and learned from her music teacher, not hated her.[9]

Like Virgie Rainey in *The Golden Apples,* sibyls, Medusas, and women musicians have played important roles in earlier literature by women, of whom Willa Cather, Edith Wharton, Kate Chopin, Sarah Orne Jewett, Mary Wilkins Freeman, Elizabeth Stoddard, Augusta Evans, and Madame de Staël are especially important for readers of Welty. It is necessary to discriminate, however, between the cautionary scenes of instruction prominent in nineteenth-century sentimental romances that sometimes feature women artists, such as Augusta Evans's *Vashti; or, "Until Death Us Do Part"* (1869), and the truly empowering scenes of instruction that are centerpieces of women's local color literature, a somewhat separate, realist tradition that partakes of romance conventions but tends to parody and revise them.[10]

The classic example of a scene of instruction in the American local color tradition is in Jewett's *The Country of the Pointed Firs*, set in a rural town in Maine not completely unlike Welty's Morgana, Mississippi. Coming from a large eastern city, the narrator immediately is struck by the way in which one of the women, Mrs. Todd, has made a professional as well as a social identity for herself: she is the town's herbalist and its social arbiter. But she quickly becomes a figure of mythic power as well, a vision of a woman in the midst of a community of men and women entirely in control of her own identity: "She stood at the centre of a braided rug, and its rings of black and gray seemed to circle about her feet in the dim light. Her height and massiveness in the low room gave her the look of a huge sibyl, while the strange fragrance of the mysterious herb blew in from the little garden." At the end of the story cycle the narrator's last glimpse of Mrs. Todd shows that she has internalized her solitary strength: "her distant figure looked mateless and appealing, with something about it that was strangely self-possessed and mysterious. . . . [A]t last I lost sight of her as she slowly crossed an open space on one of the higher points of land . . ." (Solomon 51, 150). The narrator may be leaving, but her tutelage in self-reliance has been completed.

Descendants of Jewett's Mrs. Todd can be seen in the stories of Willa Cather and Katherine Anne Porter, particularly Old Mrs. Harris in Cather's story by that name in *Obscure Destinies* and Grandmother in Porter's Miranda stories, among others. Porter characteristically treats her version of this character ironically: her stubbornness and sentimentality are inextricably a part of her heroism. The unwavering strength of Cather's matriarchs seems almost superhuman in comparison. The young heroines of "Old Mrs. Harris" and "Old Mortality"—Vickie Templeton and Miranda—learn from these women, but there are no straightforward scenes of instruction or farewell as there are in Jewett. The girls learn from these older women largely without knowing that they are doing so, and their last scenes with them, ironically, find them asserting their own independence against what they take to be their antiquated and oppressive influence. But their very rebelliousness shows that they have absorbed their mentors' strength of character; and it is only later in their lives, usually after their mentors' deaths, that they look back and see how much they owe. In Cather's eloquent words, "when they are old, they will come closer and closer to Grandma Harris. They will think a great deal about her, and remember things they never noticed . . ." (158).

With many American women writers, the heroic matriarch tends to be not an artist or a musician but a spinster or a divorced or widowed woman who through her own efforts has gained special status working in her community. Welty's richest examples of the scene of instruction, however, tend to involve the teaching of music.[11] The reason that women musicians play such an important role in Welty's stories may be because of the influence of two works by Willa Cather that are about women artists, *The Song of the Lark* and the stories in *Youth and the Bright Medusa*. These works offer a complex combination of the cautionary scenes of instruction featured in romances such as *Vashti* and the empowering scenes of instruction that characterize some women's local color writing.

Cather's novel *The Song of the Lark* portrays the life of an opera singer based on Olive Fremstad, and it is considerably more sanguine than her stories about women artists in *Youth and the Bright Medusa*. In Welty's essay on Cather in *The Eye of the Story,* she praises *The Song of the Lark,* among other novels, in the midst of a discussion of how Jewett taught Cather to "find your own quiet center of life and write from that" (48); Welty sees it as a novel of an artist's rebellion and self-discovery—how she trains herself to be reborn. The most important role models for its heroine, Thea Kronborg, are her music teachers. The first is Professor Wunsch, whose name in German means *desire*. A homeless musician trained in Europe, he supports himself in Colorado with only a few students, of whom only Thea has any real talent. He boards with a family at the edge of town and has bouts of depression, violence, and alcoholism. Like Miss Eckhart, he is a "wanderer" (*Lark* 23) whose career ends in madness, with his trying to chop down an orchard and dove-house while (as in "June Recital") children watch the events from their second-story bedroom windows. Thea's second teacher is Andor Harsanyi, a successful musician in Chicago. Welty singles out his credo in her essay: "every artist makes himself born. It is much harder than the other time, and longer" (175).

Thea Kronborg's story is not a cautionary tale to her women readers but a (potentially) revolutionary one: Thea's success teaches them to question how identity is defined, not merely to choose from among the patterns that society offers. The epigraph for Cather's novel ("It was a wond'rous storm that drove me," from Lenau's *Don Juan*) could be the epigraph for "June Recital," especially the scene in which Miss Eckhart plays Beethoven during a thunderstorm. And when Thea sings Frika's part from Wagner's

Das Reingold, Cather describes her "distant kind of loveliness for this part, a shining beauty like the light of sunset on distant sails. She seemed to take on the look of immortal loveliness, the youth of the golden apples, the shining body and the shining mind" (447). Such a passage is a precursor to all the images of radiant and powerful heroines in *The Golden Apples,* from Snowdie MacLain at the beginning to Virgie Rainey at the end, as well as a source (along with Yeats's "Song of Wandering Aengus") for its title. Furthermore, when Welty alludes to this passage by Cather, she joins it with Cather's other vision of the woman artist forced by her society to be a "bright Medusa": Miss Eckhart may be a heroic quester like Aengus and Perseus, but she is also characterized at the end of "June Recital" by her flaming hair—the "grave, unappeased, and radiant" Medusa's-head of her madness that forever remains the frightening alter-ego of the woman artist (*CS* 330). No image of the sibyl's shining mind is entirely separable from the threat of Medusa's shadow, in Cather or in Welty.

Cather's inspiration for Thea Kronborg came partly from her acquaintance with Olive Fremstad, partly from Henry James's stories about art and artists, and partly from Augusta Evans's *Vashti.* As Ellen Moers has pointed out (287–92), another important influence was not an American work at all: it was Madame de Staël's *Corinne; ou, L'Italie* (1807), the most famous nineteenth-century novel about a woman artist. De Staël's heroine was an improvisatrice in Rome, a national poet-sibyl who spontaneously composed and recited verses during great public exhibitions. She is thus a kind of modern Cumaean sibyl whose prophetic and revolutionary arts include literature as well as music. De Staël's Corinne, moreover, did not fit into any of the social roles played by other women in the novel; rather, her arts inspired a revolutionary transgression of social roles. Several passages about Corinne's public performances portray her as a sibyl exactly in the mode of Domenichino, with black hair, beautiful blue drapery flowing from her shoulders, and a rich Indian fabric wrapped turbanlike around her head.

Most of the sentimental romances popular in the nineteenth century offer a hypnotically powerful forgery of a Corinne-like heroine to their women readers, however. Edna Earl in *St. Elmo*—the heroine of the best-selling nineteenth-century romance that Welty satirized in *The Ponder Heart* and shows her mother gently mocking in *One Writer's Beginnings* (7)— appears to combine the intelligence of Corinne with the morality of an upright American girl; but actually she is much closer to Corinne's half-sister and rival in the de Staël novel, the thoroughly proper embodiment of what would become the conservative Victorian ideals of true womanhood. Here is Evans's revealing description of Edna Earl: "The young face, lifted toward the cloudless east, might have served as a model for a pictured Syriac priestess. . . . The large black eyes held a singular fascination in their mild sparkling depths, now full of tender loving light and childish gladness; and the flexible red lips curled in lines of orthodox Greek perfection" (8). Disguised behind this stylized profile is a heroine completely lacking Corinne's revolutionary power even as she masquerades with her beauty and at least some of her authority. Other women who more blatantly aspire to Corinne's power, such as Salome Owen in *Vashti*, are punished for their ambition. Such features of the sentimental romance give special force to Gilbert and Gubar's point that the feminist scene of instruction must involve a traumatic but liberating displacement of one kind of cultural text for another that has been dismembered and forgotten. The sibylline references in Welty's stories show precisely that process. They identify and then transgress the sentimental romance's portraits of dutiful daughters as angels and powerful women as monsters that all twentieth-century women writers (particularly southern ones) have inherited. But Welty's references to sibyls also identify moments in women's writings—especially in American local color literature—that have subverted that inheritance and firmly place Welty's work within that tradition. In effect, her stories teach her readers to change the ways in which they may resist confining cultural texts—showing them how to evolve from identifying with Medusa to identifying with a sibyl, from self-destructive rage and guilt to empowering acts of disguise and revision. It seems particularly just that as contemporary readers are recovering and remembering a lost tradition of nineteenth- and early twentieth-century women's literature, Eudora Welty should be so instrumental in teaching us how to understand their prophetic power.

How Not to
Tell a Story

Eudora Welty's
First-Person Tales

Eudora Welty's fiction overflows with gifted, loquacious storytellers; it resounds with their voices. So, for me at least, it is surprising to realize how few of the stories are actually told in the first person.[1] Welty is much more likely to depict storytelling as a kinetic exchange, an unpredictable process of reply, response, and mutual invention. *Losing Battles,* with its "fray" of voices (*CS* 368), is the epitome of this process.

In that novel, one of the Beechams' main strengths (however terrifying) is their capacity to draw everyone and everything into a communal, continual story which becomes their own, as when they invent a paternity for Gloria which makes her one of the family. Such storytelling is a constant interchange, a game which everyone can—and must—play. A great moment of *Losing Battles*, weighted with danger and possibility, occurs when Lady May Renfro, the baby whose genealogy has been "decided" by the previous day's round of storytelling, finds her own voice, and thus begins her own life as a storyteller. Opening her eyes, "She put her voice into the fray, and spoke to it the first sentence of her life: 'What you huntin', man?' " (*CS* 368). Her sentence is a question, which demands a response: a story.

But occasionally, Welty has created a character who spurns such a communal storytelling. In such cases, we readers are unforgettably bombarded with direct address. This occurs most memorably in two great, singular stories: "Why I Live at the P.O." and "Circe."

The narrator-protagonists of these stories, Sister and Circe, frame their tales as definitive assertions of their own commanding visions; they brook no interruptions and no replies. Both women tell stories because they have been confronted with a version of experience they refuse to accept. For both are pitted against rivals who insist on being protagonists. These rivals, Stella-Rondo and Odysseus, aggressively advance their own tales and their own heroism. Circe and Sister can combat them only be reinventing their worlds. And they do so by preempting the story's voice for their exclusive use. In each case, that voice belongs to a single woman, uncomfortable with the place she finds herself assigned in others' narratives. Circe, the nonhuman sorceress, and Sister, the incapacitated woman, deny humanity by refusing the communion of storytelling. But they also act to preserve themselves, by grappling with conventional female plots which would constrict them. Their failures as storytellers, and as heroines, are among Welty's most stunning successes.

Sister's very title, "Why I Live at the P.O.," is an act of appropriation; it asserts that *she* is the center of attention and that the reason for her domicile is of pressing interest to us. But then in her first sentence we learn that she has seized the power of narration because someone else snatched the role of protagonist: her prodigal sister, Stella-Rondo, who makes a spectacular reappearance at the family home on Independence Day—with a surprise two-year-old in tow. Against such peremptory claims for attention, Sister fights for control, by means of her narrative. Virtually the only information she imparts about her sister's absent husband, for example, is that *she* "went with" him first. The very scene of Stella-Rondo's return, dramatic as it must have been, is omitted. Instead, in Sister's first dramatized scene she places herself at the absolute center of the household, "over the hot stove," trying gamely to perform feats of domestic magic and to "stretch two chickens over five people and a completely unexpected child" (*CS* 46).

For Sister, her family is the world, and the optimal position for herself, as her tale begins, is the traditional domestic locus of power: feeding the family. Her family's importance is so self-evident to her that she does not think to tell us what their surname might be. Almost all Sister's relatives— Mama, Papa-Daddy, Uncle Rondo, and Sister herself—are referred to only by names which designate family relationships. The exception, of course, is Stella-Rondo. She is named for a star and a man (her mother's brother), and by stealing Mr. Whitaker from her sister, she managed to accomplish what Sister has not—to project herself outside the family house and the state of Mississippi. When Stella-Rondo acquired a daughter, she determinedly named her in the language of a larger world, outside the self-referential family vocabulary. Her child is Shirley-T., for Shirley Temple.

Newly equipped with daughter, Stella-Rondo is formidable competition for her sibling. According to Sister, she can lie effectively at the drop of a hat, discrediting Sister in the most humiliating ways. She arrives back home equipped with the paraphernalia of sexual experience, notably a seductive trousseau and a child. But Stella-Rondo denies that she is the child's biological parent. To admit that she bore Shirley-T. would be to acknowledge that she was subject to the uncertainties and indignities of conception and pregnancy, and that admission might also subject her (and her child) to the stigma of an out-of-wedlock pregnancy. She prefers to present herself as an adoptive parent, who exercised the powers of choice. If she is lying about Shirley-T.'s parentage, as seems likely, Stella-Rondo denies her own involvement in one of the most common female stories. By asserting that Shirley-T. is adopted, Stella-Rondo places herself in a position of clear-cut power which biological motherhood cannot afford: without the encumbrances of sexual passion and pregnancy, she chose her time and her child, as surely as she chose Shirley-T.'s defiant name.

When Stella-Rondo eloped with Mr. Whitaker, it must have seemed to Sister, and to all of China Grove, Mississippi, that she was this family's shooting star, its wanderer, its questing protagonist. But now she appears a fixed star, instead—returned to her place in the family constellation. Presumably, Mama once made the same return with her two daughters. For Mama too lives in *her* parental house, and there is no mention of the man who fathered Stella-Rondo and Sister. Stella-Rondo's return brings on a set of reversals, repetitions, and complications so disturbing for Sister that she must grapple for retrospective control of the situation by means of her plotted monologue.

Sister comprehends that plot is power; it is for her, as in Peter Brooks's definition, "the logic and dynamic of narrative, and narrative itself is a form of understanding and explanation" (10). Thinking back over the events of the last few days, Sister gropes for an explanatory arrangement of those events, a plot which will reinforce her version of the self she wishes she were. She once had a secure place and was "getting along fine," as she asserts in her first sentence. She was well entrenched as postmistress and as dutifully domestic daughter. But when Stella-Rondo came back, Sister found herself a defending protagonist, locked in combat with her antagonist.

The plot-battle which ensues is conducted almost entirely through language. Sister's monologue itself is a highly elaborated weapon. According to her, Stella-Rondo puts up an unfair fight, for her weapons are lies. She tells her uncle and grandfather that Sister made mocking or critical remarks about them. But by Sister's account, it was Stella-Rondo herself who said the words she attributes to Sister—for example, Stella-Rondo actually said that Uncle Rondo "looked like a fool" as he swayed across the lawn in a peach silk kimono. Sister is especially infuriated by this treachery; she admonishes her audience, to make sure we don't miss Stella-Rondo's duplicity, asking, "Do you remember who it was really said that?" (*CS* 52).

In Sister's story, she presents herself as the speaker of a solicitous language, that of the loving housekeeper who makes heroic domestic efforts to take care of everything and everyone, sweetly warning her drunk uncle against dripping ketchup on her sister's silk lingerie. By her inspired lies, Stella-Rondo robs Sister of her own (hypocritical) caretaking language—and thus of the secure position she thought she had. Stella-Rondo's lies are the instrument by which she reshapes Sister's story. And the lies also isolate Sister, as a single woman, by destroying her alliances with male power. Just as she once stole Mr. Whitaker, by lying to him that Sister "was one-sided" (*CS* 46), she now steals the allegiance of Papa-Daddy and Uncle Rondo.

Under the pressure of Stella-Rondo's attack, Sister tries to win points with a display of domestic faculty. But her efforts are souring by the minute, turning as tart as the green-tomato pickles she stirs up on the Fourth of July—"Somebody had to do it" (*CS* 50), she claims. A less essential food than green tomato pickle can scarcely be imagined, and Sister's effort to consolidate her powers at the stove cuts no ice with Mama, who "trots in. Lifts up the lid and says, 'H'm! not very good for your Uncle Rondo in his precarious condition, I must say. Or poor little adopted Shirley-T. Shame on you!' " (*CS* 50).

Sister's response is "That made me tired." And well she might be. It is Independence Day, but she is at the stove, expected to suit her cooking to whatever kinfolk might turn up, in whatever condition. She ends her account of her kitchen efforts with an admission of defeat—no longer claiming authority but, instead, asking for pity: "I stood there helpless over the hot stove" (*CS* 51). She has become that most threadbare of domestic clichés—a mocked, overburdened, hearth-bound Cinderella, ripe for a godmother.

Sister makes one major effort to fight Stella-Rondo by her own methods. She attempts to discredit her sister's trump card—Shirley-T. Realizing the child has not spoken since her arrival, she deliciously imagines "something perfectly horrible" and asks, " 'Can that child talk?' " The most fitting debility Sister can imagine for her new niece is to rob her of the defending, denying, shaping powers of speech. But Shirley-T. wins the engagement by yelling in a deafening "Yankee voice," " 'OE'm Pop-OE the Sailor-r-r Ma-a-n!' and then somebody jumps up and down in the upstairs hall. In another second the house would of fallen down" (*CS* 51).

Shirley-T. has asserted her otherness from Sister and her invulnerability in every possible way: she is adopted, and not blood kin; she has all her faculties; she is a Yankee, not a Mississippian, and she is strong enough to bring the house down—or so it seems to Sister. And the child identifies not with a woman, but with a strong man, Popeye the Sailor, another figure from the mass culture which gave Shirley-T. her name. It is a complete rout for Sister—and from a two-year-old!

The last straw comes when Sister loses her last ally, Uncle Rondo, to

Stella-Rondo's "lies." Angrily, Uncle Rondo throws a lit string of fire-crackers into Sister's bedroom. Stella-Rondo's lies have already destroyed Sister's credibility with her family; the language by which she maintained her sense of her own dignity and power under their roof is no longer effective there. The firecrackers are not only phallic—aggressively male—and antidomestic; they are also pure, explosive, inhuman sound, absolutely outside Sister's control. And she prides herself on her sensitivity to noise.

Sister's response to the firecrackers is the turning point in her plot. This is the moment when she sees herself as most helpless; she says, "there I was with the whole entire house . . . turned against me." She describes herself in terms which emphasize her youthful *female* vulnerability: she is a "young girl" along in her bedroom, traumatized by an explosive invasion. But Sister refuses to subside as a helplessly violated victim. Instead, she recasts herself as a hero. The source of this renewal is her essential self-possession: "If I have anything at all I have pride" (*CS* 53).

Sister's story is fueled by that pride. Her family is no longer a haven or a receptive audience. So she changes her locale—she moves into "the next-to-smallest P.O. in Mississippi," where (thanks to Papa-Daddy) she holds the position of postmistress. By deciding to move and then by incorporat-ing that decision into a story, Sister rescues herself; she becomes her own fairy godmother.

Once she has decided to move, Sister describes herself in newly decisive language. She "marches" through the house, "snatching" her possessions. Stella-Rondo is now routed, reduced to tears at the thought that a family boycott of the P.O. will cut her off from her husband. Mama exclaims helplessly, " 'Oh, I declare . . . to think that a family of mine should quarrel on the Fourth of July, or the day after, over Stella-Rondo leaving old Mr. Whitaker and having the sweetest little adopted child! It looks like we'd all be glad!' " Mama extols the sentimental ideal of the family. She believes in holidays and games (her solution to family discord is " 'Why don't you all just sit down and play Casino?' " [*CS* 53, 55]). If villains exist, they are outside the family, as is "old Mr. Whitaker." Although she may assume the postures of power under her father's roof, shaking her finger at Sister over the stove, she is incapacitated for movement and action in a larger world, for she "trots" about with only tiny feet to support her 200 pounds. Mama's daughters have little choice but to conclude that staying home could mean for them what it did for her—triviality and ineffectuality.

Gathering up her movable possessions, Sister says to Mama with new independence, " 'You 'tend to your house, and I'll 'tend to mine' " (*CS* 54). The new force of her language contrasts with Mama's. She says, leaving, " '*He* left *her*—you mark my words. . . . That's Mr. Whitaker. After all, I knew him first. I said from the beginning he'd up and leave her. I foretold every single thing that's happened' " (*CS* 55). Thus Sister pronounces herself a spiteful oracle and demonstrates that she has exchanged places with her sister. Now Stella-Rondo is the displaced victim; now Sister is the adventuring protagonist, setting out to occupy a new world.[2]

In her new world, the P.O., Sister has a title which is not familial, as an agent of the U.S. Mail. As postmistress she should, ideally, facilitate China Grove's exchange with the distant outside world. Thus she is also allied with the U.S. male, for in this story the world of distances is associated with men. For example, Uncle Rondo "was in France" (CS 53), and it was he who financed Sister's one major journey, to Mammoth Cave. When a woman travels, it is with the aid or provocation of a man. When Mama, impressed by Sister's new oracular authority, questions her about where Mr. Whitaker has gone, Sister replies, " 'probably to the North Pole, if he knows what's good for him' " (CS 55).

Sister's own short journey to the P.O. has led, she claims, to a happy ending: "Oh, I like it here. It's ideal. . . . I want the world to know I'm happy" (CS 56). But the ideal world she asserts she has created in her five days of domestic life at the P.O. is as far from the hectic bustle of her roomy home as the North Pole—and as chilly. The last thing Sister collected from her home was the kitchen clock. She has appropriated and brought with her domestic time, as an immigrant woman might carry household rituals into a new country. But Sister has simply created a miniaturized version of the family house, crammed with the hideous appurtenances of domesticity, arranged to her own perverse taste, "everything cater-cornered, the way I like it" (CS 56).

Whatever the faults of Sister's family house, it was at least a model of domestic process. Nothing was stale or static there; everything was in a constant state of change and renewal. Allegiances shifted, and shifted again; a wanderer reentered as prodigal. Sister's ideal world at the P.O. is created by rearranging an especially motley selection of domestic props. But her arrangement is fixed. And thus process is thwarted.

The process of the U.S. Mail is thwarted too, for Sister's family, by her account "the main people of China Grove," refuse to patronize the P.O.; and many townspeople, taking sides in the dispute, have "quit buying stamps just to get on the right side of Papa-Daddy" (CS 56). Sister and the P.O. are a bottleneck; the exchange of communication, of storytelling, and of domestic life at its best, has become impossible. Sister has "won"— by the last page, she has shaped and narrated her own self-centered tale, and she has denied Stella-Rondo's rival version. Sister concludes triumphantly, with a declaration of independence: "And if Stella-Rondo should come to me this minute, on bended knees, and *attempt* to explain the incidents of her life with Mr. Whitaker, I'd simply put my fingers in both my ears and refuse to listen" (CS 56).

Obviously, Sister has found no real independence. Instead, she has denied some of her own deepest impulses. One of those impulses is her sense of the centrality of family to human life, to which her language often attests. (She refers to Judgment Day itself as an occasion for meeting one's "whole family" [CS 53].) Another of Sister's deepest impulses is to hear. Insatiably curious, she habitually eavesdrops around her family home. But now she boasts of stopping her ears against her sister's voice, shutting out the one story she most wants to hear. Finally, Sister has incapacitated herself as storyteller. For her true subject was the conjunction of her sister's life and her own, the pattern of rivalry, speech and silencing, setting forth and return which they mutually wove. Just as Stella-Rondo earlier destroyed the authority of Sister's voice, Sister now refuses Stella-Rondo a hearing. And she is her own victim: fingers in ears, she is rendered deaf.

Sister's story is a triumph of rearrangement. But in that very triumph, she has ignored what Eudora Welty calls "a storyteller's truth: the thing to wait on, to reach there in time for, is the moment in which people reveal themselves. You have to be ready, in yourself; you have to know the moment when you see it" (Eye 354). The story Eudora Welty wrote is very different from the one Sister tells, for it captures/invents Sister in her very moment of self-revelation, which is the telling of this story. But recognizing revelation is beyond Sister's powers. She is not "ready, in herself" for that discovery.

The first sentence of "Circe" tells us that we have come upon a storyteller more cultivated and more reflective than Sister, but one who shares her essential situation. Circe must contend with an intrusion into the well-ordered world she has created and governs—her household. Sister begins, "I was getting along fine . . . until . . ." (CS 46, emphasis added). Circe is getting along fine, too; her house is impeccable and her pigsty is full of former men, transformed by her infallible recipe.

As Sister's tale is a response to the stories Stella-Rondo told about her, Circe's tale counters the Odyssey version of herself. In Homer's narrative, she was an episode, a stage in a man's quest. Now, like Sister, she seizes centrality; as the title attests, this is her story.

As the story begins, Circe is sewing in her tower room. "Needle in hand," she says, "I stopped what I was making" (CS 531). Her position is traditionally feminine: waiting, in a house. However occupied with domestic tasks, like her sewing, Circe is constantly aware of the sea and the men it might bring to her island. She boasts of her self-possession, epitomized in her practical magic, which promptly translates thought into fact. "Men are swine: let it be said, and no sooner said than done" (CS 533). This magic is expressed through her traditional female role, as domestic woman; it is her delectable broth which subdues and transforms all men, and her magic wand itself is a broom. Yet Circe needs a constant supply of male mortals to confirm her powers. So, when Odysseus's men swarm toward her house, she speaks "the most dangerous word in the world": " 'Welcome!' " (*CS* 531).

One of the most obvious differences between the two stories I am discussing is their language. Sister's language is the product of Welty's infallible ear; its rhythms are absolutely credible as small-town Mississippi speech, and it seems the only imaginable language Sister could speak. But Circe's voice seems oddly contrived—sometimes self-conscious, sometimes literary, sometimes breathtakingly lyrical. The problem is that Circe is immortal; human speech is not her native tongue. A part of her yearns to discover the mystery of mortality, which men bear into her house. So she speaks a language of hospitality they understand: "Welcome!" Yet her welcome is a betrayal of hospitality's deepest meanings, for when the men come in, her first act as a hostess is to offer the broth, which traps them. And later, when Circe again attempts human language as the men are grieving for a dead sailor, her efforts frighten them away from her island forever.

When Circe encounters, among the new crop of men, one who will not succumb to her spell, she knows that her enchantment has "met with a hero" (*CS* 532). The island is a world controlled by Circe. But a hero has his own powers. Circe is first aware of Odysseus as a magical resistant presence in the room she thought was empty after her new swine had trotted away. She says, "I felt something from behind press like the air of heaven before a storm, and reach like another wand over my head" (*CS* 532). Wand is matched against wand. Circe moves to another form of magic—seduction, with elaborate domestic embellishments, including a luxurious bath, laundry service, and supper in a golden bowl. But the subjugation is finally her own: Odysseus will not accede to her domestic order and eat his supper until she restores his men to their mortal forms. When, at the end of the first day, they climb to the tower room together, Circe and Odysseus speak sorcerers' shoptalk "of signs, omens, premonitions, riddles and dreams." To Circe, her new lover is a "strange man," because he is so much like herself, "as unflinching and as wound up as I am." Yet "his short life and my long one have their ground in common. Passion is our ground, our island" (*CS* 534). Passion is also their common language.

For such a lover, Circe spreads out the panoply of her island's riches: all the charms of nature made delicious by domestic faculty. She extends her resources, putting "the house under greater stress for this one mortal than I ever dreamed of for myself" (*CS* 534). Circe feeds the sailors "a god's breakfast" and cleans up after them, but all her efforts are taken for granted. She laments, "Tell me of one that appreciated it! Tell me one now who looked my way until I had brought him his milk and figs" (*CS* 534).

Here, Circe petulantly echoes Sister's complaints about her unappreciated labors at a hot stove. Her language has lost the beautifully certain cadences of the story's first paragraphs. Earlier, as the men arrived, she felt omnipotent as she fed them and put them in their place (the pigsty). But now she is reduced to the position of an unappreciated drudge. For the men know what they did not know on their arrival, that Circe's power is not absolute. A male hero can reverse it.

From the first, then, Odysseus and Circe are both lovers and combatants. And one of their major areas of contention is time. On their first day together, Odysseus begins to tell Circe stories, confirming his heroism. (Eventually, Circe herself will become a story, with which Odysseus will entertain a king's banquet.) He boasts to Circe of vanquishing "the monster with one eye—he had put out the eye, he said." But the owl, overhearing outside Circe's window, reports that the Cyclops's eye is growing back, to be extinguished again by yet another man. Odysseus presents himself as protagonist of a tale of decisive, effectual action; *he* put out the eye, for good. But the owl reminds us of another version of the tale, cyclical and regenerative. Circe is impatient with both. She says, "I had heard it all before, from man and owl. I didn't want his story, I wanted his secret" (*CS* 533). His secret was only initially the herb that allowed him to escape Circe's transformation. Essentially, it is his mortality itself, engine of his restless, questing humanity.

Circe's time is very different. Her rituals repeat endlessly, just as the grapes ripen on her vines again and again. In one sense, their dispute is between mortal, end-stopped, and immortal, endless, time. Circe's deepening involvement in this dispute is indicated as the time frame of her narrative intersects with Odysseus's sense of time. After breakfast on what would seem by Circe's account to be the second day of the men's stay, Odysseus says, " 'We are setting sail. . . . A year's visit is enough.' " And he gives her "a pecking, recapitulating kiss," as if he is setting the final seal on an episode. (In his tale, the *Odyssey*, Circe appears as a finite episode.) But she counters with a barrage of seductive caresses, and he delays his men, saying, " 'Tomorrow' " (*CS* 533). Thus they battle for time. And when the men finally depart, it is mortality that spurs them: the sailor Elpenor's careless, passionate death. As they leave, Circe speaks from the door where she had first welcomed them, in what she thinks is "epitaph . . . the idiom of men." She tells them to write on the gravestone, " 'I died of love' " (*CS* 536). That frightens them so much that they drop the body, unburied, and run for their ship. That one could die for a woman's love and remain forever planted on Circe's island is a thought they will not stay to confront.

In another sense, the combat between Circe and Odysseus may be seen as a battle of feminine versus masculine time. According to Kathryn Allen Rabuzzi, the traditionally feminine occupation of housework, when performed as ritual and invested with emotion and commitment, "makes the individual a player in a scene far older and larger than her individual self." Any committed housekeeper, then, shares Circe's situation. "No longer does she participate in profane historical time; instead she is partici- pating in mythic time" (96). In Welty's story, Circe's mythic time and Odysseus's heroic time collide, as has happened with countless pairs of female and male lovers.

Sister, in her self-defeating triumph, reestablished domestic time at the P.O., with herself as heroic and solitary protagonist. She told a shapely story. But the shape of Circe's tale is imposed by the men, who choose to arrive and to depart by their own schedule. For Circe herself, the story ends with a nightmare phantasmagoria of shattered time. During the men's last days with her, she tries to reassert her own domestic rhythms. But she is disoriented: "it was as though I had no memory." Overcome by "tor- ment," she hallucinates the loss of her powers: "I believed that I lay in disgrace and my blood ran green, like the wand that breaks in two. . . . I awoke in the pigsty, in the red and black aurora of flesh, and it was day" (CS 536). Circe is pregnant with Odysseus's son—she herself is transformed, as the pigs once were. And even nature wears the harsh colors of flesh. Here Circe's language regains its beauty. But now its power comes not from certainty and control, but from the authenticity of her despair.

An immortal woman pregnant with a mortal male child embodies within herself two conflicting kinds of time. An abandoned Circe, her nerves still raw with love, is painfully aware of the extent and limits of her own powers. She knows the story of the men after they leave the island; probably she has always known it. But she cannot intercede in the story's unwinding. So she mourns that "foreknowledge is not the same as the last word" (CS 536).

Sister made a last word for herself, self-destructive and demented as that word may seem. But Circe's tale subsides in frustration and despair. To whom can she speak? The island girls laugh at her now that she has let herself be made a fool by love. Odysseus and she could commune on their island of passion—but he is gone, and she must stay. Now Circe identifies with the fixed female figures in the sky, such as Cassiopeia, tied "to the sticks and stars of her chair" (CS 537). To the moon, Circe says, " 'Why keep it up, old woman?' " (CS 536). There is no answer.

Circe's isolation seems endless, as multiple as her own multiplying vision. The men may find satisfaction, "strange felicity," in the completion of a story. But Circe, who sees with both mortal and immortal, male and female vision, will never be satisfied. She ends her story trying to find a human emotion—grief, which would let her express and expel her feelings. But grief is waiting for Odysseus, not for her; she will never find and kiss its "dusty mouth" (CS 537).

In Welty's fiction, storytelling at its best is a process which works like a tool to explore and discover. The process never ends. The Beecham reunion extends it, year after year. In "The Wide Net," it is symbolized by the net itself, a periodic communal dredging for truths larger than any man could bring up alone. And in "Powerhouse," the process is a constant, improvisational meditation on love and death which moves seamlessly from play into art. Sister denies that process by preempting a voice and transforming herself into protagonist and hero. Circe at first seems to speak in a voice equally confident, backed with all the shaping resources of her magic. But she loses control of magic, island, and tale. No one is there to answer. Circe cannot tell a human story, as the Beechams do, because she is not human. And Welty's triumph, with "Circe," is that in assuming the voice of a sorceress she forces her human readers to see their own mortal condition from outside. The rending and beautiful mystery of this tale is not magic, but humanity. For women especially, the story offers multiple resonances. Here humanity is presented in male terms; Odysseus is quintessentially human. But he is also quintessentially masculine, and many women readers may feel themselves more intimately connected with Circe, whose immortal femininity mirrors many mortal female lives. The first person, direct address further dramatizes the immediacy of Circe's situation.

At the same time, Welty also uses Circe to demonstrate the collision of male and female storytelling traditions—one progressive, quest-based; the other cyclical, taking its rhythms from nature and from the continuing rituals of housekeeping. Many women readers may find a version of their female humanity reflected in Circe, as she contends with male patterns on her domestic island.

Sister, too, struggles with the female possibilities her world offers. In both their stories, cyclical time must confront the trajectory of an individual will. And although both women are deeply rooted in cyclical time, which goes beyond the limits of any individual life, they lust for the satisfying finality of a "last word." Thus their stories cannot join the process of storytelling. Circe and Sister deny that storytelling's subject is what it is also subject to: flux, change, partiality, collaboration, losing battles. All the maddening and necessary stuff of human communication and community. The first person is antithetical to that process. In these two tales, Welty has used it as an oblique window on what she has called her own "continuing passion" as a *writer* of stories: a way of parting "a curtain, that invisible shadow that falls between each other's presence, each other's wonder, each other's human plight" (*Eye* 355).

The human and nonhuman plights of Sister and Circe are embodied in their first-person tales. After "Circe," Eudora Welty has thus far turned to the first person only once more—in the chilling late story, "Where Is the Voice Coming From?"[3] There the speaker is a bigot and a murderer; his "last word" is a gunshot which makes him a fugitive. In a sense, it is a logical sequel to the monologues of Sister and Circe, those moving and desperate demonstrations of how not to tell a story.

3

Visible Connections

"Everybody to their
own visioning"

JAN NORDBY

G R E T L U N D

THE TERRIBLE AND
THE MARVELOUS

Eudora Welty's
Chekhov

The 12 September 1982 *Atlanta Journal and Constitution* calls Eudora
Welty the Chekhov of the South. This is not a new notion for readers
familiar with critical works on Eudora Welty's achievement; several critics,
most notably Chester Eisinger, Alun R. Jones, and Ruth Vande Kieft,
maintain her indebtedness to the short fiction of the Russian master. But
so far nobody has taken the trouble to compare the two writers in order
to establish what is meant by phrases such as a Chekhovian kind of realism,
in the Chekhovian mode, and the like.

Chekhov has always had many admirers and imitators among English
and American writers. Some of the best were Katherine Mansfield, James
Joyce, D. H. Lawrence, Katherine Anne Porter, and Ernest Hemingway.
All of these employ some Chekhovian modes, but Eudora Welty has been
able *to combine* more essentially Chekhovian elements in her fiction than
anybody else writing in English and yet consistently speak in her own
voice and out of her own time. Some of these Chekhovian elements are
enumerated and explained in this essay. I am not suggesting that there is
a secret combination formula of Chekhovian ingredients to be rediscovered,
since the main ingredients are indefinable. It takes imagination, sensibility,
and compassion of a special order to express the Chekhovian topics and
craftsmanship in fiction. The kinship is finally based on kindred perspectives. Chekhov's best work is in short stories that appeared under his own
name between 1886 and 1903. This mature work can be compared to
the fiction that Welty has published since 1936. In her essay "Reality in
Chekhov's Stories," Welty refers to seventeen of the stories written during

that seventeen-year period. I have made the same stories the main basis for my study of the affinities between the two writers.

Both writers seem to have had some difficulties in fully sustaining a long narrative drive. They are at their best with just the suggestion of their vision. Their long efforts often read like a series of scenes or stories and are difficult to distinguish from short story cycles. This is true of some of the lengthy Chekhov stories referred to in Welty's essay: "The Steppe," "The Duel," "An Anonymous Story," and "Three Years" (*Eye* 61–81). And even though Welty's *Delta Wedding* is considered a novel, it does show a tendency toward episodic narrative. In *Losing Battles*, the tendency has become a flaw that mars the book. Welty is clearly at her best when she can string her stories together loosely, as in *The Golden Apples*. Chekhov's so-called short stories are often longer than her so-called novels, and in general there is little agreement among critics on maximum length for a short story. Traditional attempts at defining the distinction between short story and novel do not seem to apply to the fiction of Chekhov and Welty. Even when they allow themselves many pages, they do not necessarily supply the large context; situation and scope are not necessarily developed; and everything is not always resolved and accounted for. This does not mean that their fiction observes established criteria for the short story. They are rarely satisfied with the presentation of a slice of life or the achievement of a single effect; nor do they always look for the compact structure customarily assigned to the short story. In other words, it is not very helpful to see their fiction as a development in the history of the short story as a genre, and it is too limiting. What Welty shares with Chekhov is a way of looking at ordinary events and people—rather than extraordinary events—and a way of writing of private joys and sorrows. They refuse to impose an artificial form on the formlessness of the lives they describe, and the fiction is a reflection of the formlessness. In their fiction, character is a more profound subject than situation or structure, and place can be almost a character; so it is no wonder that traditional distinctions between short story and novel are useless when applied to their fiction. And in this essay no such distinction has been imposed on their writings.

Chekhov often wrote of the steppe and small Russian towns; Welty often writes of the Natchez Trace and small southern towns. They can both paint a convincing portrait in few words, and both look for the visual detail to help them do this. And Chekhov was as interested in the painters of his day as Welty is interested in photography. Both people their fiction with an impressive range of diverse characters; but always there are his doctors and her teachers. They also share an unexpected severity of vision, for they are in no sense of the words gentle or safe writers. They both recognize the existence of the marvelous and the terrible, and they see life as inviting and frightening at the same time. They seem to suggest that to enjoy one side of life fully, one must be constantly aware of the other.

Compression is a word that describes the artistic technique that Chekhov and Welty have mastered. They often compress many observations into a single, trivial detail, and there is much apparent trivia in their fiction. In "On the Road," which is fairly short, Chekhov devotes some lines to a potboy: "all at once the door creaked and the potboy, in a new print shirt, came in. Limping on one leg, and blinking his sleepy eyes, he snuffed the candle with his fingers, put some more wood on the fire and went out" (8: 203). The potboy is not important in the story, but the limping boy matters as a human being, and the pot, the limp, *and* the new print shirt affect us. At the end of the story it becomes clear that the everyday impressions are not irrelevant but necessary conveyors of emotions. The details also serve to convince us that it is the real world we have been reading about. "Making reality real is art's responsibility," as Welty wrote in "Place in Fiction" (*Eye* 128), and this is what Chekhov was able to do with his potboy. The crucial information may be offered as an apparently trivial detail, and there may be no other clue in the story. This is, of course, perfectly true to life, where the important events are not pointed out, and their importance is perhaps only realized later. The use of the detail in fiction reflects the way we observe the world. We notice the detail that tells us about another's life because our apparatus of perception predisposes us to notice and be convinced by the detail. When Olenka in "The Darling" receives a telegram about her husband's death, Chekhov convinces us of the reality of this telegram by misspelling one word and by putting in a word without meaning: "Ivan Petrovitch died suddenly to-day. Awaiting immate instructions fufuneral Tuesday" (1: 8). Who will question the reality of a telegram with one misspelled and one incomprehensible word? Welty's tribute to Chekhov stresses his use of such details.

Chekhov and Welty also share character-creating genius. They imagine people whose actions and appearance are so convincingly drawn from life that they persuade us of their existence and their relevance for our understanding of our lives. They refuse to psychologize and abstract the lives they create. In Chekhov's "Ariadne," the brother of Ariadne has found and read a letter from Lubkov, his sister's lover: " 'From that letter I learned that she is very shortly going abroad. My dear fellow, I am very much upset! Explain it to me for goodness' sake. I can make nothing of it!' As he said this he breathed hard, breathing straight in my face and smelling of boiled beef" (1: 46). We may question the existence of a man who talks to one of his sister's admirers in this stilted manner. But we are easily convinced that a man whose breath smells of boiled beef *would* read his sister's mail. In the story "Keela, the Outcast Indian Maiden," Welty writes in the Chekhovian mode. It is a small black boy who parades as the Indian maiden. He eats live chickens in a traveling show. The man who finally liberates the boy from the freak show is remembered as " 'a tallish man with a sort of white face. Seem like he had bad teeth' " (*CS* 41). The bad teeth, which the man may have had, have no other function in the story than to convince us of his reality.

Chekhov and Welty establish the humanity of their characters by having them long for what they cannot have, be it gooseberries or Moscow, love or Morgana; but mostly the power of custom, habit, or routine defeats their fragile longings. We learn this not through detailed accounts of their thoughts, but through observation of the characters and by listening to them. At times, humanity in all its vanity is brought to life in brief character-izations, but we are not permitted to forget that we are reading about individuals who matter to the writer. When we see a glimpse of Dr. Startsev in "Ionitch," we realize the extent to which he has cut himself off from his own emotions by the change in his physical appearance: "Startsev has grown stouter still, has grown corpulent, breathes heavily, and already walks with his head thrown back" (3: 90). We can easily imagine the obese and unhappy Dr. Startsev on his way down the street of Chekhov's town of S. And we can sympathize with Mrs. Flewellyn in Welty's story "The Wanderers," "who had caught the last breath of her husband in a toy balloon, by his wish, and had it at home still—most of it, until a Negro stole it" (*CS* 435).

Dr. Startsev and Mrs. Flewellyn are, of course, particularly unfortunate and even somewhat ridiculous; but there are plenty of heroic characters in stories by Chekhov and Welty. Dr. Osip Stepanitch Dymov of "The Grasshopper" risks his life in an attempt to save a boy with diphtheria by sucking through a tube to clear the boy's throat. Dr. Dymov dies. And Dr. Richard Strickland of Welty's "The Demonstrators" perseveres in his life's work of helping whites and blacks in Holden, Mississippi, in spite of the dangerous racial climate of the 1960s. But we are not asked to sit in judgment of these characters; we are just asked to believe in them and to try to understand why they are, what they are. Both writers work with undercurrents of suggestion, so we may not notice at first that we are actually discovering facets of our own selves; for surely there is a bit of both the unfortunate and the heroic in all of us. The message is clearly that we should be more tolerant and take pleasure in the variety.

The moods of Chekhov's and Welty's narrators are often surprising: they do not claim to be detached and objective, and they are certainly not self-effacing or restrained in the telling of their stories, and their stories reveal their own emotions. It is obvious that their responses to objective reality, if there is such a standard, have a tendency to be distorted and inconclusive. There are several introspective and unreliable narrators in Chekhov's stories (for example, the aging professor of "A Dreary Story"); and Welty has the young girl at the lake in "A Memory" so preoccupied with herself that she sees everybody else as being perfectly disgusting. There are similarities between Chekhov's self-revealing narrator of "The House with an Attic" and Welty's talkative beautician of "Petrified Man." But the most obvious parallel is between the narrator of Chekhov's "An Anonymous Story," Stephen, the footman as he calls himself, and Sister of Welty's humorous story "Why I Live at the P.O." In their confessional narratives they reveal the core of their humanity. Our interest is captured and held by the gradual revelation of the narrator's state of mind, which obviously matters much more than the stories they tell.

The careful arrangement of selected details and the emphasis on the individual life often cause the overall plot development to be vague in the fiction of both Chekhov and Welty. They tend to rate character development above the organization of the action. No matter how dramatic the event may be, it still seems to occur by chance; as when Laevsky in "The Duel" comes into a room and sees "Kirilin, and beside him Nadyezhda Fyodorovna," the woman Laevsky lives with, who should not be *there* and certainly not with the good-looking police captain (2: 128). There is no obvious attempt to find a motive or a reason for what happens. The life we see is arranged so that it will suggest the whole rather than explain it, and as in life there are many distracting details.

It is not the plot of Welty's *The Ponder Heart* that is interesting; in fact there is not much of a plot in this short novel. What is important is the suggestion of daily life in Clay, a small town in Mississippi, and the life of Miss Edna Earle, as it is suggested in her self-revealing monologue. It is not that Welty's fiction is lacking in dramatic incidents: a young man stabs his pregnant wife; a man kills his fellow hitchhiker with a beer bottle; a racist shoots a black leader; a girl is raped by several men; and two blacks are stabbed to death with ice picks. There is no attempt to avoid the dramatic incident; but the drama and the violence are never in the stories to entertain. The focus remains squarely on the growth of the individual characters, and the dramatic events serve to tell us about them. Powerhouse, in the story named for him, has many listeners when he claims, "I got a telegram my wife is dead" (CS 133). Surprisingly, his listeners are not really concerned about what this message will mean to the leader of the band. Instead, they begin to question the existence of such a telegram. Powerhouse only suggests, and his audience is free to interpret his claim as they like. Powerhouse finally admits that the truth is "something worse," and Welty leaves her readers with that suggestion. The vagueness of the plot and the many never-confirmed suggestions allow the fiction to remain an open structure with space for growth in the reader's imagination.

Chekhov's work is not didactic in general, but at times he goes out of his way to voice his indignation. In "Peasants" he exclaims: "how lovely life would have been in this world, in all likelihood, if it were not for poverty, horrible, hopeless poverty, from which one can find no refuge!" (6: 288). And the whole story can be read as an indignant protest against the hopeless situation of the Russian peasants of his day. But the truly Chekhovian element is the parenthetical "in all likelihood," for he knows that helping people out of their poverty would not in itself be enough to assure mankind a "lovely life." Nevertheless, he is always conscious of people less fortunate than himself and tells us of hardship, hunger, and workers in the brickyards whose singularity is obscured in red dust (7: 164). The awareness of desperate need does not lead Chekhov to harass his reader by constant exhortation, but he does include thinly veiled discussions of social issues in his fiction. On the other hand, he is well aware of the difference between the writer as artist and the writer as social crusader. In "An Artist's Story," he tells us of Leda, who despises the artist and narrator of the story: "She did not like me. She disliked me because I was a landscape painter and did not in my pictures portray the privations of the peasants, and that, as she fancied, I was indifferent to what she put such faith in" (1: 160). The artist was not indifferent, nor are Chekhov or Welty. They do not crusade in their fiction, yet they faithfully render the social reality they see. Welty, the writer, does not propose social reforms, yet the realist and artist cannot afford to exclude from her vision the hardship she sees about her. In her story "The Whole World Knows," she observes: "A load of Negroes came over on the water taxi and stepped out sulphur-yellow all over, coated with cottonseed meal. They disappeared in the colored barge at the other end, in single file, carrying their buckets, like they were sentenced to it" (CS 388). Whether the humanity is covered by red brick dust or sulphur-yellow cottonseed meal, it is difficult to pretend that this writing praises the status quo. The picture of the social conditions is an indictment in itself. There is overt social criticism in some early Welty stories such as "Flowers for Marjorie" (especially in its first version), which is set in New York during the depression, and "The Whistle," which is also about the 1930s, but set among poor tomato farmers. "Where Is the Voice Coming From?" and "The Demonstrators" present Welty's artistic vision of the 1960s and civil rights issues. In several ways these stories resemble the stories Chekhov wrote in criticism of his Russia of the turn of the century. But for both writers what is important is not so much that people are starving or being treated cruelly, it is what happens to them as human beings under such circumstances. They both know that human nature is to some extent shaped by the social structure we find ourselves in and that a good artist cannot afford to ignore this fact.

Welty's novel *Losing Battles* is a stark portrayal of the situation for Mississippi farmers in the 1930s. Although everything is described leisurely and with humor, the description is realistic enough to imply criticism of the farming programs, or the lack of them, at the time. The events of the novel occur during the summer of 1930, so it will be a long time before the situation will improve for the farmers. Yet Welty does not accuse, preach, or crusade in the novel; she just portrays the situation in Banner County as it was. In an interview, I once asked Miss Welty whether it is at all possible for a novelist to avoid crusading. She answered by explaining why Steinbeck bores her and why Chekhov does not: "The real crusader doesn't need to crusade; he writes about human beings in the sense Chekhov did. He tries to see a human being whole with all his wrong-headedness and all his right-headedness. To blind yourself to one thing for the sake of your prejudice is limiting" (*Conversations* 226).

Instead of crusading, Chekhov and Welty accept and celebrate life in all its forms; and their characterizations demonstrate how unpredictable and selfish people are. When we are introduced to ordinary people close up and in the middle of the petty affairs of everyday life, the effect is often comic and pathetic. And both Chekhov and Welty are chroniclers of the human comedy. Grandfather Ilarion in "Ariadne," who is called upon every day because he is so "amazingly intelligent," does not become less interesting when we learn that he has been dead for some time. It is also an amusing scene in "Gooseberries" when Alehin welcomes his guests by informing them: "I must go and wash, for I almost think I have not washed since spring" (5: 273). When he washes the water turns brown, then dark blue, and finally the color of ink. Yet Alehin is one of the most likable of characters in Chekhov. Both writers accept their characters as they are, and their compassion is always felt in the humor and the satire. Welty has written her share of humorous scenes. One of the funniest is in *The Ponder Heart* when Grandpa Ponder takes Uncle Daniel back to the asylum in Jackson and gets himself detained instead, by mistake. And there is a fine comic scene in *Delta Wedding* which involves Troy Flavin, who is marrying into the Fairchild family:

> He started out and then stock-still asked Ellen, "Is she ironing *money?*" "Why, that's the payroll," said Ellen. "Didn't you know Aunt Mac always washes it?" "The payroll?" His hand started guiltily toward his money pocket. "I get the money from the bank when I drive in, and she hates for them to give anything but new bills to a lady, the way they do nowadays. So she washes it." (95–96)

There is a measure of social satire and indirect criticism in this passage. As it is with most humor in fiction, it is not really funny unless it stings. But the acid social comment is faithfully kept in the guise of humor, and the humor is there to be appreciated.

One of the favorite targets for the satire of both writers is religious hypocrisy. Chekhov lets his most devout couple strike down an irritating cousin with a bottle of Lenten oil in "The Murder" (7: 121). And with all the religious intolerance displayed in Welty's *Losing Battles,* it is singularly gratifying that a storm picks up the local Methodist church and sets it down, all in one piece, next to the Baptist church. The Baptists of Banner gleefully help their Methodist neighbors tear down the dislocated church. The boards are carried back across the road, so that the church can be reassembled "where it belonged" (*LB* 238). Chekhov is often more severe in his satire on religious hypocrisy. In *The Eye of the Story* Welty remarks (77) on a passage from Chekhov's "In the Ravine," where there is a priest at the dinner after the funeral of an infant, who was killed with boiling water:

> . . . the guests and the priests ate a great deal, and with such greed that one might have thought that they had not tasted food for a long time. Lipa [the mother] waited at table, and the priest, lifting his fork on which there was a salted mushroom, said to her: "Don't grieve for the babe. For of such is the kingdom of heaven." (6: 230–31)

The shallowness of his pity for the mother is exposed in that revealing detail. The target is never any one religious denomination, but always it is religious hypocrisy, which parades in many disguises. In Welty's "Moon Lake" there is a certain Mr. Nesbitt, who seems to be related to Chekhov's fork-swinging priest: "Mr. Nesbitt, from the Bible Class, took Easter by the wrist and turned her around to him and looked just as hard at her front. She had started her breasts. What Easter did was to bite his right hand, his collection hand" (*CS* 347). In her satire of orphan-bites-deacon, Welty goes for the religious jugular of the hypocritical Nesbitt: "his collection hand."

In both Chekhov's and Welty's visions, man is often trapped in sad isolation. With compassion they show how we may try to break the isolation only to learn that the inability to communicate seems to be inherent in life. Our natural state seems to be a vain longing for love and togetherness, whether it is symbolized by a cherry orchard in Russia or a plantation home in Mississippi. Professor Nikolai Stepanovitch of "A Dreary Story" finds himself in an existential void. Lecturing has become a substitute for sex, and emotionally he is a bankrupt. When the young woman Katya becomes as "dry and cold" as the old professor himself, he has become separated from the only person that still meant something to him. He is not so far gone that he cannot see the tragedy of the change in Katya; but as he realizes what is important in life, he becomes increasingly unable to communicate and remains emotionally paralyzed. There are several such characters in Welty's stories. In his transient life as a salesman, Tom Harris feels isolated from his customers. He lives the life of an observer even when he should be most deeply involved; and as if once removed from himself, he notes the events of his life with the interest of a bystander. Although "The Hitch-Hikers" features a murder and its effects, the focus is on the salesman and the slow death of his emotions. The story reads as a moral warning: do not end up like Tom Harris!

The most poignant and famous case of isolation and the failure of communication in Chekhov is his "The Lady with the Dog." The character Gurov desperately needs to tell somebody that he has fallen in love and to communicate his joy of the discovery that he is able to love. One evening he cannot resist telling a fellow cardplayer about this important change in his life, but he is met with total indifference:

> " 'If only you knew what a fascinating woman I made the acquaintance of in Yalta!'
> The official got into his sledge and was driving away, but turned suddenly and shouted:
> 'Dmitri Dmitritch!'
> 'What?'
> 'You were right this evening: the sturgeon was a bit too strong!' " (3: 17–18)

For Gurov this is a strange and inadequate response; but it seems to be the only communication we can count on. Welty has Shelley Fairchild in *Delta Wedding* speak for her through a diary entry: "Does the world suspect? that we are all very private people? I think one by one we're all more lonely than private and more lonely than self-sufficient" (84). This isolation seems to be our natural state in both Chekhov and Welty.

According to both writers, the only way to overcome loneliness is through love. The husbands may come and go in Chekhov's "The Darling," but Olenka's need for love endures. Without it, people would not even try to break out of their isolated world of suppressed emotions. In Welty's "At the Landing" Jenny is unable to reach Floyd, but she is convinced that there is love, and she asks herself: "Ought I to sleep?" For she knows that it was love that might always be coming, and that "she must watch for it this time and clasp it back while it clasped, and while it held her never let it go" (*CS* 253). Welty's best story of an attempt to break out of isolation is probably "A Piece of News": "Mrs. Ruby Fisher had the misfortune to be shot in the leg by her husband this week." This is what another woman of the same name reads in a Tennessee newspaper. She imagines the dramatic incident with herself as the victim, for she is bored in her marriage and longs for more attention from Clyde, her husband. But she is also trying to escape basic human loneliness; and it is her attempt to break her isolation by reaching out to Clyde that has universal significance. There is a moment when husband and wife have a chance to bridge the gap between them: "they looked at each other. The moment filled full with their helplessness. Slowly they both flushed, as though with a double shame and a double pleasure. . . . Rare and wavering, some possibility stood timidly like a stranger between them and made them hang their heads" (*CS* 16). The moment cannot last, but it is valuable in itself; for it works as a confirmation that Ruby and Clyde need to be able to go on together. The mood at the end of this story is not unlike the mood at the end of "The Lady with the Dog." Anna and Gurov realize that their future promises to be difficult. They are both married to somebody else, but they understand that their love will force them to stay together (3: 28).

Even if it is not a storyteller's function to champion one cause or another, it is the hope of a writer ultimately to transcend the mere plot of his story. Both "The Steppe" and "The Wide Net" demonstrate that one who drags the river with a wide net must expect to catch a variety of life. And one who decides to dive down into the stream and touch bottom, like Ivan Ivanovitch in the river at Mironositskoe or like William Wallace in the Pearl River, will find that the world is more than just objectified reality on resurfacing. In her essay on Chekhov, Welty explains: "In the river, Ivan has experienced happiness of such purity that it is forgetful of self" (*Eye* 76). This is also what the storyteller is after in the expression of vision.

In *The Ponder Heart* Miss Edna Earle may claim that she is only a go-between and that she hardly ever gets a word in for herself, but she tells the story of the Ponders and imposes her vision on it. Implied in the vision there is a message. Chekhov and Welty *are* didactic in that they insist on one message: enjoy the gift that is life; never waste life. We should accept life as the dying narrator does in Chekhov's "An Anonymous Story," when he says: "The sun doesn't rise twice a day, and life is not given us again— clutch at what is left of your life and save it" (3: 255). It is with this determination to explore life that Welty's young woman leaves the Innisfallen and goes ashore in Cork full of cautious optimism and curiosity. In this important respect the ending of "The Bride of the Innisfallen" has its obvious parallel in the ending of Chekhov's story "Betrothed." Nadya, who is the betrothed of the title, is full of life and high spirits when she leaves behind her native town and her husband-to-be, and in her mind "rose the vista of a new, wide, spacious life, and that life, still obscure and full of mysteries, beckoned her and attracted her" (11: 75). The preservation of the desire to live and experience fully is crucial. The mystery and the exoticism that man longs for are within reach, as Chekhov's black monk and Welty's lady with the purple hat indicate. But we seldom take the advice of the black monk or follow the lady with the purple hat, as we fear losing our self-respect or even our sanity. The public point of view demands that we rid ourselves of black monks and purple-hatted ladies from New Orleans. The point made by both writers is that to kill off these figures of the imagination may be too high a price to pay to be considered sane by our neighbors. Closing our eyes to the life of possibility is a waste of life itself.

Chekhov's fiction is full of tragically wasted lives, but Grigory in "Sorrow" is an extreme case. When he is on his way to the hospital in a blizzard, he feels something for the first time in years. As he listens to his dead wife's head banging against the side of the sledge, he tries to remember the years of his married life: "His wedding he remembered, but of what happened after the wedding—for the life of him he could remember nothing, except perhaps that he had drunk, lain on the stove [another translation has simply: "lain about"], and quarreled. Forty years had been wasted like that" (9: 149). Grigory is found in the snow; and when he wakes up in the hospital, he discovers that his arms and legs have been amputated. The doctor tells him to stop crying, as he has already lived his sixty years, which should be enough for anybody. Grigory argues that he would like to live another five or six years, but the doctor replies: "What for?" and leaves the ward. The last sentence of the story seems to be in the voice of Chekhov himself: "It was all over with the turner!" (9: 151). Grigory has wronged his wife and wasted his life, and he gets no second chance. The absolute absence of sentimentality is typical of Chekhov, and it is also typical of Welty. In "Death of a Traveling Salesman," the salesman R. J. Bowman realizes how rootless, materialistic, and lonely his life has been when he compares it to the life he encounters in a Mississippi cabin. The tragedy is that when Grigory and Bowman realize that they have wasted their lives, it is too late to do anything about it. Bowman is *not* offered a choice between his own isolation and the possibility of love. Instead, and without a trace of sentimentality, Welty lets him die: "He sank in fright onto the road, his bags falling about him. . . . He covered his heart with both hands to keep anyone from hearing the noise it made. But nobody heard it" (*CS* 130). Or, as Chekhov might have put it: good-bye to the salesman. In an unpublished part of my interview with Miss Welty from 1978, she said, "I just finished reading all of Chekhov again that I could. I mean all the stories. And you don't cry in those; although you could because it is so encompassing, at the same time they are not sentimental." These same words apply as well to her own stories.

In this essay I have been content to celebrate the likenesses of perspective and to establish affinities between the art of Anton Chekhov and the art of Eudora Welty. Some of their deepest connections are expressed in the advice they give to us. At the end of his long story "The Duel," Chekhov gives two cheers for life: "In search for truth man makes two steps forward and one step back. Suffering, mistakes, and weariness of life thrust them back, but the thirst for truth and stubborn will drive them on and on. And who knows? Perhaps they will reach the real truth at last" (2: 172). Welty shares this cautious optimism and refers to this passage in her essay on Chekhov (*Eye* 81). In "The Wanderers," the last story of her main work, *The Golden Apples,* she writes:

> Virgie never saw it differently, never doubted that all the opposites on earth were close together, love close to hate, living to dying; but of them all, hope and despair were the closest blood—unrecognizable one from the other sometimes, making moments double upon themselves, and in doubling double again, amending but never taking back. (*CS* 452–53)

In her use of the convincing detail and compression, in her art of characterization, in her psychological realism, in her rendition of loneliness and how to overcome it, in her humorous vision of people and their illusions, in her subtle development of social issues, in her emphasis on imagination, sensibility, and compassion, in her warning against the wasted life, and in her cautious optimism about the future, Eudora Welty combines many essential Chekhovian elements in her fiction and deserves the praise and recognition in the epithet the Chekhov of the South.

DAUN

KENDIG

REALITIES IN
"SIR RABBIT"   A Frame Analysis

In "Reality in Chekhov's Stories" Eudora Welty reminds her readers that
" 'real,' as in 'the real world,' does not, as we know, mean invariable, or
static, or ironclad, or consistent, or even trustworthy. What is real in
life . . . may be at the same time what is transient, ephemeral, contradictory,
even on the point of vanishing before our eyes. So it isn't just *there*" (*Eye*
63). Welty's stories also assert again and again that reality "isn't just there"
as an objective fact; rather "it comes to us through the living human being"
(*Eye* 63). Although the notion operates in much of her work, *The Golden
Apples* is perhaps the most extensive exploration of this theme. Set in the
fictive town of Morgana, Mississippi, which in name alone calls up the
illusory fata morgana, each story in *The Golden Apples* turns on some facet
of the individual's enigmatic sense of reality.

Intrigued by the same notion in a very different discipline, sociologist
Erving Goffman found himself asking not "what is reality?"—as if it were
"just there"—but "under what circumstances do we think things are real?"
(2). He was particularly interested in William James's and, later, Alfred
Schutz's position that there are multiple realities, rather than only one. In
Frame Analysis, Goffman developed an analytical vocabulary to explore
the nature of these various realities. This vocabulary serves as a kind of
magnifying glass, revealing the subtle, taken-for-granted, minute details
constituting the individual's sense of reality.

Before defining specific terms however, we should consider the system's
relevance to literary analysis. Though Goffman's concerns were psychoso-
cial, many of his examples and explanations drew from film, theater, and

literature because these scripted works, particularly those exploring multiple realities, provided such clear examples of complex framing. Consequently, frame analysis should be particularly insightful with a story like "Sir Rabbit" from *The Golden Apples*. As the shortest and perhaps most consistently comic story of the cycle, "Sir Rabbit" has received only nodding attention from most critics.[1] At the same time, the story's brevity provides a manageable model for examining some of Welty's more complex framing techniques in this and longer works in the cycle. Much of the attention this story *has* received revolves around whether or not Mattie Will's seduction was real or imagined. While frame analysis may not end the controversy once and for all, it will certainly demonstrate why it is so compelling.

Goffman defines a frame by explaining that when we come to a situation, we ask, consciously or not, "what is going on?" We appeal to the frame for an answer. A *frame* is a culturally or community-determined definition of a situation that organizes things like appropriate activity, objects, participant roles, and interaction patterns. These organizational premises help us to determine, among other things, a situation's reality status. *Primary frames* set off literal situations that we interpret at face value. They are the self-explanatory or most basic situations in a culture, so intrinsic to our way of seeing and understanding the world that they have become invisible through familiarity. We rarely stop to question how or why we behave as we do in these most basic contexts; instead, our interpretation of primary frameworks tends to be tacit and frequent. As a result, it is only when one of these assumptions is amiss that we question, and consequently notice, the framework. When an already-meaningful activity in terms of some primary framework is systematically transformed into an activity with a different, nonliteral meaning such as a dream, joke, game, or story, the framework is called a *keying*. For example, what may initially look like a literal car accident, or a primary framework, may at second glance be a simulation of a car accident to teach emergency workers. In this instance the structure of both situations is the same in terms of objects (ambulances and wrecked vehicles), participant roles (victims and rescue workers), and appropriate behaviors (testing vital signs and treating symptoms). But the style differs since the primary framework demands the actual life saving operations while the keying simply demonstrates the steps of the process without, for example, actually injecting a shot or setting a bone. More significantly, the meaning differs since the primary framework is about saving lives while the keying is about testing skills and procedures. *Retransformation* uses the keyed framework as a model for reworking and is consequently one step further removed from the original interpretation provided by a primary framework. A retransformation of the previous example would occur if a videotape of the simulation was used to train future paramedics. Each subsequent keying or rekeying adds a *layer* to the activity. We learn from the number of layers how many times the activity has been transformed (theoretically) and how many steps the present activity or utterance is removed from the original or literal meaning. As an example of the relationship among these terms, consider the current trend in television commercials that uses an actor to play an actor filming a commercial. Here the primary framework, or literal activity, that serves as a model is a person spontaneously commenting on a product. This is keyed into a commercial, which uses an actor giving a scripted rendition of the product's value. This conventional commercial is then rekeyed in a version that shows a commercial in production complete with a view of cameras and technicians acting as if they were taping the event. This framework has three layers: the literal experience of casual conversations, the keyed experience of a commercial based on casual conversation, and the rekeyed experience of a commercial simulating the production of a commercial. Notice that each transformational layer bears a resemblance to the primary framework but that each also evokes completely different, nonliteral meanings.

Goffman argues that individuals do not create frames. Instead, we learn frame expectations as part of the socialization process. The fact that we can usually recognize what is going on and behave appropriately further suggests a shared understanding of interactive patterns. This means, however, that for a frame to exist, its cues must be clearly and conventionally established and the individual participants socially competent and attentive to these cues. Since a frame organizes both the meaning of an event and subjective involvement in it, the frame can break either through misframing of meaning or flooding of involvement. *Misframing* results from ambiguity, error, or dispute, while *flooding* results from inappropriate shifts in participation status. Paradoxically, these threats to frame stability can actually have very positive results; for they encourage intense involvement in making sense of the situation. Goffman explains that if "the whole frame can be shaken, rendered problematic, then this, too, can insure that prior involvements—and prior distances—can be broken up and that, whatever else happens, a dramatic change can occur in what it is that is being experienced" (382). This kind of negative experience is not foreign to the literary world either. Brecht's explorations of alienation techniques, as well as Pirandello's exploration of appearance and reality, turn on the same idea. So too, the use of unreliable narrators and unreliable reflector characters alert readers to frame vulnerability that forces them to become actively involved in making sense of events. As a result, the technique frequently signals complex frame structures that demand close participant involvement.

Both Goffman and Welty are intrigued by the complexity and vulnerability of the individual's experience of reality. Both are sensitive to the tension between the individual's competence to recognize and interact in community-generated frameworks and the individual's inclination to do so through a filter of unique interests and expectations. Welty explores this tension in "Sir Rabbit" through a richly and mysteriously layered framework that is ever threatened by its perceiver.

Most narrative fiction by nature develops at least two transformational layers, since readers experience events on the dramatic layer of the characters' represented world and on the epic layer of the narrator's storytelling situation. In "Sir Rabbit," Welty transforms the story on both of these layers.

The dramatic layers reflect Mattie Will Sojourner's immediate, spontaneous, personal experience. In many ways, she presents an ideal challenge to the tension between community-generated frameworks and individual competence to interpret them. As a country girl, she lives at the geographical, social, and intellectual outskirts of the community. So while she revels in what she knows, her knowledge is limited. What she knows, of course, is the King MacLain of legend, both who he is and "the way [he does]" (CS 331). Based on this understanding, she, as a young woman in the woods, assumes she must be ripe to enter the legend and, through it, the community.

On the dramatic layer, two distinct events occur at two distinct times: at fifteen, Mattie Will submits to a spring tumble with the MacLain twins; as an adult, she yields to an autumn seduction by their father. But Mattie's limited competence and primed expectations frame both events as legendary MacLain seductions. Although the two events are stylistically different, Mattie perceives structural similarities that suggest a common framework. This perception is most notable in her expectation of a surprising appearance, an overwhelming presence, and a transforming power.

Upon seeing someone peer around a tree, the fifteen-year-old Mattie Will thinks she recognizes a familiar rogue's behavior and announces, "Oh-oh. I know you, Mr. King MacLain!" (CS 331). Of course, for all of her confidence, Mattie Will is wrong in this instance; but years later, when King MacLain identifies himself from a distance, she still must recognize him not by something as mundane as his word, but by an enchantingly familiar whistle: "Mr. MacLain even *whistled* with manners. And with familiarity. And what two men in the world whistle the same? Mattie Will believed she must have heard him and seen him closer-to than she thought. Nobody could have *told* her how sweet the rascal whistled, but it didn't surprise her" (CS 334). In both encounters "King" seems magically to reveal himself to Mattie. But in the first instance naive anticipation, not an enchanting appearance, traps Mattie Will. In the second encounter, however, King's seductive whistle exceeds her expectations.

Mattie moves from identifying King MacLain to actually confronting him; and in each instance, the result is so overwhelming that it renders her an easy victim. In the first case she is confused suddenly to confront "the two meanies that she'd never dreamed of instead of the one that would have terrified her for the rest of her days" (CS 331). But they "didn't give her a chance to begin her own commotion. . . . One of the twins took hold of her apron sash and the other one ran under and she was down" (CS 332). When Mattie Will realizes that it is the twins, not their father, the frame breaks momentarily for her, since the premises governing the organization and meaning of the experience collapse. The twins take advantage of her confusion; and for a while Mattie seems to distance her immediate involvement in the situation as she analytically monitors her response and realizes, "she might have felt more anger than confusion, except that keeping the twins straight had fallen her lot" (CS 332).

In her encounter with King MacLain, however, she is disoriented by his very presence. In fact, "when she laid eyes on Mr. MacLain close, she staggered, he had such grandeur and then she was caught by the hair and brought down as if whacked by an unseen shillelagh" (CS 338). In this instance, it is not a framing error but flooding that threatens Mattie Will's hold on the framework. Having spent much of her life dreaming of this moment, Mattie finds the current reality of King MacLain's presence so overwhelming that once again her grasp on the frame momentarily flutters.

Mattie Will also expects to be transformed by the experience, both through the role she assumes and through the notoriety of the legend. In each scene, for example, she reflects upon the responsibility implicit in her role. As she moves beyond confusion to realize her role in the first incident, she thinks prophetically, "from now on, having the visit go the visitor's way would come before giving trouble" (CS 322). But her role for King MacLain demanded even more: "like submitting to another way to talk, she could answer to his burden now, his whole blithe, smiling, superior, frantic existence. And no matter what happened to her, she had to remember, disappointments are not to be borne by Mr. MacLain, or he'll go away again" (CS 338). Mattie understands the implications of her role in each instance because of her familiarity with the frame.

She realizes too that the significance of each event goes beyond the fleeting literal moment; for she is now a part of timeless, legendary reality. Just by putting the event into words, she calls it up again. She suspects, of course, that her husband would not appreciate her adventures, legendary or not. In fact, Junior would naively want to deny the reality and suppress the story of her first encounter with such grandeur.

Tumbling on the wet spring ground with the goody goody MacLain twins was something Junior Holifield would have given her a licking for, just making such a story up, supposing, after she married Junior, she had put anything into words. Or he would have said he'd lick her for it if she told it *again*.

Poor Junior! (*CS* 333)

With King MacLain however, the legend is so well established that there are already words for Mattie: "she was Mr. MacLain's doom, or Mr. MacLain's weakness, like the rest, and neither Mrs. Junior Holifield nor Mattie Will Sojourner; now she was something she had always heard of" (*CS* 338). For Mattie Will, becoming "something she had always heard of" means that she, formerly an insignificant country girl, can finally be a part of the community because she is now a part of one of its most vital legends.

It is not clear that both events are physically the same, since the encounter with the twins sounds like an inexperienced game of grope and tumble, while the scene with King sounds passionate. Yet Mattie Will recognizes a common frame in the organization of experience: for her, both are legendary MacLain seductions. Mattie is ready and willing to identify the frame because she knows all about King MacLain and "the way [he does]" with country girls like herself. She experiences, consequently, what she expects: magic and transformation. The twins' sudden appearance seems magical at the time, but it is no match for King's enchanting whistle. Similarly, she is overwhelmed first to confront not one large but two small MacLains and then to confront not a mortal charm but a godly grandeur. Finally, upon entering the frame, she takes on a role that transforms her from the insignificant Mattie Will Sojourner to the woman responsible for pleasing first the twins and later King. In assuming this role she becomes part of a legendary reality that supercedes her mundane literal existence.

Mattie Will's dramatic layer of the framework shows her experiences in Morgan's Woods as spontaneous, immediate, and personal. The narrator's epic layer, however, approaches these events from a broader realm. As an authorial narrator, she knows the shape and significance of the whole and attempts to focus that for the reader by keying mythic behaviors.

Narrative description of the scene with Mattie Will and the twins seems to key some ancient fertility rite. While the sexual exploration alone might account for this association, the scene's language and imagery also place in the foreground ceremonial behaviors and seemingly primal bonds with nature. The event occurs "under the dark tree with its flowers so few you could still count them, it was so early in spring" (*CS* 331). As they unbuckled their knickers, the boys jingled as they "trotted up and down through the gully like a pony pair that could keep time to the music in the Ringling Brothers', touching shoulders until the last." Then the boys moved in and made a jangling circle around her before bringing her to the ground. Despite their lively approach, they seem pensive, and Mattie Will notes that "they didn't have a smile between them; instead little matching frowns were furrowing their foreheads." As the twins explore, Mattie notices the sun that "[took] hold of their arms with a bold dart of light" and of the "soft and babylike heads, and the nuzzle of cool noses" (*CS* 332). Years later she recalls the boys as "young deer, or even remoter creatures . . . kangaroos." The story closes with Mattie thinking, "they were mysterious and sweet—gamboling now she knew not where" (*CS* 341).

Several features contribute to the ritual quality of this scene. The boys' approach, with their rhythmic and coordinated movement, their trotting and circling pattern, and the jingling accompaniment of their knickers, sounds like a ritual dance. This is reinforced by Mattie's tendency to think of the boys in animal terms, referring to them as ponies, deer, and kangaroos, and to their behavior as trotting, nuzzling, barking and gamboling. Though very little is spoken, everyone seems to know what to do; and often the cue seems to come from the natural world. As they tumble to the ground, they are prompted by "old foolish worms . . . coming out in their blindness." The sun takes hold of their arms, rests on their heads. The crows hover nearby and when "one crow hollered over their heads . . . they all got to their feet as though a clock struck" (*CS* 332). Even their final act of sitting in a circle with a communal bag of candy sticks which they "sucked and held . . . in their mouths like old men's pipes" is so rich in sexual allusion that it creates a more stylized ritual keying complete with intimations of ceremonial smoke.

While these general ritualistic qualities heighten the scene's impact, the concentration of motifs from Celtic mythology, particularly its Beltene celebration, suggests a systematic keying that focuses the scene's signifi-cance. Although there is no evidence that Welty consciously knew or patterned this specific ritual, the abundance of Beltene symbolism in this scene cannot be overlooked. The roots "bel," for shining or brilliant and "tene" for fire suggest a distinct solar character for this festival, and the scene generally is ablaze in sun imagery (MacCana 64). Between spring and summer, on the eve of May first, this outdoor fire festival honored the divinities with fertility rites to insure the productivity of the land and animals for the coming year. During the celebration, people danced in a circle that moved sunwise, from east to west.[2] The deer or stag, as well as the horse, symbolized virility and was thought to have divine powers. In fact, in Staffordshire, people still enact the fertility dance of the horns, a relic of pagan worship now controlled by the local church. In this ritual, circular, interweaving dance patterns *symbolize* fertility, while the lively rhythm and movement presumably *promote* fertility in people, animals, and crops.[3] Finally, while Celtic goddesses frequently took the form of birds, three in particular appear as crows, the sisters Morrigane, Bobd and Macha (Markale 113).

In the second encounter, King MacLain appears to Mattie some time in October, and much of the initial description endows him with the godlike ability to appear and disappear partially and elusively. For example, as Mattie tries to keep track of him, she notes that "he showed for a minute and then was gone, . . . while the white glimmer . . . then . . . passed behind another tree . . . and the invisible mouth whistled from east right around to west . . ." (*CS* 333–34). First his voice is "far away for a moment," then "suddenly loud upon them. They saw part of him. . ." (*CS* 334–35). When Mattie *does* see him in full, "he looked like the preternatural month of June" (*CS* 337).

A number of scholars have noted that the actual seduction scene clearly parodies Yeats's poem, "Leda and the Swan." By paraphrasing several essential phrases to maintain Mattie's distinctive style and perception while still echoing Yeats's text, the scene provides a delightful keying. For example, Yeats's poem opens with "a sudden blow" while Mattie is "whacked by an unseen shillelagh"; where Leda is "a staggering girl" under the great beating wings, Mattie Will "staggered" in the presence of King's grandeur; and while Yeats's persona asks rhetorically, "did she put on his knowledge with his power?" Mattie simply realizes that "she had to put on what he knew with what he did" (*CS* 338). King MacLain's parodic role emerges gradually with scattered references that associate his behavior and appearance with the mythic white bird. For example, Mattie describes King's linen shoulders as "white as a goose's back in the sun" (*CS* 338). After the seduction, Mattie notices that, "a dove feather came turning down through the light that was like golden smoke. She caught it with a dart of the hand, and brushed her chin; she was never displeased to catch anything" (*CS* 339). While the light, like golden smoke, faintly mirrors the shower of gold affair, the rest of the passage confirms earlier suggestions that if this scene differs from the mythic core, it is in how each woman perceives her role. For Leda is presented as a frightened victim, but Mattie Will has enthusiastically fulfilled her life's dream. Finally, the reader can almost see the massive wings flap as King "beat his snowy arms up and down" to chase Mattie Will away (*CS* 340).

After her seduction, Mattie returns to Junior and his friend Blackstone, but a trancelike quality has fallen on the scene. The use of abundant narrative significantly slows the reader's sense of time so that the characters seem caught in a timeless netherworld, while the behaviors described reinforce the hypnotic suggestion. As the dog trots mindlessly back and forth from licking the seat of Blackstone's pants and Junior's "stone-like hand," Mattie Will realizes that "for ages he might have been making that little path back and forth . . . but she could not think of his name, or would not, just as Junior would not wake up" (*CS* 339). She wanders off only to come upon the now-snoring King MacLain and thinks "he snored as if all the frogs of springtime were inside him—but to him an old song. Or to him little balls, little bells for the light air, that rose up and sank between his two hands, never to be let fall" (*CS* 340).

Just as the seduction rekeys Yeats's transformation of the Zeus and Leda myth, the larger scene further keys Celtic mythology. In fact, if Mattie Will's seduction by the twins draws from Beltene motifs, consider how her seduction by King draws from the other great Celtic open-air celebration. Observed on the eve of November first, Samhain marked the transition between the old and the new year. The celebration, however, was neither part of the old nor the new year. Instead, it was a liminal time between time. This curious chronology marked not only the suspension of temporal boundaries but also those between living and dead, mortal and immortal, visible and invisible. The Celts treated it as a time charged with preternatural energy (MacCana 127–28). This then, may account for the "right time" that King appears (*CS* 340), his godlike invisibility and grandeur, and the trancelike, atemporal quality of the scene. The Samhain celebration passed from east to west in the direction of the dying sun, which is perhaps why King's enchanting whistle follows this course and sets the scene in motion. In addition, several Celtic stories tell of divinities that change from human to swan form, particularly during the Samhain festival (MacCana 237). The rituals were held at a sacred site, usually an oak grove since this was a sacred tree for the Celts.[4] Is it any wonder then that King MacLain has a favorite spot under a large oak tree where he meets Snowdie and probably Mattie Will? Even her closing contemplation of the now-sleeping King seems to draw from the Celtic belief that during Samhain, fairies moving from one fairy hill to another accompanied by bells and elf horns were suddenly visible to mere mortals. Mattie hears in King's snores this ancient fairy music and seems mesmerized by a fairy incantation about the fertile and magical Sir Rabbit.

Despite the abundance of Celtic ritual motifs, both scenes are very loose rather than close keyings. Here, as elsewhere in the cycle, Welty repeatedly disrupts the mythic pattern and so discourages easy parallels. Like the elusive King MacLain, these Celtic motifs tease us as they flash and vanish through the story, so that we can never claim easy frame stability. We cannot even claim with certainty that Welty knowingly patterned these specific rituals. We can, however, examine the effect they have on our perception of the story. Much of the ambiguity of this mythic layer occurs because the imagery is so natural and consistent with the literal scene. This supports Welty's contention that she uses mythology not for allegory but because it permeates our lives and imagination (*Conversations* 189, 313). Because both scenes occur in the woods, for example, it makes literal sense that the trees, the birds, and the sun would be present. But as Welty animates and even personifies many of these images, they develop a magical participation reminiscent of their ancient, mythic portrayal. In trying to make sense of the scene, we seek other cues that might confirm this framework. As images from Mattie Will's literal, everyday reality correspond with motifs from ancient mythology, we begin to perceive the everyday world in a magical, mystical context. This juxtaposition can create several diverse effects. For example, when Mattie Will's homespun associations contrast with mythic awe, a comic irony occurs: the twins' sober approach compared to a Ringling Brothers' circus pony act, King's shoulders compared to a goose's back. At some points, however, Mattie's associations tend to intensify the literal moment with mythic reverberations. For example, when she sees the sun take hold of the twins' arms "with a bold dart of light or rest on their wetted, shaken hair, or splash over their pretty clothes like the torn petals of a sunflower," the sun seems to bless the boys and empower the scene as it was thought to do in the ancient ritual. These free and natural associations demonstrate how these myths pervade the everyday world, how we reach to these magic realms to understand the magic in our literal reality.

While Mattie Will's perceptions contribute to our sense of magic, we cannot always trust them. In fact, a framing error opens the story, immediately alerting the reader that this character poses ever-new challenges to identifying a stable and coherent framework of understanding. Yet despite the perceptual and psychological limitations of her focalization, Mattie plods blithely and confidently on. While readers inevitably follow her, they do so at the risk of their credulity.

Mattie Will is cognitively and emotionally limited in a number of ways. As a country girl, she has been to town and recognizes people who live there, but she demonstrates that she is not familiar with them. For example, she does recognize the twins and remembers that they are about her age. She even remembers that they used to have a pop stand in the summer. At the same time, she must not get to town frequently, for she is amazed that they are almost grown. It seems that many of Mattie Will's conclusions about town folk are based on very limited associations. In fact, her insights seem to grow from her imagination rather than from experience; for though she begins with firsthand experiences or generally recognized facts, she tends to romanticize from there. For example, she knows that King's wife, Snowdie, is an albino and that her husband "roamed the country end on end . . . (CS 336). Most notably, Mattie has an extended memory of the time Snowdie came to look after the family when Mattie Will's parents were ill. Mattie moves, however, from this genuinely warm memory to a rather melodramatic image of Snowdie MacLain as the town's inspiration:

> She was . . . always, a sweet-looking Presbyterian albino lady. Nothing was her fault. . . . Going down the aisle she held up her head for the benefit of them all,

while they considered Mr. MacLain a thousand miles away. And when they sang in church with her, they might as well have sung,

> "A thousand miles away.
> A thousand miles away."

It made church holier. (*CS* 336)

If her image of Snowdie is this idealized, it is little wonder that she sees King as she does.

Despite her limited knowledge and experience, Mattie Will thinks of herself as quite worldly. This of course, is when she is most likely to make framing errors. She is, for example, determined to behave as if she understands and is in control of events, although she rarely is. In the opening scene she boldly announces to King MacLain that she knows who he is and what he does. Then she thinks, "When it came down to it, scared or not, she wanted to show him she'd heard all about King MacLain and his way" (*CS* 331). In her determination to cover for her limited experience, she paradoxically demonstrates her vulnerability. Even when she realizes within seconds that she does not know King MacLain as well as she had thought, she only "took back what she said" mentally. And despite even this, she did not quite learn a lesson from the experience; years later she is ready to blame her error entirely on the twins: "But it wasn't fair to tease me . . . to make me think that first minute I was going to be carried off by their pa" (*CS* 333). Not only is she willing to pass the blame, she is just as ready to confront King MacLain the next time around. When Junior remains stubbornly skeptical and cautious, she brushes him off saying, "Don't be so country" (*CS* 336).

Mattie also knows how to use her relationship with Junior. From her perspective he seems domineering, slow, and stubborn. While she caters to his ego one minute, she scorns him the next. She simultaneously fears he will "lick her" if she tells of her romp with the twins; but she pities this naive attempt to control her or the legend with her sigh, "Poor Junior" (*CS* 333). When he remains skeptical of King MacLain's identity, she "pretends" to be as slow as he is and later commends his bravado by whispering "looks like you scared that man away. Wonder who it was" (*CS* 335). Mattie stopped wondering about King's identity with his first whistle; and when he invites her into the open, she scorns Junior's objection and country ways, asserting her imagined worldliness. Even when Junior faints in fear, Mattie rationalizes her indifference by criticizing his fear as egocentric and his fall as stubborn: "Big red hand spread out on his shirt (he would always think he was shot through the heart if anybody's gun but his went off). Junior rose in the air and got a holler out. And then— he seemed determined about the way to come down . . . no man more set in his ways than he . . . he kicked and came down backward" (*CS* 337).

Despite these faults, we cannot help but like Mattie Will, perhaps because we identify with her frame vulnerability. At the same time, the accumulated errors, exaggerations, and questionable value judgments alert the reader not to take Mattie Will's perceptions at face value. Instead, we face ambiguity and doubt at every turn. While some critics argue that the scene with King MacLain is actually a daydream, there is not enough evidence to give the framework even this dubious security. For every argument establishing a fantasy, there is an equally strong literal explanation.

Merrill Maguire Skaggs has argued that only a fantasy could account for the apparent inconsistency in King MacLain's behavior. She contrasts his geniality toward the Holifields in this scene with his insolence toward Old Man Moody and Fatty Bowles in "June Recital"; she notes also his begging and pleading here with his sneaking and grabbing at Katie Rainey's funeral. Finally she contends that he was not in the habit of hunting in these parts and that even if he were, he would not do so from his unlikely perch while dressed in a white suit (232–34). While this is an interesting argument, it has several problems. King was not cordial to the Old Man Moody and Fatty Bowles in "June Recital" because he did not have to be. They had nothing he wanted; in fact, they were in his way. Similarly, he has no cause to beg at the funeral. At the same time, he does know how to turn on the charm to get what he wants. In "Shower of Gold," Katie Rainey warns, "Beware of the man with manners," for he could be "just as nice as could be. . . . Just as courteous," and yet be "outrageous to some several" (*CS* 264). There is also significant evidence from other stories that King MacLain was indeed in the habit of hunting in these parts, though perhaps not for literal birds. His dress, location, and request could be literal since the one thing we do know about him is that he is not conventional. Since we only know what various narrators choose to tell us, perhaps he frequents this area more than folks know (or have told us up to this point). In fact, some of the discussion in "The Wanderers" suggests that he turned up more than was commonly realized to bestow gifts (and perhaps do a little hunting). Junior suspects that King MacLain is out hunting for young women; and several of the other stories, particularly "Moon Lake," allude to the living evidence of similar hunting expeditions. If this is the case, his apparel, location, and behavior make perfect sense.

Marie Antoinette Manz-Kunz argues more convincingly for the fantasy key: abundant narrative description in this scene acts to suspend time while it permits readers to trace King's movement through the woods as a glitter or glimmer magically appearing and disappearing (91–92). While this argument is persuasive, it is just possible that from Mattie Will's fixed focalization point a clear view of King MacLain is often blocked by foliage, causing him to appear and disappear abruptly. It is also possible that Mattie's heightened awareness and disorientation may create a slow-motion effect. Patricia Yaeger simply assumes the scene is a fantasy and then considers why other readers might disagree and interpret it as an actual encounter. She concludes that these readers confuse Morgana's ideology—as she outlines it—with the town's contradictory reality. While Yaeger's resulting interpretation of the story is provocative and insightful, it is ultimately a diminished reading since it is based on the essentially unprovable assumption that the incident is a fantasy and proceeds to limit the possible readings to that conclusion.

Was Mattie Will *really* seduced by King MacLain? Perhaps the issue is not whether the seduction is real or imagined but why its ambiguity is so compelling. In the opening scene, Mattie's psychological focalization results in misframing. As the story progresses, Mattie grows older but continues to demonstrate her psychological vulnerability to King MacLain. Eventually readers anticipate another error. By the time King MacLain appears, we expect the error before it occurs; the same primed anticipation makes us suspect Mattie Will of seeing King because she expects to do so. When the narrator offers no clear evidence to confirm or deny the framework, we are caught between what we expected and what we experienced. But what did we experience? All that we know has come through Mattie Will's conscious experience, mediated by the narrator. Based on this we know that for her the seduction was real; beyond this we can only speculate. While this ambiguity may be unsettling to some readers, it serves a variety of functions. For one thing, this reading encourages us to experience the story on at least two layers of reality at once. As a result the framing is much richer and more complex. In addition, while it furthers Katie Rainey's notion of King's mythic status, it does so without granting resolution. The illusion is maintained. Finally, this stubborn ambiguity takes us back to one of the cycle's central themes. As Welty has explained in another context, "ambiguity is a fact of life. A fiction writer's responsibility covers not only what he presents as the facts of a given story but what he chooses to stir up as their implications; in the end, these implications, too, become facts in a larger fictional sense" (*Eye* 160).

As this discussion demonstrates, frame analysis focuses the multiple frames of reality in "Sir Rabbit" so that we can better understand how they interact to affect the reader as they do. Although two distinct events occur in this story, they unfold with such structural similarity that we begin to interpret and reinterpret one based upon the other. While this correspondence is at work on the dramatic layer, the narrative presentation draws on imagery and word choice that suggest a faint keying of Celtic rituals. These sources lend an air of mystery and magic to events while creating a timeless and universal significance for the frameworks. In the midst of all of this, Mattie Will's psychological vulnerability poses a perpetual threat to frame stability so that even in the most literal moments we are reminded that "what is real in life . . . may be at the same time what is transient, ephemeral, contradictory, even on the point of vanishing before our eyes . . . it isn't just there" (*Eye* 63).

CHERYLL

B U R G E S S

From Metaphor
to Manifestation

The Artist
in Eudora Welty's
A Curtain of Green

"This could never have been a popular view," admits Eudora Welty, referring to Willa Cather's lifelong opinion that "[a]rtists . . . are perhaps greater, and more deserving to be made way for, than other human beings" (*Eye* 59). While she attempts to understand and to explain why Cather sets apart the artist in value, Welty herself strikes a humbler pose. Whereas Cather's novels introduce numerous semiautobiographical artists, characters of commanding stature, Welty's corpus contains very few portraits of the artist. She does not vaunt her role, even from behind the veil of fiction.

Despite such personal modesty, Welty generously praises the accomplishments and extols the special gifts of other authors—Jane Austen, Henry Green, Katherine Anne Porter, William Faulkner, and Willa Cather, to name but a few. Moreover, Welty's essays on writing prove her to be an artist highly conscious of her craft, respectful of its demands. These critical statements on art and artists lead to fresh readings of Welty's own stories, helping us recognize artistic impulses in characters not explicitly identified as artists. Such insights deepen our understanding of the characters while at the same time suggesting how Welty, as artist, perceives herself. If she is too self-effacing to paint overtly autobiographical portraits of herself as artist, Welty is nevertheless too fascinated by the process of artistic creation to resist treating the subject altogether.

Reading Welty's earliest collection, *A Curtain of Green,* with eyes alert for references to storytellers reveals numerous characters who do literally tell stories. Leota, the hairdresser in "Petrified Man," Steve, in "Keela, The Outcast Indian Maiden," and Sister in "Why I Live at the P.O.," tell stories at some length. But these unsophisticated characters are not artists in disguise. To find Welty exploring the nature of her role, we must turn to the tantalizing passages that invite consideration as metaphors for the art of storytelling. For example, the girl in "A Memory," looking at the world through the small frames made by her fingers, suggests the compositional techniques of focus and framing. Mrs. Larkin, in the title story, "cutting, separating, thinning and tying back . . . the clumps of flowers and bushes and vines" (*CS* 108), parallels in her gardening the task of a writer: editing, organizing, deleting, and controlling her words and sentences and paragraphs. Perhaps most impressively, the jazz improvisations that Powerhouse composes on the piano both accompany and suggest themselves as musical equivalents to the performance of creating a story.

These metaphors for storytelling might fruitfully be used to elucidate the creation of stories. One might discuss such considerations as framing one's story, pruning away irrelevances, improvising a plot line, reiterating an idea, creating variations on a theme, and controlling rhythm and cadence of language. I propose, however, a slight change of focus, shifting emphasis from the craft of writing to the character of the writer. If Welty plants metaphors of story writing in her fiction, doesn't that in some sense cast the corresponding characters in the role of author or artist?[1] The girl in "A Memory" and Mrs. Larkin in "A Curtain of Green" are not artists as Welty is an artist. Yet something suggests that we consider them as such.

I would like to show that excerpts from Welty's essays support the intuition that framing and gardening may be read as metaphors for story writing or artistic creation; that studying characters who do these things as authors or artists offers valuable insights into the stories; and that in seeing where these characters fall short as artists—where the metaphors break down—we can better understand Welty's conception of the artist. Finally, I shall discuss Powerhouse, both as he is in contrast to the girl in "A Memory" and Mrs. Larkin of "A Curtain of Green" and as the single fully realized artist in this collection of stories.[2]

Welty's essays represent a mature crystalization of the ideas about art that she explored through metaphor in her early fiction and are a good place to seek explication of those metaphors. In "Place in Fiction," Welty elaborates on her notion of frame: "Place, to the writer at work, is seen in a frame. Not an empty frame, a brimming one. . . . [The writer] is always seeing double, two pictures at once in his frame, his and the world's, a fact that he constantly comprehends; and he works best in a state of constant and subtle and unfooled reference between the two" (*Eye* 124–25). The concept of two pictures, the author's and the world's, reappears in subsequent essays; Welty believes in the notion of a duality of perception and of the artist's power to fuse the two impressions into a story which is both reality and illusion: a picture of the author's reality under the "pleasing illusion that it is the world's" (*Eye* 125).

The girl on the beach, squaring her vision with her hands, looking out at everything through the small frames made by her fingers, shares the artist's impulse to see double, to act as both "observer and dreamer" (*CS* 76). While she dreams of the moment when her hand brushed against the wrist of her secret love, she watches the outward world: "children running on the sand, the upthrust oak trees growing over the clean pointed roof of the white pavilion, and the slowly changing attitudes of the grown-up people" (*CS* 151). As long as the outside world does conform to her private reveries, the girl can bask in this mood of artistic absorption, where people cluster in "attitudes" (*CS* 77), and the picture is tinged with the rosy wash of her ineffable passion. A dirty stain blotches the girl's composition, however, when an ugly family of bathers plant themselves disarmingly near her, and the man "includes" (*CS* 78) her in his smile. She wishes they were all dead.

We've seen artistic traits in the girl, but when the grotesque bathers lumber into her framed field of vision, the girl's power of fusion fails utterly. She cannot integrate the family into her framed composition. An observation by Welty on failed fiction may tell us why:

> The bad novel of today is unhappily like the tale told to the analyst. It is not communication, it is confession. . . . It is self-absorbed, self-indulgent, too often self-pitying. And it's dull.
>
> Surely what is indicated is for us not to confess ourselves, but to commit ourselves. Only when the best writer on earth is ready and willing . . . to commit himself to his subject can he truly know it—that is, absorb it, embrace it in his mind, take it to his heart, speak it in plain words.[3]

Nina Carmichael, in "Moon Lake," shows precisely this kind of willing commitment when she thinks, "It's only interesting, only worthy, to try for the fiercest secrets. To slip into them all—to change. To change for a moment into Gertrude, into Mrs. Gruenwald, into Twosie—into a boy. To *have been* an orphan" (*CS* 361). The girl on the beach, however, is too self-absorbed and self-indulgent to take the bathers to heart; consequently, she perceives only externals and relates only vulgarities like "Fat hung upon [the woman's] upper arms like an arrested earthslide on a hill" (*CS* 78). Until she commits herself to others, learns to accept the imaginative challenge of scenes incompatible with her dream of the touch, the girl will be able to paint only a single picture, write that one dull novel, see the world through the unsympathetic eyes of a child.

In both "A Memory" and "Moon Lake," Welty may be tracing her own development as an artist to a childhood passion for observing life. The girls of both stories possess the artistic gift of perception—"a capacity for receiving [life's] impressions" (*Eye* 128); they share the desire to find secret meanings in ordinary gestures, to wait breathlessly for the moment when people reveal themselves; and they both by nature transform sight into insight, view into vision. Nina, however, is further along in terms of artistic growth than the unnamed girl: she no longer "form[s] a judgment upon every person and every event which came under [her] eye" (*CS* 75) but yearns instead for her "heart to twist" (*CS* 346), striving to imagine herself into other's lives. Likewise, the adult narrator of "A Memory" has apparently outgrown the childhood need for absolute conformity to her ideas, as it requires an effort of memory to imagine herself back to those days of terrified withdrawal. In these stories, Welty suggests that artistic sight is not merely given but learned and that it involves an "open mind and . . . receptive heart" (*CS* 130), a willingness to include the ugly, the threatening, the painful, the foreign into one's field of vision and into one's heart.

In "A Memory" and "Moon Lake," Welty's young protagonists experiment with modes of perception; they are not yet impelled to create art, to communicate their visions in concrete form. "A Curtain of Green" concerns composition, not perception. In one sense, Mrs. Larkin can be said to author her own garden. She controls its shape; she determines whether it will sprawl in profuse growth or, as her neighbors would prefer, adhere to the bounds of propriety for an effect of restfulness. In her garden, Mrs. Larkin cuts, separates and ties back her plants, and yet, the narrator tells us,

> To a certain extent, she seemed not to seek for order, but to allow an overflowering, as if she consciously ventured forever a little farther, a little deeper, into her life in the garden.
> She planted every kind of flower that she could find or order from a catalogue—planted thickly and hastily, without stopping to think. (*CS* 108)

The overflowering ground of Mrs. Larkin's garden metaphorically echoes Welty's statement about a story: "The story is a vision; while it's being written, all choices must be its choices, and as these multiply upon one another, their field is growing too. The choices remain inevitable, in fact, through moving in a growing maze of possibilities that the writer, far from being dismayed at his presence on unknown ground . . . has learned to be grateful for, and excited by" ("How I Write" 245).

The words *field, growing,* and *ground* in this essay about story writing underscore Welty's tendency to think of stories as analogous to gardens. In contrast to the writer stirred by possibilities, Mrs. Larkin is neither grateful nor excited. Although she submerges herself daily in a labyrinth of potential choices, she seems to make none. Perhaps she has not decided where she will direct her story. Welty writes that the "multitude and clamor and threat and lure of *possibility* . . ." guide the author's story "most delicately" ("How I Write" 245). Mrs. Larkin seems deliberately to allow possibility, in the form of lush vegetation, to multiply and compound; but she does not stop to think or pause to plot. Her garden, then, rather than representing a completed story or even a story in progress, seems to be a metaphor for a story's unconscious origin. Indeed, Welty's account of the workings of a mind on the verge of producing a story closely resembles Mrs. Larkin's garden:

> The dark changes of the mind and heart, where all in the world is constantly *becoming* something . . . are not mapped and plotted yet . . . and their being so would make no change in their processes, . . . or schedule or pigeonhole or allot or substitute or predict the mysteries rushing unsubmissively through them by the minute. . . . The artist at work functions . . . without . . . the least power of prevention or prophecy or even cure. ("How I Write" 242)

The view of Mrs. Larkin as a writer groping for a story is a helpful one for understanding her plight. An author is one who has the power to manipulate fate: if the author wants a sunny day, she can create one; if she wants a happily-ever-after ending, she can write one. Mrs. Larkin once tried to exercise this power of authorship in real life when she watched the chinaberry tree crash down and kill her husband. She spoke softly, "You can't be hurt" (*CS* 214). But her husband was killed. Again, she conjured the protective words "You can't be hurt" in an attempt to change the event, rewrite the ending, but without effect. When we see Mrs. Larkin in the garden, tearing away at the foliage with her hoe, it is in furious rage at her powerlessness: it seems that there is no story she *can* write. The crisis, when she holds the hoe poised high, ready to strike Jamey, seems to be a moment in which she can grab the pen and gain a measure of control over what has been inexorable fate. If she could not author her husband's life, at least she can author Jamey's death.

But, according to Welty, something is drastically wrong with Mrs. Larkin's conception of authorship. Where Mrs. Larkin would create a story to "compensate," to "punish," to "protest" (*CS* 111), the novelist, Welty maintains, "does not argue; he hopes to show, to disclose. . . . [He] works neither to correct nor to condone, not at all to comfort, but to make what's told alive" (*Eye* 149, 152). An author's mission, Welty seems to say, is not to control but to record, not to exercise power in the interest of changing the world, but for the sole purpose of making "feeling felt" (*Eye* 105). "Life *is* strange," she writes. "Stories hardly make it more so" (*Eye* 128). And this is so: chinaberry trees *do* kill husbands. Mrs. Larkin fails as an artist when she wants to reenact "the workings of accident, of life and death" (*CS* 110). The chinaberry tree's fall would be reenacted; with her hoe, she would fell Jamey: she would act rather than observe. Welty, in contrast, succeeds as an artist because she makes us feel Mrs. Larkin in action, makes us feel "her life in the garden" (*CS* 108).

Both the girl in "A Memory" and Mrs. Larkin in "A Curtain of Green" can be discussed as artists by virtue of the fact that their gestures—the girl's framing and Mrs. Larkin's gardening—may be interpreted as metaphors for aspects of the creation of art. A twofold advantage accrues from such a reading: recognizing an artistic *impulse* in the characters provides a context in which to understand their actions, while seeing why they nevertheless fail to *be* artists—where their actions deviate from the terms set in Welty's essays—deepens our understanding and provides an index by which we can measure and appreciate the real artist. Treading this indirect pathway, that is, via metaphor, to gain access to the nature of the artist seems justified in the case of Welty; for as noted, her characters are mostly ordinary, unsophisticated, inarticulate people, who, although they may tell stories, have little or no interest in art. Powerhouse, a jazz improvisationalist in the story bearing his name, is conspicuously different and therefore attracts and merits our attention. No metaphor need be adduced to identify him as an artist; the whole story joyously proclaims his power.

What inspired Welty to overcome her usual reticence in this singular celebration of an artist? She recalls that she launched this daring experiment in fiction—completely outside her usual orbit—in a single burst of energy after having heard Fats Waller play at a dance in Jackson (*Conversations* 297). Welty told interviewer Linda Kuehl that in "Powerhouse," "I tried to write my idea of the life of the traveling artist and performer—not Fats Waller himself, but any artist—in the alien world" (*Conversations* 94). In this portrait of Powerhouse, a black, male, jazz musician on one level, "any artist" on another, Welty presents in highly animated, nonanalytical measures some ideas about storytelling and storytellers that her later essays state formally.

I have spoken earlier of Welty's vision of an artist as one who fuses two perceptions, his own and that of the rest of the world. She reasserts this belief in another delightful passage, which may help to describe the uncanny force of Powerhouse's narrative:

> Some of us grew up with the china night-light, the little lamp whose lighting showed its secret and with that spread enchantment. The outside is painted with a scene, which is one thing; then, when the lamp is lighted, through the porcelain sides a new picture comes out through the old, and they are seen as one. . . . The lamp alight is the combination of internal and external, glowing at the imagination as one; and so is the good novel. (*Eye* 119–20)

And so is the good jazz improvisation, one might add, where soul resonates with rhythm to cast a musical spell. Powerhouse's story projects its blazing internal light—what Welty elsewhere describes as "that initial, spontaneous, overwhelming, driving charge of personal inner feeling" (*Eye* 125)—through its external narrative shape.

His impromptu story seems to emanate out of the mood created by the sad strains of the "Pagan Love Song." "You know what happened to me?" Powerhouse asks. When the bass fiddler Valentine hums a response, Powerhouse produces the theme that he and his band members will collaboratively develop as the night lingers on: "I got a telegram my wife is dead" (*CS* 133). Powerhouse varies the music in order to accentuate the words of his story, playing 4:4 time to the four words of the telegram, "You wife is dead," and triplets to reinforce his triple, "Tell me, tell me, tell me" (*CS* 133–34). Soon Scoot, the drummer, and Little Brother, the clarinetist, join Valentine and Powerhouse in propelling the story into existence. Scoot demands to know the name of the person who sent the telegram and thus inspires Powerhouse to invent Uranus Knockwood, assigning a name and eventually a definite shape to the vague sense of fear that eats away inside him when he is away from home. Little Brother insists that Gypsy wouldn't do a thing like jump out the window and kill herself. Paradoxically, Little Brother's skepticism makes at least part of the story more real: by questioning Gypsy's actions, he attests to her identity.

Although they stop playing the waltz to break for intermission, the band continues to play with the story, resurrecting it in the Negrotown World Café. Powerhouse answers Little Brother's solicitous doubts by heaping up more and more external details, as if the more completely a scene can be visualized, the more convincing it will be. A story, of course, need not be literally true; but in order for it to be true emotionally, its imagined world must become the reader's illusion. The circle of black onlookers willingly suspend disbelief, moan with pleasure as Powerhouse's story takes shape. He imagines Gypsy's feelings of loneliness and fear, the footsteps outside her room in the night, her jump—". . . Ssssst! Plooey!"—and Uranus Knockwood watching her fall, stepping in the mess, and carrying her away.

Uranus Knockwood, that "no-good pussyfooted crooning creeper" (*CS* 138–39), may have begun as a projection of Powerhouse's private fears; but finally, as Welty notes of great works in general, he "transcends the personal" (*Eye* 132). A collective chorus of black voices give him his final shape: "He take our wives when we gone!" / "He come in when we goes out!" . . . / "You know him." / "Middle-size man." / "Wears a hat." / "That's him" (*CS* 138). When all are in a wonderful humor, Powerhouse ends the story by exorcising this haunting character, sending an imaginary telegram back to him: "What in the hell you talking about? Don't make any difference: I gotcha" (*CS* 140).

The crowded dance hall and crammed café of "Powerhouse" contrast with the sparsely peopled beach of "A Memory" and the secluded garden of "A Curtain of Green." Neither the girl on the beach nor Mrs. Larkin share their predicaments with another soul. The artistic issues that Welty explored in those stories did not include a writer's relationship to readers. In "Powerhouse," however, she remains acutely aware of the rapport between performer and audience, or, by extension, between writer and reader. Unlike the animated black onlookers in the World Café, the white audience in the dance hall receives Powerhouse's story with mute impassivity, no murmur, no titter, just as earlier in the evening "nobody dances" (*CS* 258) to his music; only his band members participate in the story's germination. In the face of such unresponsiveness, the story soon fizzles and the band disbands for intermission.

But Powerhouse is unable just to relinquish his story—the teller must tell his tale. The blacks in the café, pressing in "gently and bright-eyed" around him, attend to Powerhouse's story with stirs of delight, "Ya! Ha![s]," sighs, halloos of laughter, moans of pleasure, and other contributions of their own. In that charged atmosphere, Powerhouse's story burgeons into truly gory proportions. Although a writer cannot interact with his readers in the same way that a performer can play off of his audience, the writer, according to Welty, still "assumes at the start an enlightenment in his reader equal to his own, for they are hopefully on the point of taking off together from that base into the rather different world of the imagination" (*Eye* 152). Writing, like jazz, is a collaborative performance.

As his story demonstrates, Powerhouse has been able to overcome some of the artistic problems that blocked both the girl in "A Memory" and Mrs. Larkin in "A Curtain of Green." The girl could not find a way to cope with the threatening presence of the beach family. In an artistically fatal reaction she tightly closes her eyes. While the girl strives not to see that which threatens her, Powerhouse makes his fears visible for all to see, even gives them a name. Whereas Mrs. Larkin loses herself in her overflowering garden and seems unable to face its bewildering maze of possibility, Powerhouse manifests the artistic excitement that Welty describes, eager to advance his story by trying first one choice then doubling back to discard, alter, embellish, only to plunge onward in new directions. Furthermore, Mrs. Larkin would use art to strike out against a strange life, while Powerhouse glories in and exploits the very strangeness of it. As Welty affirms, the novelist "believes the insoluble is part of his material too" (*Eye* 152).

Finally, the real artist can be identified from the metaphoric one by motive. Welty explains that the story writer does "everything out of the energy of some form of love or desire to please" ("Reading and Writing" 54). Even though Powerhouse performs in an "alien world," he "gives everything," even for an audience of one (*CS* 133). In contrast, Mrs. Larkin never gives away a single one of her flowers, nor does she share her thoughts with Jamey; the girl on the beach also hoards her vision of the touch in the most private recesses of her mind. Ultimately, what distinguishes Powerhouse from the girl and Mrs. Larkin is his overbrimming love and his benevolent desire to send everybody—whites as well as blacks—into rapturous "oblivion" (*CS* 132). Not every writer or artist is necessarily motivated by love for others and a desire to please, but apparently these motives are basic for Welty. Her conviction is best expressed in her own words: "And so finally I think we need to write with love. Not in self-defense, not in hate, not in the mood of instruction, not in rebuttal, in any kind of militance, or in apology, but with love" (*Eye* 156).

DANIÈLE

PITAVY - SOUQUES

OF SUFFERING
AND JOY

Aspects of
Storytelling
in Welty's
Short Fiction

"All narration is obituary in that
life acquires definable meaning only
at, and through death. . . . We seek
in fictions the knowledge of death,
which in our lives is denied to us."
Peter Brooks

"Most good stories are about the interior of our lives," says Eudora Welty
(*Eye* 30). This is something she has known since she wrote her first short
story, "Death of a Traveling Salesman"; something she has ceaselessly
explored, story after story, each time carrying her exploration further along
that perilous track, entering that strange country, that hinterland which
is death's territory. Because hers is serious fiction, Welty's reader feels
challenged and compelled to leave the ordinary level of simple delight that
usually rewards the reader of short fiction, to question the very nature of
life's innermost adventure. If some of her stories haunt the imaginative
reader forever, puzzling and disquieting, shattering "those universal false
dreams, the hopes sentimental and ubiquitous, which are not on any
account to be gone by" (*Eye* 36), it is because such stories force us to
acknowledge the truth of our identity.

The essential nature of our identity, the truth of what it means to be an
individual, psychoanalysis has told us, involves suffering *and* language. To
speak and to suffer are two moments of a *singular* act, since both are the
"cause" of the subject: in them and through them the subject is questioned.
We remember the way Jacques Lacan summed up Freud's discovery before
an audience of psychoanalysts in Vienna in 1955: "*it speaks,* and, no doubt,
where it is least expected, namely, where there is pain" (*Selection* 125). In
this famous reappraisal, Lacan was stressing the importance of Freud's

discovery by showing how it shifted the true center of the individual from where the whole humanistic tradition had placed it—in thinking—to suffering. Thus the *cogito ergo sum* must be replaced, Lacan said, by the formula: "I am not, there where I am the plaything of my thought; I think about what I am, there where I do not think that I am thinking" (183). Without oversimplifying the statement by rewriting the *cogito* as "I suffer; therefore I am," we should stress the emergence of language where and when the subject suffers. Suffering thus becomes the distinctive mark of humanity, even what defines us as human beings, since it is precisely *in* suffering that words originate, later language, and still later, writing.

Just as "the unconscious is structured like a language" for Lacan (232), words necessarily come in organized speech, Freud insisted; language is constituted by laws. Likewise, the expression of suffering follows some narrative pattern, and the construction of the sentences reflects some inner journey of the soul. No wonder then that it has long been the privileged territory of those artists—poets, painters and writers alike—who could see furthest and probe deepest into human destiny. They were also the ones who were ready to embark on the aesthetic adventure such patterns and organization provided them with. Eudora Welty is among them. To show how suffering is both method and subject, I have chosen three stories from *The Bride of the Innisfallen* to emphasize the development of Welty's technique, with special reference to two earlier stories—"Powerhouse" from *A Curtain of Green* and "At the Landing," the final story in her collection *The Wide Net*.

It seems appropriate to begin with Powerhouse, the jazz musician whose best music expresses pain and suffering, since he is the figure who represents both the production of Eudora Welty and the critical work in this book. Another reason to begin with "Powerhouse" is that along with other stories in *A Curtain of Green,* it is emblematic of the writer's craft.

The story sets a pattern for storytelling, opposing the *producer* of jazz music, as he is perceived by a white audience, to the *production* of this music when Powerhouse plays for his own people. Later, the portrait is completed when the narrator creates the appropriate background—a black café mysterious as a sea-cave ("but that's what they looked like, when the door was open; of course, I'd never been inside one") and puts a canvas on his easel— the death of Gypsy ("I just felt it was something very private, that went on in just this way, every night, and need never be made public,"[1] Eudora Welty told me recently). What matters is the elected theme: *death* for this most private, most internalized, "closest to the eye" composition. It's perfectly obvious death here has nothing to do with the private life of the musician's wife, if he has one. It simply is, par excellence, the theme of the creative artist. Yet, this composition on death with its theme and variations ends in joy, the pure joy of artists composing together a work of beauty, transcending in the very act their mortal human condition. Death is truly experienced in its grief, but the implicit act of faith shown here is of the same essence as the tragic joy experienced by Beethoven writing his *Ninth Symphony* or Mozart composing his *Requiem*—something that admits transcendence.

A number of close-ups on Powerhouse's mouth—"vast and obscene" in the white audience's view of it—leads to its transformation into a vast oracular mouth. Two explicit references to the sibyl confirm this reading: "Then all quietly he lays his fingers on a key with the promise and the serenity of a sibyl touching the book" (131); and "Who could ever remember any of the things he says? They are just inspired remarks that roll out of his mouth like smoke" (141). The artist is the one the gods have elected to voice what cannot be said. And just as the mysterious sounds produced by the Sibyl at Cumae, together with those volumes of smoke, were undecipherable unless one was aware of the code, some interpretation is needed to grasp the full meaning of what the short stories reveal.

Suffering, says Denis Vasse, is experienced as disruption. It is a rupture in the course of time, the shattering of our self-image. We no longer are who we believed we were, our future is definitely altered, gone are the comforting, fabricated projections behind which we had hidden until then; we become fascinated by the very vanishing of our selves into lethal waters (*Le Poids* 11–13, 26–27).

Yet, at the same time, suffering is a cry, which manifests our desire to live in spite of all new obstacles. And this cry implies that we are becoming aware of the Otherness to which we are ultimately summoned. By freeing us from false images, suffering enables us to hear the cry of the suppressed self. The mirror, which had complacently sent us back the image we had built of ourselves, is now shattered, and words that were frozen on its surface can at last be heard (Vasse, *Le Poids* 30–46).

We experience something similar in our relationship with the other. The first movement toward the other is based on need. "Need is of the same order as assimilation or consumption: it is a transforming power that reduces or destroys its object. Yet in man need is never pure need," Vasse says. "It bears the mark of the spirit when it becomes the desire for the other, which originates in need but is not reducible to it. To desire the other is to want him for what he is and I am not, to *renounce* him as pure object of my need" (*Le Temps* 20–21). In so doing, the subject takes a leap in the dark and suffers a momentary loss of balance in the act of reaching toward the Other. We note that this Other is not necessarily another individual but may be the hidden, hitherto unacknowledged side of our own self.

I want to stress here the similarity between the psychic process and the creative act. In the attempt to reach this Other, at least trying to accept it for what it is—that part which can never be properly understood—there is a risk, a momentary loss of balance, which likens it to the creative process when the artist takes a leap; for Eudora Welty, this necessary loss of balance has meant literary creation ever since she wrote "Acrobats in a Park" in 1935.

All three stories from *The Bride of the Innisfallen*, "No Place for You, My Love," "Circe," and the story that gives its title to the volume tell of trapping people who refuse to be trapped, listening to the secret voice that speaks of the human desire to acknowledge fully one's essential duality, take the leap in the dark that would enable an individual to reach full humanity. The first stage is centered on suffering, the second on the emergence of some form of language, and the third on mortal mystery which, as Circe puts it, "only frailty, it seems, can divine" (*CS* 533). Each story privileges a different stage: suffering with "The Bride," the emergence of language in "No Place" (paradoxically, the body as language is what is acknowledged here), and mystery with "Circe." The strange beauty of such stories is their unfolding in space, their taking place literally in a haunting place—Welty's and absolutely unique.

Welty wrote of the protagonist in "No Place for You, My Love," explaining that "the story told . . . of a girl in a claustrophobic predicament: she was caught fast in the over-familiar, monotonous life of her small town, and immobilized further by a prolonged and hopeless love affair; she could see no way out" (*Eye* 111). To some extent—because after all they come to share the same experience—her male companion on this ride is caught in middle age, immobilized by the nets of matrimony and the loss of creative imagination.

The young woman fears—and justly so—that her affair with a married man is obvious; she would like to conceal this image of herself which she projects outward because she cannot totally identify with it. She is "immobilized" by the need of her lover as much as by her own need, a need that seeks the other as the same. Theirs is not a two-way relationship, merely a duplicated relationship, one that can only foster violence, as the bruise attests.

In the same way, the American girl in "The Bride of the Innisfallen" is unhappy, and so are most passengers on the train. They suffer because they are trapped—not so much by a situation as by the opinion the others have of them. They feel used, the victims of need, which tends to appropriate them. Gradually, the American girl comes to realize her husband wants to possess her, body and soul. In this carefully composed short story, Eudora Welty explores different forms of relationship within marriage, building her text upon more and more serious offenses until marriage, which here stands for any relationship with the other, becomes a duel. One of the keywords of the story is *destroyed*. The man from Connemara uses this language when he speaks of his bird, which his wife overfed out of jealousy: "He was destroyed by a mortal appetite for food you'd call it unlikely for a bird to desire at all" (*CS* 504). Later, the same character speaks of the squire stabbed by his wife and how the pair haunts the castle: "She comes first because she's mad, and he slow—got the dagger stuck in him, you see? Destroyed by her" (*CS* 505). Likewise, the language used by the heroine in analyzing her own predicament expresses want: "Love with the joy being drawn out of it like anything else that aches—that was loneliness; not this. *I* was nearly destroyed, she thought" (*CS* 517). Thus *destroyed* signals a relationship based simply on need; it tends to devour the other and is some form of cannibalism or vampirism, as the numerous references to food in the story attest.

The narrative technique used in "Circe" presents the problem from the other side of the mirror, in reverse, or *en creux*. Eudora Welty said to Albert Devlin and Peggy Prenshaw: "We were passing Sicily and all of those other islands where Circe was supposed to be. And I thought, 'What would it be like to be condemned to live forever?' To see everybody that you love die and not be able to feel anything about mortality or the preciousness of the moment. That must have been what she felt" (19). Because she is immortal, Circe fails to understand the weight of a mortal body full of needs and desire and in her scorn is bent on reducing men to mere animals. She fiercely tries to destroy this "mortal mystery" that "if [she] knew where it was [she] could crush like an island grape" (*CS* 533). In her lust for power, Circe is but the other side of possessive love. At the same time, because she is rooted in her island, she fails to understand Odysseus's aspirations as they are symbolized by his wanderings. She mistakes the hero's tale for sheer arrogance when it is in fact his ultimate attempt at denying death. For what is a legend-making exploit but a refusal to be reduced to mere body?

Thus all the characters are trapped by that primary form of love which is the need for the other. Part of the plot is to send them on a journey, which is both the means by which they can reach higher awareness and the symbol of the experience they undergo.

The function of the journey is to bring these people to an awareness of their true selves. It is a painful process which forces them out of their hiding place into public light. It entices them to put some distance between themselves and everyday life too, to step into margins, the better to see their true position in the world.

The woman in "No Place," so desperately trying to hide her grief and hopelessness, is forced to exposure. "The vain courting of imperviousness in the face of exposure is this little story's plot," Welty writes (*Eye* 113). The whole New Orleans adventure makes her conspicuous, first in the restaurant, because of her northern look, her ridiculous hat and earrings, then on the ferry, when she steps up onto the tiny bridge and loses her hat. The dubious quality of her involvement becomes obvious, as a revision to the first draft stresses:[2] Welty replaced "here was a woman hopelessly in love" by "here was a woman who was having an affair"; and she added further down "so people think they can love me or hate me just by looking at me" (CS 465). Later, when the pair puzzles customers at Baba's Place, she is mistaken for this stranger's mistress, and the bruise she had so carefully hidden under her hat becomes visible. She is also forced out of her prison by the furious speed of the ride, which contrasts with the slow rumination of her thwarted life. The very violence of the ride releases her from her protective shell, as all kinds of creatures swarm the roadside.

In this strange country, Welty's "south of South," known categories no longer apply. Hence, the importance of *margins*. We are literally between two worlds, water and earth mingle inextricably, the Mississippi River "felt like the sea and looked like the earth under them" (CS 470): "There was water under everything. Even where a screen of jungle had been left to stand, splashes could be heard from under the trees" (CS 472). Flowers become traps for the unwary. Such distinctions are also blurred psychologically and physically: "At length, he stopped the car again, and this time he put his arm under her shoulder and kissed her—not knowing ever whether gently or harshly. It was the loss of that distinction that told him this was now" (CS 479).

The marginal country, no longer solid ground but not yet the ocean, is psychologically that free land, or hinterland where we are freed from the ties of rationality and able to invent new modes of thinking. The delicate balance on which this place is poised is the symbol for the jumping-off place. Only from such a place can any new human relationship start, because it is only by deliberately losing one's balance, so to speak, that we can plunge headlong into deeper understanding.

In "The Bride of the Innisfallen," the long train and boat journey through the night, when all travelers are isolated from the rest of the world, is another version of this progress through margins. Significantly, the final landscape of the story is the shore or the mouth of the river. A house located at this crucial margin looks out into the hills as well as to the sea; the onlooker is inside as well as outside:

> I may walk for ever at the fall of evening by the river, and find this river street by the red rock, this first, last house, that's perhaps a boarding house now, standing full-face to the tide, and look up to that window—that upper window, from which the mystery will never go. The curtains dyed so many times over are still pulled back and the window looks out open to the evening, the river, the hills, and the sea. (CS 518)

Here the American girl can at last decide to become herself and sever all ties with the past.

The two perfect strangers who went together on the ride in "No Place" come to a true experience of the Other. The kiss, then later the embrace in the car, are the signs of a full reconciliation with the radical otherness—what is necessarily apprehended through the body. This embrace is almost devoid of sexual desire; it acknowledges on a higher level the fullness of individuals created as body and soul. "The cry," says Welty, "that rose up at the story's end was, I hope unmistakably, the cry of that doomed relationship—personal, mortal, psychic—admitted in order to be denied, a cry that the characters were first able (and prone) to listen to, and then able in part to ignore. The cry was authentic to my story: the end of a journey *can* set up a cry, the shallowest provocation to sympathy and love does hate to give up the ghost" (*Eye* 114). What the trip gives them—and it is a great gift—is the intimation of that higher dimension present in everyone, in ourselves as well as in those around us. Because they are enabled to see themselves differently, they feel joy, pure exhilaration in the case of the many, who can contemplate again the freshness and buoyancy of youth:

> As he drove the little Ford safely to its garage, he remembered for the first time in years when he was young and brash, a student in New York, and the shriek and horror and unholy smother of the subway had its original meaning for him as the lilt and expectation of love. (*CS* 481)

As for the woman, her relationship is bound to be altered, for the better. The narrator suggests this when "a figure in the lobby strolled to meet her" (*CS* 480), since she is delivered from her obsessive narcissism and is free to invent by herself and for herself a new relationship. She is "cured of her fright," as an early draft suggested.

The American girl of "The Bride" experiences joy too; she allows pure exhilaration to win over her shyness: "Out of joy I hide for fear it is promiscuous," she says, a few minutes before she decides to take that leap, "without protection," as Welty added for *The Collected Stories*. Fully affirmative, the tale ends superbly: "The girl let her message go into the stream of the street, and opening the door walked without protection into the lovely room full of strangers" (*CS* 518).

An earlier version of this joy, with almost sinister overtones, brings "At the Landing" to its close. Eudora Welty, it seems, had not yet quite reconciled herself to what was already a haunting theme and pattern of her fiction. The narcissistic prison is there; so is a first painful initiatory journey that forces Jenny out of protective, complacent self-images. In her brief encounter with Billy Floyd, she first acknowledges her need and his need of her, nurturing the body first. Then after he has left her, she feels exposed, like the woman in "No Place": "when the house was clean again she felt that there was no place to hide in it" (*CS* 253). She then embarks on a symbolic journey, well aware that she will come in the end upon that Other, who is the ultimate aim of her quest:

> it was only a sense of journey, of something that might happen. She herself did not know what might lie ahead, she had never seen herself. She looked outward with the sense of rightful space and time within her, which must be traversed before she could be known at all. And what she would reveal in the end was not herself, but the way of the traveler. (*CS* 254)

At the end of the journey she has lost her ordinary human face; she has undergone some transmutation. The superb engulfed landscape that she walks through before coming to the Landing, so reminiscent of Ariel's song in *The Tempest*, reinforces this view of transformation. "The original smile that now crossed Jenny's face, and hung there no matter what was done to her, like a bit of color that kindles in the sky after the light has gone" (*CS* 258), denies death in a way. This text, which concludes a difficult collection of short stories, asserts that man can live only where life intrudes, that is *in suffering*—in the shadow of death. It also asserts that man can "die death," as Denis Vasse says, in the only place where it can be apprehended, *in the light of life* (*Le Poids* 187).

Thus, the artist's territory is this margin, this in-between country. The French sociologist Edgar Morin speaks of a no-man's-land between what we can conceptualize and express rationally, the mapped Cartesian world, and what we *cannot* know—this "real" that far exceeds human understanding. Man's only possibility, Morin says, is to explore this no-man's-land, as it is the place for thought, for artistic creation, for scientific progress.[3] This no-man's-land, "l'arrière-pays," as the poet Yves Bonnefoy calls it, has always been Eudora Welty's privileged country, her territory. In it, she metaphorically projects her quest. Already present in "Death of a Traveling Salesman," it finds its most realized expression in "No Place for You, My Love." With this text, we are invited into a very ancient place where animal species of the primeval age have survived; it is a legendary place also, where one walks over the bodies of sprawling giants, where the imagination is confronted with mythic battles, the slaying of the dragon by Saint George (this is what the man thinks when he sees the crocodile on the ferry). And beyond fairy tales and legends from the lives of saints, we come to the great myths by which we poetically transcribe our fears and hopes.

This country is strangely reminiscent of the country of the Three Gray Women in Hawthorne's tale "The Gorgon's Head," the title Welty had originally chosen for "No Place." This "very wild and desert place, overgrown with shaggy bushes, and so silent and solitary that nobody seemed ever to have dwelt or journeyed there" (Hawthorne 1176), stretches between the world of the living, where Perseus comes from, and the country of the Gorgons where he is going. It is also very much like the wild forest through which Young Goodman Brown was journeying on that fateful night. Through associations such as these, I would suggest that Eudora Welty belongs to that highest of all American literary traditions which concerns itself with what Gwendolyn MacEwen calls the dark pines of the mind ("Dark Pines under Water").

I like the connection with Perseus, whom I regard as the key figure of the artist in Welty's fiction. Around him revolves a cluster of words such as *vaunt*, which Eudora Welty recently defined for me as a *leap*. This leap is what we do when we renounce ourselves, the better to become ourselves; when we resolve not to be loved that we may better love. It is also the risk taken again and again in any creative act. An artist who merely records what we all experience—"the proper separation between man and wife"— fails in the creative mission and teaches us nothing, produces at best good popular fiction. An artist who tries merely to reconcile us to suffering would be some kind of priest or sister of charity and would again fail in the mission. The great artist calls the public to see suffering not as a necessary or unavoidable evil but as a challenge (I would, of course, except horror), which restores integrity to man's secret, that very secret which Circe longs to know. Denis Vasse tells us that "this secret lies in the contradiction out of which his desire is born. A living creature, man knows this: he is mortal and he is endowed with speech; yet he knows nothing of death or speech" ("*Ce secret réside dans la contradiciton d'où naît son désir: vivant, il se sait parlant et mortel, sans savoir ni ce qu'est la parole, ni ce qu'est la mort*" [*Le Poids* 43]).

4

Endurance and Change

"Travel is part
of some longer continuity"

NOEL

P O L K

Going to Naples and Other Places in Eudora Welty's Fiction

It is, I think, worth noting that Eudora Welty's classic meditation on the subject of place in fiction was first delivered as a lecture at Cambridge University in England and subsequently published in Duke University's student literary magazine, the *Archive,* in 1955, the year of the publication of *The Bride of the Innisfallen,* a book of stories which runs deliberately away from the southern literary industry's almost exclusive preoccupation with southern settings and characters and customs. Further, if the beginnings of *Place in Fiction* can be traced, as I think they can, to Welty's acerbic January 1949 letter to the *New Yorker* attacking Edmund Wilson's review of Faulkner's *Intruder in the Dust,* it is worth remarking that the inception of her public thinking about "place" is also curiously coincident with her first trip abroad, on a renewed Guggenheim Fellowship in 1949–50, and with the publication in the autumn of 1949 of "Put Me in the Sky!" (renamed "Circe" for its narrator and central character and included in *The Bride of the Innisfallen*). This story, divested completely of any concern with particular time and particular geography, occurs in a purely literary "place" created by and whose boundaries are marked by the conjunction of *The Odyssey* and Welty's imagination. Finally, if we accept "Ladies in Spring" as a Mississippi story (its setting is not specified), then only three of the seven stories in *The Bride of the Innisfallen* are set in Mississippi, and one of those three, "The Burning," is in fact set in a Civil War Jackson that could have been no more a part of Welty's actual, observable experience than the lives of Circe and Odysseus. Thus we note, in *The Bride of the Innisfallen,* her seventh book of fiction, a deliberate abandonment of her native Mississippi as the setting, the "place," of her fiction, precisely during a period when her nonfictional theorizing on the subject seems—or at least has been taken—to be holding her literary feet firmly, and perhaps a bit sentimentally on Mississippi soil.

Yet "place" in Welty's work has almost never been more specifically definable than "Mississippi," and even that "place" is not so specific a place as Yoknapatawpha County, say, moving as it does from the Natchez area to the Delta to any number of sites vaguely located somewhere we take to be Mississippi perhaps more because we are told it is Mississippi than because of anything endemically "Mississippi" in the stories themselves. The words *Mississippi* and *the South* have in fact become so evocative of all the myths and clichés of southern culture that we frequently respond to them without thinking, supply our own images and emotions when we see them, and create as we read certain specifics of those "places" that the actual words of the text do not give us. In fact only nine of the seventeen stories in *A Curtain of Green,* Welty's first book, have a specifically named or identified setting in Mississippi, and all but one of the others ("Flowers for Marjorie") we assume to be in Mississippi simply because we know that the story is by Eudora Welty and that she writes *about* Mississippi. Moreover, not all of the stories specifically named as set in Mississippi are otherwise identifiably Mississippi: nothing in the physical details of Alligator, Mississippi, for example, leads us inevitably to identify the setting of "Powerhouse" as Mississippi, and it is probably worth pointing out that the more important parts of that story take place in the World Café. Such stories as "A Curtain of Green," "A Memory," and "A Visit of Charity," are decidedly unlocalized and unregional in setting and language and, from what we can tell from the general nature of their physical details, could easily be thought of as taking place in many other parts of the United States. When she wants to, of course, Welty can describe a particular, identifiable landscape as sensitively and realistically as anybody writing; numerous passages in the fiction and, especially, her eloquent encomium to Rodney, Mississippi, "Some Notes on River Country," leave no doubt about this. Given her capacity to describe Mississippi with photographic accuracy when she wants to, we ought to be able to assume that when she does not do so, she refrains from deliberate choices dictated by the needs of the work at hand. In point of fact, then, "place" as setting in Welty has never meant just a faithful reproduction of a particular place in a particular time, and it is a mistake that the southern literary industry has too frequently made to make fetishes of the southern landscape and culture. Such fetishism has too often led reviewers and critics, who ought to know better, to confuse the source with the product, the matter with the imagination working upon it, and to assume that the southern writers' connections to their geographical roots are essential to the quality of their writing.

This assumption is, of course, at best spurious: consider, for example, that although she writes warmly of Jackson in her various memoirs, Welty but rarely writes about Jackson itself in the fiction, almost not at all by name. She does locate the first version of "Where Is the Voice Coming From?" in Jackson, but she changed the name to Thermopylae in the version finally published. Likewise although other Mississippi "places" figure in her fiction, she in fact relies heavily upon settings and characters she had encountered and taken photographs of during her travels throughout the state while she was employed by the WPA in the mid-thirties: settings and characters she had viewed—with love and sympathy and extreme interest, of course—from the perspective of an outsider, of one who had lived in Wisconsin and New York, of one coming in from somewhere else today and going somewhere else tomorrow, someone in transit: from the perspective of one who could participate in their lives primarily through the power of her imagination. As she wrote in "Place in Fiction":

> The open mind and the receptive heart—which are at last and with fortune's smile the informed mind and the experienced heart—are to be gained anywhere, any time, without necessarily moving an inch from the present address. There must surely be as many ways of seeing a place as there are pairs of eyes to see it. The impact happens in so many different ways.
>
> It may be the stranger within the gates whose eye is smitten by the crucial thing, the essence of life, the moment or act in our long-familiar midst that will forever define it. The inhabitant who has taken his fill of a place and gone away may look back and see it for good, from afar, still there in his mind's eye like a city over the hill. (*Eye* 130)

That is, of course, precisely the position of many of her characters—the travelers, the wanderers, the rootless, the escapees—who spend their lives in transit and, like R. J. Bowman, long for such rooted stability as they imagine the "placed" to have; or, like King MacLain and his sons, try to escape from such places and such placed. Whatever raw material Welty's Mississippi provides her, then, as author, as observer, the value of such attachments to place for the people she writes about depends entirely upon who is doing the evaluating and where he or she stands.

Granting that she is not judgmental about her characters, and granting that she writes out of love, Welty is nevertheless completely unsentimental about them and never idealizes any of them out of the reality of their lives and their relationships, and she never invests place—a character's location in time and space—with any particular exhilaration or strength or magic annealing power. More often than not it is a point of confinement, of limitation, of isolation against which the character must function. Some years ago I noted that *Delta Wedding* was by no means the portrait of a "Cloud-Cuckoo Land" that Diana Trilling had called it, nor yet a "simple comedy of rural manners." It is rather, I suggested, "a subtle and tough-minded rendering of all the tender savagery of family relationships: of the ferocious possessiveness of love. For underlying all the sweetness and light in that novel, underlying all the wedding preparations, the family visits back and forth, the night lights and the quilts, underlying all that togetherness and all those protestations of love is a rather grim substructure of violence and imprisonment" which holds the family together perhaps even more firmly than the love does (Polk, "Water" 99). The same is more or less true, as I also suggested then, of the Vaughn-Renfro clan in *Losing Battles,* although I am no longer so sure that it is love so much as sheer desperation and muleheadedness that hold that family together.

I rather liked Carol Manning's argument that *Losing Battles* is a parody of certain aspects of the southern tradition in literature: "parody . . . underlies the work as a whole. While the novel is first and foremost a convincing and amusing story about a particular family, on a second and subtler level it is a parody of values often called southern and of conventional literary incidents which depict them. . . . Two objects of parody," she claims, "are the values of family devotion and unity" (143). The method of the parody is precisely to take those values associated with the southern "place" to their logical extremes, to show what happens when a family—and, I'll argue, any of the groups of relationships and associations forming the concentric rings radiating outward from home—makes fetishes out of those values, worships them as ends sufficient to themselves, and so in effect hides behind them, hoping to stave off anything foreign, anything traveling and therefore suspect.

The Renfros' and Vaughns' and Beechams' hatred, their fear, of the outside world is demonstrated in their treatment of Gloria, who is problematic for them since although she is an outsider, and pointedly refuses to be a Beecham, she is nevertheless Jack's wife and the mother of his daughter and so must be dealt with in some way. They are delighted at the possibility that she may after all be Jack's first cousin, since that would make her one of them, even though their marriage would be thus legally incestuous. Their reaction is to initiate her into the family; many southerners have had their faces stuck into an opened watermelon, a ritual of play something like throwing snowballs or dropping ice down someone's back. But what the Renfro women do to Gloria is particularly vicious; Welty's language describes it as, in fact, nothing less than a sexual violation, a rape:

> . . . a trap of arms came down over Gloria's head and brought her to the ground. . . .
>
> She struggled wildly at first as she tried to push away the red hulk shoved down into her face, as big as a man's clayed shoe, swarming with seeds, warm with rain-thin juice.
>
> They were all laughing. "Say Beecham!" they ordered her, close to her ear.

They rolled her by the shoulders, pinned her flat, then buried her face under the flesh of the melon with its blood heat, its smell of evening flowers. Ribbons of juice crawled on her neck and circled it, as hands robbed of sex spread her jaws open.

. . . they were ramming the sweet, breaking chunks inside her mouth. . . .

"Come on, sisters, help feed her! Let's cram it down her little red lane! Let's make her say Beecham! *We* did!" came the women's voices. . . .

The aunts were helping each other to their feet. Gloria lay flat, an arm across her face now, its unfreckled side exposed and as pale as the underpelt of a rabbit. (*LB* 269–70)

The scene is one of the most violent in all of Welty's works, and it is in no way celebratory of any sense of southern "family." The only comfort she gets from her mother-in-law, Miss Beulah, is a brutal "Gloria Beecham Renfro, what are you doing down on the dusty ground like that? Get up! Get up and join your family, for a change. . . . go back in the house and wash that face and get rid of some of that tangly hair, then shake that dress and come out again. Now that's the best thing I can tell you" (*LB* 270–71). By forcing her to eat this particular fruit, her family feeds her, indeed, but violates her in the very feeding. And part of the violation is that in so feeding her they hope to close the family circle around her, to contain her alienness within it.

The Vaughn-Renfro-Beecham reunion, then, is in most ways a sham: it is a *re*-union, of course, which assumes dispersal and fragmentation, and indeed except for Beulah Beecham Renfro, the Beecham family is scattered throughout the state, many of them wandering; even their parents met mysterious deaths trying to escape from that family "place." There is considerable evidence of their ignorance, even of illiteracy: there is no evidence that the Beechams communicate throughout the year, and we are told numerous times that none of them writes a comforting letter to the family hero, Jack, while he is in Parchman, not even to let him know when his beloved grandfather dies, much less makes the trek across the state to visit him. Thus this family's "unity" is an illusion, an article of faith rather than of substance, and all their fine talk a ritualistic paean to a unity that in fact does not otherwise exist. There is savage irony in Beulah Renfro's name: Beulah's land in *Losing Battles* is no biblical heaven but rather a land of smug, insular, self-righteousness. Its communities call themselves Peerless, Wisdom, Upright, Morning Star, Harmony, Deepstep, and Banner, which Miss Beulah calls "the very heart" of Boone County (*LB* 18); its citizens, so far as we can tell from the Renfros, are none of these things. Across the river, where Miss Julia Mortimer, the mortal enemy of their insularity and ignorance, taught her school, is Alliance, a name implying the values of true community that the Beechams, with all their talking, simply lack. Connecting Banner and Alliance is a very rickety and untrust-

Noel Polk

worthy bridge which was constructed about the time Miss Julia came there
to teach. The Boone County weekly newspaper is *The Vindicator;* the ritual
of reunion is an exercise in vindication—of themselves, or each other, of
their state—and not in celebration or love. From this point of view, *Losing
Battles* is a study of the effects of such single-minded, self-righteous insularity as the Renfros exemplify, and it may be read as a devastating critique
of Welty's native "place," her native state of Mississippi and, not coinciden-
tally, of the clichés of southern literary study. Place, then, any particular
place, is not necessarily all we've cracked it up to be, and a great deal of
the specific energy of Welty's fiction derives from the conjunction of
character with place: the moment of truth occurs when the wanderer
confronts the threshold, going in or coming out. Most characters in one
place want desperately to be in another place and expend a good deal of
energy trying to get there, even if they do not necessarily know where
"there" is or what they hope to find when they get there. I need not remind
you that Miss Julia Mortimer actually dies "in the road" (295).

In 1974 Welty published an essay entitled "Is Phoenix Jackson's Grandson Really Dead?" In this significant essay, she simply dismisses the question, often asked by her readers, as not having anything to do with the
story's meaning: "The grandchild is the incentive," she wrote:

> But it is the journey, the going of the errand, that is the story, and the question
> is not whether the grandchild is in reality alive or dead. It doesn't affect the
> outcome of the story or its meaning from start to finish. . . .
>   What I hoped would come clear was that in the whole surround of this story,
> the world it threads through, the only certain thing at all is the worn path. . . .
> The path is the thing that matters. (*Eye* 160–62)

As we have already noted, many of Welty's most interesting stories are
about characters in transit, from her first published story, "Death of a
Traveling Salesman," to the final story of *The Bride of Innisfallen*, "Going
to Naples." Many plots involve the intrusion of an outsider into another
character's defined place, in ways that force a radical confrontation with
the assumptions that govern that place; sometimes the focus of the story
is the intruder, sometimes those intruded upon. Sometimes the intruder is
completely alien to the place, as is Faye, in *The Optimist's Daughter;* sometimes the intruder is one who has exiled him- or herself, who has escaped
and returned, as Laurel has done in the same novel.

For Welty's characters, place is at worst a trap, an omnivorous insatiable
enemy; at best it is fluid, shifting, distant. "Place" in the first story of *The
Bride of the Innisfallen*—the distinctive country south of New Orleans—is
specifically *"No Place"* for love: but it is precisely the strangeness of that
"place," its distinctiveness, its remoteness from their ordinary lives, and
their capacity to discover it as they drive, that allows the two strangers a

respite, a "Time Out" (*CS* 465), from the pressures and complications, whatever they are, that await them back home when their separate trips are over and they must return. There is likewise no "place" for love on the ship in "Going to Naples"; there is indeed No Place at all, except the journey itself. Naples, every bit as much a "place" as New Orleans, with its own unmistakable character, is here merely a destination, the end of the journey; and that is its primary significance in the story: "Going" is the operative word in the title. Quite aside from its estimable qualities as a work of fiction, qualities insufficiently appreciated largely because it is not a "Mississippi" story, "Going to Naples" is a superb illustration of the relationship, in Welty, between place and meaning.

"What can place *not* give?" she asks, and then insists: "Theme. It can present theme, show it to the last detail—but place is forever illustrative: it is a picture of what man has done and imagined, it is his visible past, result. Human life is fiction's only theme" (*Eye* 129). In Welty's view, "human life" expresses itself whatever the setting, whatever the circumstances. This is a premise she tests in "Going to Naples," which, along with "The Bride of the Innisfallen" and "Circe," is at the furthest remove of any of her stories from her familiar, her home, territory, far from the very idea of "place," since most of it takes place on a ship moving across the Atlantic Ocean. Yet it is at the same time a masterful encapsulation of many of the themes and characters Welty had dealt with in the "Mississippi" fiction: thematically it is very familiar territory.

It begins very simply: "The *Pomona* sailing out of New York was bound for Palermo and Naples" (*CS* 567), a sentence naming the journey's source and its destination and identifying the story's "place" in its first three words—"The *Pomona* sailing"—as not just the physical ship but rather its motion through markless oceanic space. The *Pomona*'s place, then, may rather be time itself than anything geographical: the view from the *Pomona*'s rear deck is of the ship's wake, its evanescent path, the fading record of where the passengers and crew have come from; the view from the front deck, until they reach sight of the European shore, is empty of all save water and sky. It is a "warm September" (*CS* 567), and the crossing is intersected by the autumnal solstice, which creates in the conjunction of water, sky, and time a storm that frees Gabriella, if only momentarily, from her overbearing mother and from the young man, Aldo Scampo, with whom, but for her mother, she might be falling in love. It is a solstice simultaneous with and symbolic of momentous changes in her life.

Two scenes merit attention here. The first is a record of Gabriella's and Aldo's burgeoning love:

> The long passage through the depths of the ship . . . seemed made for Gabriella and Aldo. True, it was close with the smell of the sour wine the crew drank. In

the deepest part, the engines pounding just within that open door made a human being seem to go in momentary danger of being shaken asunder. It sounded here a little like the Niagara Falls at home, but she had never paid much attention to *them*. Yet with all the deafening, Gabriella felt as if she and Aldo were walking side by side in some still, lonely, even high place never seen before now, with mountains above, valleys below, and sky. The old man in the red knit cap who slept all day on top of that box was asleep where he always was, but now as if he floated, with no box underneath him at all, in some spell. Even the grandfather clock, *even the map*, when these came into sight, looked faceless, part of a landscape. (*CS* 576; second emphasis added)

In this marvelous passage, Aldo's and Gabriella's love creates its own magical landscape, its own romantic "place," out of the emphatically unromantic sour smells and loud mechanical clanging of a physical setting perhaps indebted to O'Neill's *Hairy Ape*. The "faceless" grandfather clock suggests that this is Time Out for them, as the land south of New Orleans is for the strangers in "No Place for You, My Love"; and the landscape, too, and the map itself, are also faceless; time and place, then, are simply dismissed as factors bearing on the essentials of the human journey. Gabriella, we recall from the story's opening, is from Niagara Falls, the quintessential "place" of honeymooning lovers; but she, not ever having been in love before, has never paid much attention to the falls. On board, then, she and Aldo are walking through no known landscape at all but rather the universal landscape, the universal place, of romantic love, which she has also never seen before.

The *Pomona* is no Love Boat, then, and no ship of fools, but "Going to Naples" is, I would suggest, a complicatedly simple allegory of life as journey, the voyage here being from the New World to the Old, from childhood into sexual play if not specifically into sexual experience, into independence and maturity, then directly into old age and death, the destination, the destined "place" of all travelers. Intimations of this allegory are rampant on the ship: one young man is going to Naples to get married to a woman he has never seen; one older man is going past Naples to Genoa, the city, he says, of the most beautiful cemeteries in the world. Also on the ship are numerous old women, introduced very early in the narrative, who form a significant part of the story's metaphorical understructure; their faces haunt Gabriella throughout the story:

every time, there were the same black shawls, the same old caps, backed up against the blue [of the sky]—faces coming out of them that grew to be the only faces in the world, more solid a group than a family's, more persistent one by one than faces held fast in the memory or floating to nearness in dreams. On the best benches sat the old people, old enough to be going home to die—. (*CS* 568–69)

As the *Pomona* leaves New York harbor, Gabriella waves goodbye to one relatively young lady, the Statue of Liberty, saying goodbye, in effect, to the freedom and liberty of her childhood. Landing in Naples harbor, she says hello to another woman, her grandmother, whom she and her mother have traveled to see. Nonna sits, significantly, "almost in the center of everything." She is, exactly like the old women on the boat, a "little, low, black figure waiting. It was the quietest and most substantial figure there, unagitated as a little settee, a black horsehair settee, in a room where people are dancing" (*CS* 595). This description of her reminds us of Gala Night on board, in which the old ladies of the journey preside over the moment of her independence, the moment when she discovers that she can dance alone, and indeed even prefers dancing alone. They are auguries of her future, these old women going home to die, and Nonna, already in Naples, also in black, waiting for Gabriella, makes one with them, ominous, portentous:

> And there was Nonna, her big, upturned, diamond-shaped face shimmering with wrinkles under its cap of white hair and its second little cap of black silk. . . .
> Nonna drew Gabriella down toward all her blackness, which the sun must have drenched through and through until light and color yielded to it together, and to which the very essence of that smell in the [Naples] air . . . clung . . . . She gave Gabriella an ancient, inviting smile. (*CS* 595–96)

Mama Serto has the story's closing line: verbally it is something of a non sequitur, for nothing in the story's language has prepared us for it; emotionally, thematically, it is stunningly appropriate. She hears the clanging of the church bells in the heart of Naples and exclaims: "And the nightingale . . . is the nightingale with us yet?" (*CS* 600). We stop short of an automatic response—"Yes: *already* with us"—for we are struck with wonder at the magical flourish upon which the story ends so abruptly: suddenly we are in yet another place, the specifically literary place of Keats's "Ode to a Nightingale," whose melancholy preoccupation with easeful death informs the whole story, especially in its elegiac closing pages. As they leave the port, Nonna leaves first, though none too firmly; Gabriella's mother follows and, Welty tells us, "Gabriella took her place a step behind" (*CS* 600), following in their footsteps. The implication is very clear, then, that what will become of Gabriella, will, in effect, become of us all: Naples is destination; our destination, finally, is death: "See Naples and die!" Aldo shouts at Poldy, as they walk down the gangway (*CS* 594). Dicey Hastings, the young bride-to-be returned to Mississippi from "up North" for a visit, observes that the folks gathered on the front porch of her old family place, in the middle of rural Mississippi, are "quiet and obscure and never-known as passengers on a ship already embarked to sea. . . . Their faces were like dark boxes of secrets and desires . . . but locked safely, like old-fashioned caskets for the safe conduct of jewels on a voyage" (*CS* 565). This passage, barely a page from the end of "Kin," is a beautifully effective bridge from "Kin" to "Going to Naples" and connects those rooted Mississippians and others in *The Bride of the Innisfallen* not so rooted, to the *Pomona*'s travelers—they are all, in effect, on the same voyage: we are all going to Naples, Mississippians and New Yorkers, Italians and Ohioans. We are all going to Naples: wherever we start from, however we travel, however we pretend we are not going anywhere, we are all *going*.

In "Going to Naples," then, Welty's admonition (in "Place in Fiction") that "human life is fiction's only theme" is demonstrated with a vengeance, in its almost complete divorcement from geographical place, its deliberate and carefully contrived escape from the numerous and cumbersome conventions of her southern and Mississippi place, its steadfast and artistically courageous refusal to ring any of the standard literary bells that the southern literary industry has so unfairly and unusefully insisted upon hearing everywhere in her work. In this respect, "Kin" is a perfect companion-piece for "Going to Naples"; for if in the latter Welty operates at the furthest remove from the southern literary trappings, in the former she moves directly into their heart; if in the latter she eschews them as unessential to her work, in the former she invokes them all, precisely, I would say, to demonstrate the extent to which those qualities we take to constitute "place" in Mississippi, in literature, are in fact merely constructs, an artifice, a combination of art and imagination. This is, as Danièle Pitavy-Souques has convincingly shown ("Blazing Butterflies" 133–37), part of what Dicey Hastings discovers on her own journey back to her home "place," when she discovers the strangers filling the old home waiting to have their pictures taken in front of a backdrop supplied by the itinerant photographer: it was, Dicey notes, "the same old thing, *a scene that never was,* a black and white and gray blur of unrolled, yanked-down moonlight" (*CS* 560; emphasis added). The significance of that phony "scene that never was" is brought home to her when, later, she meditates on the one painting in the old house, a "romantic figure of a young lady seated on a fallen tree under brooding skies," her great-grandmother, Evelina Mackaill. Dicey's extended meditation is worth quoting in full:

> And I remembered—rather, more warmly, *knew,* like a secret of the family—that the head of this black-haired, black-eyed lady who always looked the right, mysterious age to be my sister, had been fitted to the ready-made portrait by the painter who had called at the door—he had taken the family off guard, I was sure of it, and spoken to their pride. The yellow skirt spread fanlike, straw hat held ribbon-in-hand, orange beads big as peach pits (to conceal the joining at the neck)—none of that, any more than the forest scene so unlike the Mississippi wilderness (that enormity she had been carried to as a bride, when the logs of this house were cut, her bounded world by drop by drop of sweat exposed,

where she'd died in the end of yellow fever) or the melancholy clouds obscuring the sky behind the passive figure with the small, crossed feet—none of it, world or body, was really hers. (*CS* 561)

Dicey moves from this observation into almost an epiphany of sisterhood with her great-grandmother, a bride, too, when she came to Mississippi's wilderness, as Dicey is a bride-to-be:

She had eaten bear meat, seen Indians, she had married into the wilderness at Mingo, to what unknown feelings. Slaves had died in her arms. She had grown a rose for Aunt Ethel to send back by me. And still those eyes, opaque, all pupil, belonged to Evelina—I knew, because they saw out, as mine did; weren't warned, as mine weren't, and never shut before the end, as mine would not. I, her divided sister, knew who had felt the wildness of the world behind the ladies' view. We were homesick [Dicey understands] for somewhere that was the same place. (*CS* 561)

Dicey and Evelina are sisters across the generations, both brides, both travelers, one to, one from, the same place in Mississippi, one's journey already long completed, the other's set to begin. Wherever that place, wherever that "somewhere" that both Dicey and her great-grandmother are homesick for, it has, I am sure, nothing to do with geography.

As Dicey observes, with all of Mississippi surrounding them, all of that state in all of its placeness, Evelina and then all her descendants and their neighbors stand for their portraits in front of a mere representation of a place that never was, hoping to locate themselves in time and in space, for all of posterity to see, with whatever shabby representations of place itinerant painters and photographers can bring with them when they pass through. As she leaves the old home, Dicey turns for one more look, and notices the old house, "floating on the swimming dust of evening," and looking to her like a "safe-shaped mass darkening" (*CS* 565). This is a phrase worth pondering: home, all that it means to the memory, to the past, all its accumulated meanings as our source, all of its power to sustain us, becomes, as she looks, an undifferentiated mass against the evening, a mass shaped vaguely like safety but darkening into obscurity: "home," the *idea* of home, is our location in time and space, but it is also the fata morgana, the "desert illusion" of all those things that "home" *ought* to mean but so seldom, in Welty's fiction, actually does mean.

"One can no more say, 'To write stay home,' " Welty has said, "than one can say, 'To write leave home.'. . . For the artist to be unwilling to move, mentally or spiritually or physically, out of the familiar is a sign that spiritual timidity or poverty or decay has come upon him; for what is familiar will then have turned into all that is tyrannical" (*Eye* 129).

"Should the writer, then, write about home?" she asks.

It is both natural and sensible that the place where we have our roots should become the setting, the first and primary moving ground, of our fiction. Location, however, is not simply to be used by the writer—it is to be discovered, as each novel itself, in the act of writing, is discovery. Discovery does not imply that the place is new, only that we are. Place is as old as the hills. Kilroy at least has been there, and left his name. Discovery, not being a matter of writing our name on a wall, but of seeing what that wall is, and what is over it, is a matter of vision. (*Eye* 129)

Welty's eyes are as sharp and penetrating as any in this century. And she can see that so many of the southern literary conventions of place and theme are simply backdrops, mere representations, of scenes that never were in the South or anywhere else but which have been hanging in our parlors for so long that we have quit looking at them very closely. Welty never exploits place, hers or anybody else's, for its own sake, but rather hopes, in writing about it, to *see* it anew, for the first time every time. "It seems plain," she concludes "Place in Fiction,"

that the art that speaks most clearly, explicitly, directly and passionately from its place of origin will remain the longest understood. It is through place that we put out roots, wherever birth, chance, fate or our traveling selves set us down; but where those roots reach toward—whether in America, England, or Timbuktu—is the deep and running vein, eternal and consistent and everywhere purely itself, that feeds and is fed by the human understanding. The challenge to writers today, I think, is not to disown any part of our heritage. Whatever our theme in writing, it is old and tried. Whatever our place, it has been visited by the stranger, it will never be new again. It is only the vision that can be new; but that is enough. (*Eye* 132–33)

NANCY K.

B U T T E R W O R T H

FROM
CIVIL WAR
TO
CIVIL RIGHTS

Race Relations
in Welty's
"A Worn Path"

Since such seminal studies as Robert Penn Warren's "The Love and Separateness in Miss Welty" and Harry Morris's "Eudora Welty's Use of Mythology," it has become traditional to interpret Welty's characters in terms of mythological and cultural archetypes. Welty's black characters frequently have evoked such parallels. In addition to the obvious reference to the Egyptian resurrection myth implied by her name,[1] Phoenix Jackson in "A Worn Path" has been compared to the pagan fertility figures Kore, Demeter, and Persephone, Osiris, Attis, and Adonis, as well as Theseus and Aeneas (Ardolino 1–6); knight questers such as the Red Cross Knight and Don Quixote; Bunyan's Christian, a Magi, and Christ.[2] Little Lee Roy in "Keela, The Outcast Indian Maiden" has been likened to the archetypal scapegoat Le Roi Mehaigné, the maimed Fisher King (May), the albatross in *The Rime of the Ancient Mariner* (Warren), and American Negro folk tricksters such as Brer Rabbit (Appel, *Season* 146). Powerhouse, more simplistically, has been described as "a virtual Negro Paul Bunyan" (Appel, "Powerhouse's" 222).

Although such "superimpositions" of external ideas, as Morris terms them (40), always risk distorting the text, a majority of these mythological and symbolic readings are valid because they add resonances that enrich our understanding of the characters' roles. Welty's own comments on her use of name symbolism and the influence of remembered fairy tales and myths further support such interpretations.[3] Commentaries on her black characters, however, sometimes obfuscate more than they reveal. One obvious reason is our sensitivity to the race issue, which has made it tempting to oversimplify the narrative events to fit our own conceptions of history and how the races ought to have behaved.

Recent revisionist criticism, in particular, frequently falsifies Welty's portrayals of black-white relations in earlier eras. For example, John Hardy's "Eudora Welty's Negroes," in *The Image of the Negro in American Literature,* is, paradoxically, both sentimental and satirical. Although his attitude is somewhat inconsistent,[4] Hardy views Phoenix as "a saint":

> One of those who walks always in the eye of God, on whom He has set His sign, whether ordinary men are prepared to see it or not. For we realize finally that she has done nothing for herself, for her own advantage, either psychological or material. Just because sanctity is never self-regarding, she must see herself as a sinner. But in the ultimate perspective she is, by virtue of her sanctity, exempt from the usual requirements of economic and social morality. (229)

Conversely, he argues that those who fail to see her as such are the whites, and particularly the white women. He concludes that "There is nowhere in modern literature a more scathing indictment of the fool's pride of the white man in the superiority of his civilization, of his fool's confidence in the virtue of the 'soothing medicine' he offers to heal the hurts of that 'stubborn case,' black mankind" (229). John R. Cooley, in "Blacks as Primitives in Eudora Welty's Fiction," accuses Welty of failing to "develop her racial portraits with sufficient sensitivity or depth" (27) and criticizes her for creating a primitive idyll in "A Worn Path," making it "difficult to cut through the reverence and romance which cloud the story, in order to see the babe as a pathetic image of life caught in the stranglehold of white civilization." He cynically questions whether Welty intended the story as a myth of the phoenix perishing in its own ashes (24–25).

Such polemical demythologizings conflict with Welty's persistent refusal to use fiction as a platform, particularly for political or sociological issues, as well as her downplaying and even disavowal of racial implications in her stories.[5] Even in "Keela, The Outcast Indian Maiden," "Where Is the Voice Coming From?" and "The Demonstrators," which treat racial interactions directly, she eschews authorial statement or facile solutions or dichotomies. Thus, although we condemn his act, we are brought to understand the mundane motives for a lower-class white's murder of a black civil rights worker in "Where Is the Voice Coming From?"; the guilt-ridden Steve and cynical civil rights worker in "Keela" and "The Demonstrators," respectively, are portrayed as ethically equivocal; and even such white characters as Max and Dr. Strickland, who attempt to mediate between the races and ameliorate oppression and illness, remain largely ineffectual. The blacks, too, range from virtuous victims to perpetrators of wanton violence, but most of them are merely traditional family members coping with tragedy as best they can. One of Welty's greatest achievements as a writer is that she refuses to rewrite history but rather presents individualized conflicts and tensions, in all of their disturbing ambiguity.

Although there have been some balanced commentaries on the race relations in "A Worn Path"—in particular, Elmo Howell's "Eudora Welty's Negroes: A Note on 'A Worn Path' "[6]—one aspect of the story that has not been adequately explored is the portrayal of Phoenix Jackson as an almost allegorical representation of black people's traits and behaviors from slave times to the story's present. Alfred Appel, Jr., has suggested such a reading when he describes the story as "an effort at telescoping the history of the Negro woman" (*Season* 166), but he doesn't develop it.

The most compelling reason for seeing Phoenix as an avatar of her race is her almost mythic age. When Phoenix asks the nurse to forgive her momentary senility, she explains, "I never did go to school, I was too old at the Surrender" (*CS* 148). If we assume that Phoenix was eighteen or more at Emancipation and posit the present action of the story to be around 1940, when it was written, she would be approximately 100 years old. Further corroboration for her age is afforded by her boast when dancing with the scarecrow, "I the oldest people I ever know"; the hunter also marvels that she "must be a hundred years old" (*CS* 144, 146). This extreme age serves a symbolic function of allowing her personally to have spanned the entire history of the black people from antebellum days to those just prior to the civil rights movement.

Such an interpretation requires considerable caution so as not to reduce the story to mere allegory. It is essential to emphasize—as Stella Brookes does concerning Joel Chandler Harris's Uncle Remus (47–48)—that Phoenix is not a stereotypical or stock black character but a real human portrait with a distinctive personality. In interviews and essays, Welty has explained the key image that suggested the story to her imagination:

> One day I saw a solitary old woman like Phoenix. She was walking; I saw her in the middle distance, in a winter country landscape, and watched her slowly make her way across my line of vision. That sight of her made me write the story. I invented an errand for her, but that only seemed a living part of the figure she was herself: what errand other than for someone else could be making her go? (*Eye* 161)

She conflated this experience with another on the Old Canton Road when an elderly black woman stopped to talk with her; the woman's remark, "I was too old at the Surrender," Welty tells us, "was indelible in my mind" (*Conversations* 168). The nexus of Phoenix's character for Welty seems to have been her sense of urgency, her "desperate need" to reach her goal. She notes that Phoenix's "going was the first thing, her persisting in the landscape was the real thing. . . . The real dramatic force of a story depends on the strength of the emotion that has set it going. . . . What gives any such content to 'A Worn Path' is not its circumstances but its *subject:* the deep-grained habit of love" (161).

Phoenix particularizes these attributes of persistence and enduring love through her own distinct set of decorums and devotions, such as wearing tied shoes into town and her somewhat dubious adherence to the eighth commandment (although in her own estimation she "stoops" when she retrieves a dropped coin, she does not in conning a few more pennies and accepting the "charity" medicine for her grandson). Phoenix's personality also comprises a complicated mixture of shrewdness—"Five pennies is a nickel" (*CS* 149)—and childlike unself-consciousness—shown when she talks aloud to herself and warns all of the "foxes, owls, beetles, jack rabbits, coons, and wild animals" to keep out of her way (*CS* 141). Her composite of character traits is somewhat like conflating Ida M'Toy with the bird women in "A Pageant of Birds." This complexity, along with her distinctive voice and humor (" 'Old woman,' she said to herself, 'that black dog come up out of the weeds to stall you off, and now there he sitting on his fine tail, smiling at you' " [*CS* 145]), keep Phoenix from falling into mere quaintness or caricature.[7]

Phoenix's individuality, though, does not preclude another, simultaneous, view of her as a symbolic representative of her race. Such an interpretation helps to elucidate otherwise confusing statements or situations in the surface narrative. For example, one of the more cryptic passages in Welty's fiction occurs when Phoenix walks "past cabins silver with weather, with the doors and windows boarded shut, all like old women under a spell sitting there," and she says, " 'I walking in their sleep,' . . . nodding her head vigorously" (*CS* 144). Her strong identification with these "women" (the white woman in town who ties her shoes is termed a "lady" [*CS* 147]) suggests that they are the matriarchs of her race whose dreams she views herself as proudly carrying on. Indeed, in her own almost trancelike state, she seems to gain strength from their vicarious vision of her persisting in the landscape while they doze.

The content of Phoenix's dream becomes clearer at the conclusion of the story when she sees the gold-framed document (presumably a diploma) nailed up on the clinic wall, and the narrator asserts that it "matched the dream that hung up in her head" (*CS* 147). On the surface level, the document verifies that she has reached her specific dream or goal of obtaining the medicine (" 'Here I be,' she said" [*CS* 147]), though she ironically has a memory lapse about her mission immediately afterward. On a deeper level, the diploma also seems to represent her respect for education, which is reiterated later in the scene. Wonderful pathos is evoked by the formally unschooled Phoenix wishing education for herself, her grandson, and, by implication, her people. This dream also may inform part of her faith that her grandson, though frail in body, will prevail and prosper.

Viewing Phoenix as an emblem of her people also helps to explain the title, "A Worn Path," which seems to imply that others have trod and retrod the same arduous path before her. Echoes of slave times can be heard in her chant as she heads up the hill, "Seem like there is chains about my feet, time I get this far" (*CS* 143), as well as in the images of confinement and persecution, such as the barbed-wire fence, one-armed black men, and the threatening black dog. These symbolic references could refer specifically to the difficulties encountered by the blacks, as well as more generally to any enslaved or downtrodden people from the times of the early Egyptians and Greeks (from whom her name derives) on through the twentieth century.

Finally, this reading explains a number of Phoenix's encounters with whites, both real and imaginary. On the surface level, the story consists of a simple journey composed of about twelve obstacles—external or internal—which Phoenix must overcome to obtain her goal (*Season* 167). These encounters take on deeper meaning when seen as symbolic trials or tests of her faith. Robert Welker suggests this interpretation when he refers to the "visions" which sometimes tempted wayfaring knights so as to divert them from their final purpose (203–04). Likewise, Phoenix is tempted at numerous points to forestall her journey, as exemplified by the scene in which she marches across the hollow log, "like a festival figure in some parade," and then hallucinates a little boy bringing her a slice of marble cake which she finds "acceptable" (*CS* 143).

If taken literally, this vision makes little sense; however, it makes a great deal of sense if we see it as a symbolic role reversal in which Phoenix is tempted to accept the dream—the marble cake—rather than the reality of economic equality. This scene bears much resemblance to the parallel one in town when Phoenix requests the nice-smelling white lady to tie her shoes for her, which Hardy so incorrectly interprets as an "outrageous request," one of "the ways in which southern Negroes have learned to take subtle revenge on the 'superior' race, to exploit, for their own material or psychological advantage, the weakness of white pride" (228–29). On the simplest level, both scenes involve wish-fulfillment fantasies—one imaginary and the other realized—in which Phoenix probably does gain psychological pleasure from being waited upon by those whom she previously served. However, in neither does she seem vindictive toward the whites; she merely accepts with dignity what she considers her "due" (Howell 30–31; Robinson 26; and Dazey 92–93). Further, both situations carry a covert danger; for if Phoenix were to remain eating imaginary marble cake or allowing others to care for her, she would not complete her necessary journey.

Phoenix's vulnerability is also made explicit in the scene just prior to the hunter's entrance. Evoking her earlier hallucinations or misperceptions of reality, the setting is imbued with a fairy tale aura: a road which cuts "deep, deep . . . down between high green-colored banks" of the swamp, with live oaks meeting overhead, making it "as dark as a cave." The sleeping alligators and Cerberus-like black dog which suddenly rears up out of the weeds suggest covert dangers and unprovoked violence which catch her unawares: "She was meditating, and not ready, and when he came at her she only hit him a little with her cane. Over she went in the ditch, like a little puff of milkweed" (CS 145). Her inability to help herself is shown by her drifting into a dream of rescue.

Perhaps the most troubling incident in the whole story concerns her encounter with the young white hunter. At first he appears to be sympathetic as he helps her out of the ditch. Yet almost immediately the situation takes on uncomfortable undertones in the reversal of usual youth-age decorums when the hunter cheerily condescends to her as "Granny" and swings her through the air like a child. His apparent charity of dropping the nickel is also belied by his later assertion that he would give her a dime, if he had *any money* with him (CS 146, emphasis added).[8] Finally, the tone darkens with the implications of his hunting bobwhites—both Phoenix and the grandson are linked with frail birds[9]—and his seemingly sadistic act of turning his gun on her.

It is difficult not to condemn the hunter's behavior (Welty herself refers to him as a "really nasty white man" [*Conversations* 335]).[10] One way of gaining more perspective on his behavior is to interpret this scene broadly as an allegory of the racial stances of the early twentieth century. All of the hunter's actions can be explained in terms of accepted social behavior of the rural South in the 1930s and 1940s, which would have allowed a young white man—a simple "red neck" hunter—some degree of domineering byplay with the curious old black woman. Welty does not distort the man's realistic responses to Phoenix, much as, two decades later, she similarly refuses to pretty up the depiction of the equivalent lower-class white city dweller who murders a black civil rights worker (Medgar Evers) in "Where Is the Voice Coming From?".

More specifically, each of the characters' actions in this scene symbolically represents a particular stage in the pre–civil rights era treatment of blacks. For example, for an indeterminate time before the hunter's arrival, Phoenix waits patiently, merely dreaming of salvation. At one point she reaches up her hand expectantly, "but nothing reached down and gave her a pull" (CS 145). After the zeal of Reconstruction, which Phoenix missed out on because she was too old to be educated, a period of indifference to blacks' welfare persisted well into the early decades of the twentieth century. When the hunter finally arrives, Phoenix uses her vulnerability, lying flat on her back "like a June-bug waiting to be turned over" (CS 145), to obtain her simple need of being helped out of the ditch. Likewise, when the blacks so desperately required help out of the social, educational, and economic ditch, whites finally reached out a hand to aid them, though only perhaps because they appeared so helpless. The next stage is symbolized by Phoenix's having to grovel on her knees for the nickel, which the hunter avers he does not have. The hunter's threatening act of pointing his gun at her and his false advice—"stay home, and nothing will happen to you" (*CS* 146)—seem prophetic of southern whites' stance during the mid-fifties when blacks began to demand equal opportunities and dignity. Had Phoenix given in to this temptation to remain passive, she would not have obtained the much-needed medicine. Finally, the hunter fails to comprehend the dire necessity of her mission, mistakenly believing she is merely going to see Santa Claus. He is not, in a last analysis, so much malicious as insensitive (Robinson 24).

The final scene at the clinic has also drawn considerable commentary on the failure of charity—in the sense of the Latin *caritas* or Christian love.[11] Yet to see the white attendant and nurse merely as representing the callous welfare state is simplistic. The attendant, who does not know Phoenix's case, displays a clinical sort of charity, dispensed without care or personalization: "A charity case, I suppose" (*CS* 147). Yet it is noteworthy that at the end of the story she offers Phoenix a small personal gratuity for Christmas. The nurse does act impatiently when Phoenix lapses into senility, but only after five patient attempts to elicit the needed information regarding the grandson.

This scene focuses two of the most significant motifs of the story: Phoenix's unreserved love for her grandson and her hope for his future. The slightly humorous suspense afforded by her momentary lapse of memory functions to undercut the tendency to sentimentalize a tragic situation. When she finally remembers, Phoenix expresses one of the most powerful definitions of Christian love imaginable: "I not going to forget him again, no, the whole enduring time. I could tell him from all the others in creation" (*CS* 148). She is also adamant in her faith that, despite his seeming frailty, he is going to survive. The flame, bird, and windmill (Isaacs 81; Ardolino 7) imagery in the final scene reinforces the virtuous cycle by which she keeps her grandson alive through her persistent care; his need likewise gives her a reason to live. To overlook the real suffering in both their lives is to distort. Yet to interpret this scene cynically, as Cooley does, as the blacks swallowing the lye (lie) of racist condescension and occasional charity (24)—or to view Phoenix as some sort of misguided Don Quixote flapping at imaginary windmills (Daly 138)—misses the point that Phoenix, in her slow, plodding, and often interrupted course, has overcome every temptation and obtained her goal.

Thus, the truth of the racial interactions in "A Worn Path" lies somewhere between Hardy's, Cooley's, and Appel's encomiums of the blacks and excoriations of the whites and Howell's almost complete exoneration of both:

> There is no conflict between Phoenix and the white world, and there is no hate. . . . The whites who confront Phoenix reflect the usual attitudes of their generation toward the Negro. . . . [T]he charity of the whites, meager as it is, is proffered in kindliness and received as such. (Howell 31; see also Vande Kieft, *Eudora Welty* 140)

Whereas the former interpretations are too polemical, the latter is perhaps overly sanguine. The story does portray interracial tension and misunderstanding, if not overt conflict. To obtain her meager needs, Phoenix has to remain in her subservient role as requester. Although she avoids the more obvious near-parodic ploys, such as Uncle-Tom obsequiousness or Sambo antics, she does rely—consciously or unconsciously—on her shrewdness, senility, and even minor thievery. The whites also evince at least degrees of insensitivity toward Phoenix, but seemingly more out of callous incomprehension than deliberate cruelty. Finally, however, the mythic aura of the story mitigates the impact of these political issues, allowing the reader to apprehend Phoenix whole, as no single character within the story does.

THOMAS L.

M c H A N E Y

FALLING INTO
CYCLES   *The Golden Apples*

Eudora Welty has refused to call her 1949 book *The Golden Apples* a novel
and has expressed dismay and irritation at the attempts of students of her
work to prove that she is wrong (*Conversations* 43). Welty's disclaimers
notwithstanding, one can understand why critics try to place the book into
the longer genre. In part, the impulse has come from applications of the
New Criticism, with its penchant for turning prose texts toward epic and
then finding in the result a certain kind of unity, but mainly it has come
from a sincere desire to canonize an admirable piece of work within an
accepted form. Welty students want to endow *The Golden Apples* with the
prestige, the presumption of higher seriousness, and the opportunity to
win the wider audience that novels, as opposed to story collections, enjoy.
The tradition of what we know as the novel, as it happens, affords plenty
of room for a work made as *The Golden Apples* is made; and modern
criticism, especially, finds it nearly impossible to ignore several major
paradigms that draw Welty's book into a category she rejects. For example,
because of the closely linked mythological tales that lie beneath the surface
of the stories, *The Golden Apples* conforms to the "mythical method"
discussed by T. S. Eliot in his 1923 review of James Joyce's *Ulysses*. Though
we commonly regard *Ulysses* as a novel (and some even pronounce that it
is the end of the tradition), it is worth noting, in the wake of Welty's own
remarks about *The Golden Apples,* that Eliot's essay included the observation
that if *Ulysses* "is not a novel, that is simply because the novel is a form
which will no longer serve."[1]

   At the present time, however, though the term *novel* still serves for many of us, Tzvetan Todorov has stated strongly that "we must stop identifying genres with names of genres. . . . The study of genres must be undertaken on the basis of structural characteristics, not on the basis of names" (149). From such critical impulses, in fact, our notions of long prose fiction have received a salutary expansion in the last several years. The writing of Mikhail Bakhtin, especially, challenges us to perceive the ungeneric nature of what we have called *novel* and to appreciate its capacity to be open-ended, unconventional in structure, many-voiced, and parodic of all other forms including its so-called own.[2] But Bakhtin's wide net, like T. S. Eliot's very nearly coincidental one, would seem also to capture Welty's book into a specific tradition she appears to reject, whether we call it novel or not.

Welty is legendary for her graciousness, and as a professional writer living on the income from her work, she is hardly unaware of the economic rewards of novels as compared to story collections or works of undeclared unitary status. And at various times during her career she has accepted the gambit of writing what she is willing to call the novel. She has done this, she says, reluctantly, and only when a piece of work proved to possess unexpected scope or force and demanded the kind of weaving that Welty is willing to call novelistic. Nonetheless, regarding the status of *The Golden Apples,* she remains obdurate, though her statements about the book deliberately refuse to clarify her position. She tells us only what *The Golden Apples* is not: it is not a novel and it is not a collection of stories (*Conversations* 23, 43, 150, 192, 285, 326).

Welty's calm denial of conventional genre status for *The Golden Apples* betrays no uncertainty about her purposes and absolutely no disdain for this piece of writing. On the contrary, it is, she says repeatedly, her favorite work, something she loved writing; and the process of discovering the connections between the individual stories was marked by a great deal of aesthetic pleasure and excitement (*Conversations* 45–46, 86–87, 197–98, 272). Could it be, then, that she reflects a post-modernist consciousness, that she is one with Todorov about the need to cease speaking of genres with the names of genres? We must remember that, for all her gracious demeanor and her devotion to the small capital city of Mississippi as a hometown, she is not unacquainted with radical experimentation in the arts. Welty grew up enthusiastically in the Machine Age, launched herself with press camera and notebook during the late depression era, and came into her own as a writer of very polished fiction toward the end of World War II. Her work—the photography as well as the fiction—documents a number of things in her Mississippi but focuses often upon the strength, adaptability, and personal triumphs of women during difficult times. Welty's strong hold on the non-naming of her favorite long text might remind us that she is not an *epigone,* tailgating modernism as it is dragged off through the South to some weed-choked junkyard. Rather she is, as her famous letters to Edmund Wilson in the *New Yorker* (1949) and Richard Gilman in the *New York Times Book Review* (1975) strongly remind us, a sure and independent writer perfectly aware of the artistic latitudes popular critics tend to deny the artist. Could it be, then, that *The Golden Apples* is that post-modernist event, a text? Could it be that Welty herself is not just a reluctant deep-South object to which the smart signifying of post-modern criticism may be applied, but a post-modernist consciousness herself? There is some sense in such a view, and a good deal of critical value may accrue from it. Whether she knows it or not, Welty's remarks about *The Golden Apples* may express her reluctance to be in either of two camps seemingly open to her: one where the hidden and impossible standard of the Great American Novel presides and the other where the completion of a certain amount of work and the need or will to assemble that work combine to produce a volume of—however good—merely linked tales.

That is, admittedly, an overstatement of the possibilities in the 1980s, but not, I think, an absolutely unreasonable one for the 1940s, when Welty felt such excitement in discovering the relationships among the elements of *The Golden Apples*. At any rate, Welty's obduracy regarding the form of *The Golden Apples* should remind us at the very least to loosen our hold on limiting concepts and categories and to see whether she has discovered or elaborated a tradition of her own.

Evidence from the book itself, from its sources, and from Welty's comments about it indicates that she could perhaps give *The Golden Apples* a name if that name weren't apt to be misunderstood, weren't likely to be a diminution. The name obscured by Welty's reticence is, I will argue, rooted in the concept *cycle* but not necessarily expressed by the word itself. *Cycle* has of course been applied to *The Golden Apples* by previous criticism (Skaggs 220). When used previously, however, *cycle* has referred only to the context of such books as Sarah Orne Jewett's *The Country of the Pointed Firs,* James Joyce's *Dubliners,* Sherwood Anderson's *Winesburg, Ohio,* or Ernest Hemingway's *In Our Time.* For all their marvelous interconnectedness, in comparison to *The Golden Apples,* the books by the male authors cited here are not only quite loosely strung but also not so self-consciously concerned with the broad idea of cycle and things cyclic. In the same regard, and to speak of a tradition Welty strongly acknowledges, works by Sarah Orne Jewett and Willa Cather are not quite the model either. The work of these women may be more important to Welty's achievement in *The Golden Apples* than the collections by men just cited. But Jewett's localized cycle of tales *The Country of the Pointed Firs* and Cather's seven-story collection *The Troll Garden* or her grandly episodic *My Ántonia* do not immerse themselves in the cyclic as does Welty's book.

It is too much to say that any work of fiction is unique, but Welty's stance toward *The Golden Apples* indicates that even as she was writing it, she realized the singularity of her achievement and the good fortune of such singularity. Writing the Morgana stories, Welty discovered how much richer than expected were her sources and inspiration. Without will or conscious design, her imagination engaged itself with "the interconnections"—"finding the way things emerged in my mind and the way one thing led to another; the interconnectedness of the book fascinated me" (*Conversations* 3).

Not the simple notion of cycle, as in *series,* but cyclic form, cyclic phenomena, cycles of *things* became the power and the chief repetitive trope for this interconnectedness. To be sure, at the simplest level *The Golden Apples* is a cycle of stories about interrelated families in Morgana, Mississippi. As such, it is modeled after traditional stories in the realms of myth and legend that are organized around a central hero or theme. Many such cycles exist, and they in turn have been the inspiration for series, or cycles, of songs or poems similarly organized. One tradition often feeds another. Welty's book reflects this interrelatedness in several ways. The author not only weaves a story cycle of her own but also pointedly evokes cyclic tales, poems, and music from several traditions. First, there is the Celtic material that is an unconscious Morgana inheritance. People there bear Scots, Welsh, and Irish names. In addition, some of them quote or unconsciously paraphrase the poetry of William Butler Yeats, itself based on Celtic cycles of legend and myth. At the same time, and like Yeats himself, Welty underscores these folk and literary Celtic cycles by finding similarities between her characters and figures in classical mythology: the interrelated cycles of Zeus, Hercules, Perseus, Hera, Athena, and Aphrodite and the mortals who became involved in the affairs of these gods, among them a long list of women, including Andromache, Arachne, Cassiopeia, Eurydice, Helen, Medusa, and the Sibyl of Cumae.

It is also obvious that *The Golden Apples* uses a number of means to evoke the power and intricacy of musical literature from its simplest to its most sophisticated forms. *Tales from Vienna Woods, Carmen, William Tell, Tales of Hoffmann,* a Schumann "forest piece," several pieces with *dance* in the title—"Scarf Dance," "Dorothy—an Old English Dance," *Anitra's Dance*— as well as Liszt are mentioned (*CS* 290, 297–98, 303). But Welty most often alludes to that music which has evolved from cyclic form—from the simple round "Row, Row, Row Your Boat" to the sonatas and symphonies of Beethoven. She refers to the song cycles of Hugo Wolf and the musical dramas of Richard Wagner. Art song, for instance, with lyrical roots in cycles of myth and poetry and musical roots in the folklike song cycle of Beethoven entitled "To the Distant Beloved," is cited in a much-worn copy of Hugo Wolf's music owned by the exiled German, Miss Eckhart (*CS* 302). Wagner, who built his operas on folkloric and mythical cycles and wrote a great operatic cycle, is represented by a particularly appropriate work, *Tannhäuser,* which presents a fable of the longing for love in the world of the wandering troubadour—carrier of song cycles—and in the mythological Venusberg that the troubadour enters. At the simplest musical level, several stories allude to cyclic music. "June Recital" recalls the recurrent tunes used in musical instruction and played annually by children—pieces like "The Little Rocking Horse," with its imitation of the cyclic periodicity of rocking, and *Für Elise,* with its recurrent phrases. "Moon Lake" recalls the tunes, often rounds, sung by children at summer camp; and "Music from Spain" evokes the programs of folkloric and classical arrangements popularized by the great Spanish guitarist Andrés Segovia. "The Little Rocking Horse" and "Row, Row, Row Your Boat" are innocent songs enough, but they both hint of journeys like those taken or desired by Welty's wanderers; and "Row, Row, Row Your Boat" ends with the appropriate and poignant message understood by many in Morgana: "Life is but a dream."

Dreams, in fact, are part of Welty's cyclic lore, too, as are reveries, fantasies, and illusions. She writes that what "had drawn the characters together was one strong strand in them all: they lived in one way or another in a dream or in romantic aspiration, or under an illusion of what their lives were coming to" (*OWB* 99). Cassie Morrison recalls the face that always looks into her dreams; Loch's fever and the fire in Miss Eckhart's head are related. Mattie Will Sojourner churns and dreams. Ran MacLain fantasizes murdering his rival and his runaway wife. The rhythms of life in Morgana invite recurrence. Annual and weekly and daily events of all kinds recur rhythmically: croquet parties, summer camps, recitals, public speakings, Rook parties, milkings, Fate Rainey's plaintive calls as he makes a round of the streets selling his produce. Dreaming or waking, in fact, the life of Morgana is filled with cycles: Katie repeating local stories to strangers from her roadside stand, Mattie Will Sojourner dreaming at her churn, Cassie and Loch Morrison remembering different recurrent events in the old MacLain house next door, and the rites of birth and death, departure and return, that change but do not destroy the "Main Families" of Morgana, Mississippi. Even singular occurrences are perceived as repetitive. In the wake of Easter's near drowning in Moon Lake, the girls remember that Mrs. Gruenwald had told them the day before that " 'Moon Lakes are all over the world. . . .' And into each fell a girl, they dared, now, to think" (*CS* 373).

The ubiquity of Moon Lakes—made in the abandoned hooks of old river bends—reminds us that nature is many cycles, from the most remote— the wheel of the constellations in the dark night sky—to the nearest—the little, unremarked link between river, rain, and tree in the atmospheric cycle, the cycle of the four seasons (*The Golden Apples* begins and ends in October), and, figuratively, at least, the cycle of human fertility: the staining red sash on Virgie Rainey's last recital dress evokes the menstrual flow that early separates Virgie from the other girls and takes her out of the cyclic play of the annual June recitals.

Virgie becomes one of the book's wanderers, a figure associated with the rhythms of Aphrodite, which are in part those of the sea. She has an affair with Kewpie Moffitt the sailor, and in the final chapter she rises from her bath in the river like Venus coming out of the ocean foam (*CS* 439–40). But the rhythm of the sea is in tune with the moon, and the moon reappears in land-locked Morgana significantly: Moon Lake appropriately is the setting for the chaste adventures of little girls whose tethered boat keeps them chained to the shore (*CS* 356), and Cassie prepares for the hayride on which there will be singing of her favorite song, "By the Light of the Silvery Moon" (*CS* 316)—a song that resonates to the book's title and the Yeats poem in Cassie's head. These planetary associations might mean little if it were not for the rich astronomical context built into the book. For Cassie, things "divined and endured" rose, set, and even turned in the sky "the way the planets did. Or they were more like whole constellations . . . Perseus and Orion and Cassiopeia in her Chair. . . . It was not just the sun and moon that traveled" (*CS* 302). The imagery of the heavens is used especially strongly as Welty writes a closing measure for her final section. The author has acknowledged in *One Writer's Beginnings* her awareness that the word *planet* means "wanderer," recalling that the "night sky over my childhood Jackson was velvety black. I could see the full constellations in it and call their names; when I could read, I knew their myths." Perhaps she who knew the constellations by name and understood their evocations of ancient cycle stories also knew that by 1928 astronomers had, for the convenience of recording observations, officially portioned out the heavens, fixing upon eighty-eight as the total number of constellations. Whether Science was thinking of the music of the spheres I don't know, but Welty (who in 1928 would have been eleven or twelve, the age of her young piano players at the peak of Miss Eckhart's influence, and whose father was the sort to put her eye to a telescope to study the heavens) may then or later have noted the correspondence between that new heavenly number and the number of keys on the instrument by which Virgie and the other girls come to know so much: Miss Eckhart's piano.[3]

For heavenly wanderers, and no less for earthly ones like those in Welty's stories, travel is cycle, too. Mythological and literary travel tends, in fact, to be singularly cyclic. Welty has revealed that, in her imagination, story is associated deeply with cyclic travel: annual trips to her grandparents, weekly excursions in the family car, all of them accompanied by "talk," the telling of tales (*OWB* 13–15, 44). She admits to a deep emotional connection, as well as a solid practical one, between travel and story in the development and the forging of her art: "writers and travelers alike are mesmerized by knowing their destinations" (*OWB* 44). She says she admires the peripatetic: "my imagination was magnetized toward transient artists," she writes in *One Writer's Beginnings,* "toward the transience as much as the artists" (86). In her own way she became a transient artist herself, wandering depression-era Mississippi with camera for the WPA and finding frequent inspiration for fiction in her own travels. Trips have inspired some of her major subjects for writing, from the discovery of Yeats and AE in the library of the University of Wisconsin to the exploration of San Francisco that provoked Eugene MacLain's wanderings in "Music from Spain." Travel is a basis for a great deal of her fiction—from "A Worn Path" to "No Place for You, My Love"—and other stories and novels are filled with travelers, including such transient artists as Powerhouse. She renewed her own status as a transient artist during the writing of *The Golden Apples,* wandering with such a bold result that her Harcourt editor and fellow southerner Lambert Davis congratulated her heartily (and warily) on her discovery that she could write elsewhere than Jackson (qtd. in Devlin 54). And she has shared, in some ways, the wandering minstrelsy she admires by traveling to read from her works.

Even a casual reader can see that travel receives a great deal of exploration in *The Golden Apples* and that it is emphatically cyclic—both circular and recurrent. In "Shower of Gold," Katie Rainey speaks a dramatic monologue about a wanderer that makes the reader a passerby engaged by her tale. In "June Recital" Kewpie Moffitt pursues Virgie Rainey around and around the mattress in the upstairs room of the half-abandoned old MacLain house. Another rite of spring is prepared downstairs by the now-deranged Miss Eckhart, who first as exile from her native land and now in flight from the County Farm (a home for the destitute) has come a long way to reach Morgana. In "Sir Rabbit" a Sojourner, aptly named, has an encounter in the woods first with the MacLain twins and then repetitively with that priapic wanderer their father. In "Moon Lake" the little girls slip out like the twelve dancing princesses in the fairy tale, but their boat is tethered. Nearly drowned, the orphan Easter, like old Miss Eckhart a refugee from a county "home," returns from the dead. The twins Ran and Eugene MacLain make fateful circular journeys in the juxtaposed stories "The Whole World Knows" and "Music from Spain." "The Wanderers"—originally "The Hummingbirds" (Polk, "Checklist" 669)—is a title that evokes not only the journeys rounded out in that chapter (most pointedly those of King and Virgie) but also the planets—and constellations—with which the characters' lives have so many associations through mythology. As the musical element of *The Golden Apples* allows the juxtaposition of simple rounds with great sonatas and operas, the context of travel draws upon images as simple as the offstage hayride or the thwarted boat trip on a starry lake, as grand as King's rumored flight to the golden west or Eugene's actual temporary displacement in San Francisco.

The great body of myth, legend, poetry, fiction, and song built upon the subject of travel reminds us repeatedly that to travel meaningfully one must have some place to come from and to which one can return. Literary journeys are in essence, and often in fact, circular, archetypes of the eternal return to one's own sources and resources, preferably, though not necessarily, with the boon of new understandings. In *One Writer's Beginnings,* Welty writes of the "inward journey" of memory in just such terms: "forward or back, seldom in a straight line, most often spiraling. . . . As we discover, we remember; remembering, we discover, and most intensely do we experience this when our separate journeys converge. Our living experience at those meeting points is one of the charged dramatic fields of fiction" (102).

Morgana is a particularly charged dramatic field of fiction. Conceiving the locus of her stories as a small town on the Big Black River of the Yazoo Delta near Vicksburg, Mississippi, was a lucky invention. The luck was not only that its name is an expression of the fata morgana, the mirage, the illusion of the desert traveler, or that Morgana "was a whole town and everybody was sort of like a family itself" (*Conversations* 222) but also that it is allusively evocative of two of the main cycles of mythology that lie, along with so much else, behind the lives of her characters. Welty's fictional town has a double connection, through Morgan le Fay and the common Welsh surname Morgan, to the Celtic past that is an often lost heritage of many southerners, specifically those with names such as are borne by the "Main Families in Morgana, Mississippi" listed at the beginning of *The Golden Apples.* The proximity of the real Big Black River of Mississippi evokes the dark rivers of the Greco-Roman afterworld, an association underlined by the drowning there of Mr. Sissum, the Orphean cellist at whose funeral, ironically, the grieving Eurydice, Miss Eckhart, nearly falls into the open grave. This association puts a slant on King MacLain's deception when he departs town and leaves his hat on the banks of the Big Black; the obvious message is that he wants people to suppose he has drowned, but the act also suggests an epic quest that begins with a descent into hell. The context is reinforced many ways, not least by Virgie's recollection in "The Wanderers" that the now-dead Eugene is "the only MacLain man gone since her memory, after old Virgil himself" (*CS* 458). This not-so-oblique reference to Dante is reinforced by Virgie's immediate speculation that Eugene's "foreign" wife might even be a "Dago" (*CS* 458). Allusively named and allusively situated, Morgana, Mississippi, provides the sine qua non of fiction, a cosmos rich with dramatic possibilities, an intertextual area, a stage where the writer can be sure that the doings of fiction will occur. For Welty, the intertextuality of Morgana doubtless also would include Morgan City, Mississippi, a very small town in the Delta near Greenwood, and Morgantown, West Virginia, not too far from the town of Clay, where she made summer sojourns with her mother's family (*OWB* photo).

The cyclic material within *The Golden Apples* reflects the importance to Welty's imagination and her artistic vision of things cyclic, but Welty was hardly alone in the application of such a fascination. Eliot and Joyce, whose early works focused attention on the so-called mythical method, again come to mind, as does Yeats, with his adaptation of cyclic lore and his interest in the spirals of history. *The Golden Apples* appeared within the same decade as *Finnegan's Wake* (1939) and *The Four Quartets* (1943), both complexly cyclic works. Yeats, however, is probably a more important direct analogue, for it was Yeats whom Welty remembers discovering during her first phase of deliberate wandering, when she was a student at the University of Wisconsin. She dramatizes the encounter in *One Writer's Beginnings* with a fictional scene from an unpublished piece, a speech spoken by "an unhappy middle-aged teacher of linguistics who's reached a critical point in his life":

> "I happened to discover Yeats [Welty's male character explains], reading through some of the stacks in the library. I read the early and then the later poems all in the same one afternoon, standing up, by the window . . . I read 'Sailing to Byzantium,' standing up in the stacks, read it by the light of the falling snow. It seemed to me that if I could stir, if I could move to take the next step, I could go out into the poem the way I could go out into that snow. That it [the poem] would be falling on my shoulders, that it would pelt me on its way down—that I could move in it, live in it—that I could die in it, maybe. So after that I had to *learn* it," he said. "And I told myself that I would. That I accepted the invitation." (81)

Welty goes on to explain that the "experience I describe in the story had indeed been my own, snow and all, the poem that smote me first was 'The Song of the Wandering Aengus'; it was the poem that turned up, fifteen years or so later, in my stories of *The Golden Apples* and runs all through the book" (*OWB* 81).[4]

We can see plainly in *The Golden Apples* that Welty discovered in her fiction various connections between Yeats's poetry and the Celtic cycles that lie behind it, between that poetry and the cycles of classical mythology to which it often refers, and between that poetry and the astronomical and musical material which, cyclic itself, refers to the same rich contexts. If Welty's references to Yeats's poetry are thus not accidents, then clearly it is no accident that in "Music from Spain" Eugene MacLain sees in a San Francisco bookstore window "a dark photograph that looked like Emma," his wife, but was, "he read below, Madame Blavatsky" (*CS* 397).

181

Nothing is said to indicate whether Eugene knows or cares who this Madame Blavatsky is; but the reader, of course, has the chance to recognize her as the founder of the Theosophical movement and William Butler Yeats's spiritual mentor at the outset of his sustained interest in mysticism. I am not so rash as to suggest that the seven sections of *The Golden Apples* (or the magical seven miles between Morgana and MacLain courthouse) in any way reflect Welty's knowledge of the seven levels of Theosophist consciousness. I do think it likely, however, that someone with Welty's interest in Yeats, working during 1947 and 1948 on a cycle of stories that quoted and paraphrased Yeats's poetry quite freely, and sending her stories to a much-admired agent who happened to be the son of the Irish poet and Theosophist George Russell (known by his pen name AE and the "mystical friend" to whom Yeats dedicated his collection of Irish fairy and folk tales), would have noticed Richard Ellmann's 1948 biography *Yeats: The Man and the Masks*. Indeed, Ellmann's title itself may have attracted her attention; for masks, literal and figurative, play a major role in her book. Supposing she looked into it before or during the composition of the book, Welty would have read with interest this passage about Madame Blavatsky:

> The tenets of *The Secret Doctrine,* as Madame Blavatsky called her chief work, are of interest because they brought Yeats into contact for the first time with a comprehensive cosmology. Whatever else may be said of Madame Blavatsky, she did try to hold the world in the palm of her hand, and made huge generalizations about man and the cosmos which were easier for [Yeats] to credit, and more inviting, than the dogmas of the churches. Madame Blavatsky's faith had three main articles: in the first place, there was an "Omnipresent, Eternal, Boundless, and Immutable Principle on which all speculation is impossible." This was a far cry from Dr. Arnold's personal God, and in practice the Theosophists paid little attention to deity. Secondly, Madame Blavatsky asserted the universality of the law of periodicity, of flux and reflux, or, as she sometimes called it, of polarity. According to this doctrine, the world is a conflict of opposites; good and evil are as in Manichaeism the contraries without which life cannot exist, but these are not the only opposites; everywhere the armies clash, with now one, now the other triumphant. Thirdly, she proclaimed the fundamental identity of all souls with the Universal Oversoul, implying that any soul might under proper conditions partake of the Oversoul's power, and proclaimed also the "obligatory pilgrimage of every Soul through the Cycle of Incarnation in accordance with Cyclic and Karmic law." (58–59)

In Theosophy, Ellmann's explanation continued, "The soul has seven elements or principles and its evolution proceeds through existences on seven *planets* [my emphasis], each with varying degrees of matter and spirit, earth alone having them in equal quantities. There are seven races, and seven branch races and seven root races, and the soul, passing through all these, has about eight hundred incarnations, 'like beads on a string' " (59).

Undoubtedly, Yeats's five or six years of involvement with Theosophy, three of them in active membership, Ellmann explained, "left their mark" on the poet: "He had been brought into contact with a system based on opposition to materialism and on support of secret and ancient wisdom, and was encouraged to believe that he would be able to bring together all the fairy tales and folklore he had heard in childhood, the poetry he had read in adolescence, the dreams he had been dreaming all his life" (67). Theosophist ideas, Ellmann added, also contributed to Yeats's lifelong interest in periodicity, the ebb and flow of existence and the cyclical nature of history. "He had secured weapons for the attack on materialism. Theosophy had furnished him with shield and sword, and he went forth like Don Quixote," Ellmann wrote in 1948, "to tilt at the windmills of modern life" (69).

Was Theosophy an interest of Welty's, somehow imbibed from her interest in Yeats or her reading of Ellmann's *Yeats: The Man and the Masks?* Not much escapes a writer of Welty's caliber. Theosophy would have interested her simply because it had inspired an artist she much admired. In addition, her interest in Yeats would have been compounded by her strong relationship to her agent Diarmuid Russell, whose father, AE, had been a more active Theosophist than Yeats. The picture of Madame Blavatsky seen by Eugene MacLain *is* an oblique reference to an unorthodox system of knowledge from which, without the least commitment or belief, Welty might have derived some of the same artistic comfort as Yeats and others. Like Yeats and other modernists, she was an artist at war in certain ways with materialism. As Ellmann put it on the first page of the chapter he devotes to Madame Blavatsky's influence, "All over Europe and America" the young "refused to accept the universe that their scientific, materialist, rationalist, and often hypocritically religious elders tried to hand them. Science had disproved orthodox conceptions of the making of the world and of man, and had implied a threat to every traditional attitude. . . . Since Christianity seemed to have been exploded, and since science offered to western man little but proof of his own ignominiousness" Madame Blavatsky's Theosophy "offered a 'synthesis of science, religion, and philosophy' which opposed the contemporary developments of all three" and announced that modern thought was "ancient thought distorted" (56–57).

Like Yeats, from an early age Welty was familiar with mythology and its relationships to religion, folklore, poetry, music and, as we have seen, even astronomy. And whether or not one had read Max Müller or dipped into the full form or the 1922 abridgement of *The Golden Bough,* comparative mythology and its claims, even if filtered to the modern reader only by Yeats, Joyce and, Eliot, was well established as a necessary source for the writer long before Welty emerged from her apprenticeship. Like Yeats, Welty was undoubtedly delighted to find a tradition of thought and art that encouraged her to bring together the fairy tales and the folklore she had heard and read in childhood, the poetry she had read in youth, and the dreams she had dreamed all her life. It is, in fact, an attempt at resolving meaning from just such experience that she often gives her characters in *The Golden Apples*.

By contrast to the appeal to the mythological, folkloric, legendary, musical, planetary, and natural cycles, it is interesting to note that the major cycles of orthodoxy are absent from *The Golden Apples*. Where in Welty is the Christian cycle, the calendar of the Judeo-Christian year that one might expect in the doubtless Calvinist world of Morgana? Are we to believe that the observant Welty has overlooked this system? I think not. Some of the church's power is there—the women of Morgana play Rook, with its numbered cards, instead of bridge or another game requiring "sin cards" (those with the faces of kings, queens, and jacks that are used for gambling—euchre or poker). But the church's rituals are essentially invisible, overshadowed by the systems that interest and inspire Welty, as they did Yeats: cycles of gods and heroes; ancient images projected in story, song, and the night skies—humankind's potent conceptions of the relations between men and women and the world above, below, and around them, stories that reflect the emotions, illusions, trials, and triumphs of the human world and affirm the writer's and artist's task as diviner of mysteries and as revealer of a culture to itself.

As in the great epics shaped from cycles of tales, Welty's work acknowledges that the completion of a cyclic passage by a wandering human may affect life but does not insure success or knowledge. Eugene MacLain, Virgie Rainey supposes, has gone far away to learn that "people don't have to be answered just because they want to know" (*CS* 458). And for all his flight, even King MacLain must eventually die. Yet Eugene has touched the sources of enchantment in ways that Virgie cannot know. Taking his distant western journey, the trip from San Francisco to Land's End (like the Big Black River, a real landmark in its territory but also an intertextual one), Eugene has had his day with the Spanish guitarist and achieved momentary defeat of the horror in his life—the uncomprehending stare of a wife who has not been able to bear the death of their little girl. This adventure is cast in terms of the slaying of Medusa, the stealing of the golden apples, and other exploits of Perseus and of his descendent Hercules, whose cycle is employed throughout *The Golden Apples* (McHaney); but it also reflects the contradictoriness of the Celtic otherworlds, one timeless and idyllic to represent mortal perfection and the other a domain of fearsome giants against whom the hero could prove his valor (as he could not in a land of plenty where there was no strife). Significantly, the Celtic imagination associated the otherworld with Spain:

> In the Celtic beliefs the dead inhabit a region across the ocean, situated to the south-west, where the sun sinks to rest during the greater part of the year—a wonderful realm whose delights far surpass those of this world. It is from this mysterious country that men originally came. . . . For [its] Pagan name, which has no parallel in Christian beliefs, the euhemerism of the Irish Christian annalists substituted the Latin name of the Iberian peninsula, *Hispania*. From the tenth century onwards . . . it was from Spain, and not from the land of the Dead, that this mythic chief [Partholon] and his companions were made to arrive. (de Jubainville 15–16)[5]

Welty's "Music from Spain" thus might be seen as Music from the Land of the Dead. King MacLain feigns death to leave Morgana, and Katie envisions him "in the West, out where it's gold and all that" (*CS* 268)—thus conflating the American dream of an Eldorado, the gold-rush fever to California, the adventures of Perseus in seeking the golden apples of the Hesperides (associated by modern interpreters with the oranges of Spain: the "golden apples of the sun" in Yeats's poem), and the Celtic otherworld. Like the dead, King circles back home now and again on the eve of the Celtic New Year (which is also our Halloween), and finally settles down, still resisting the inevitable: but as his grandchildren know in a metaphor of their own, "When you get to be a hundred, you pop" (*CS* 468). The tubercular Eugene experiences—and King must face—the fate of those who return to see their homeland after a sojourn in the timeless otherworld of the Celtic myths: annihilation or old age. In the Celtic cycles, one returning from the Land of Youth to his homeland must not set foot to ground; if he does, he suffers the fate of Oisin—"his youth and beauty left him, and old age and decrepitude fell upon him" (de Jubainville 205–06). The twin Ran, whose travels are much closer to home but just as perilous for him and others despite the ironic diminution, is forgiven for the shame of his life by being made into a "smiling public man," to use Yeats's phrase from "Among School Children"—the town elects him mayor.

But it is with Virgie Rainey's cycle and with her final consciousness of the convergence of cyclic things that *The Golden Apples* appropriately ends. Her story is partly an analogue of that of Aphrodite, but its full import is revealed by reflection against the stories of other Morgana women of the last two generations. These women's lives correspond in turn to mythological cycles of their own: some repeat the fates of those who dared to challenge Athena or Minerva and suffered by being entangled in their own proficiencies (Arachne) or by being turned into something monstrous as a curse against their beauty (Medusa); some suffered the fate of those who dallied, or did not dally enough, with the gods and demigods, and who were raped, destroyed, pushed toward despair, made prophetic and unintelligible, given immortality but not ageless beauty, or apotheosized in the natural world or the starry heavens (Cassiopeia, Io, Leda, Danae, Andromache, the Sibyl, and so on). These are tropes with which Virgie and doubtless many other women can identify. Virgie knows these stories, and she hates the ones that lead to death through betrayal or loss or despair, all of which she must have experienced in her own life before returning home. In the last section, she settles the affairs of her mother's completed existence and sits down to decide what to do next herself.

The closure of *The Golden Apples,* often quoted, is a poetic statement of Virgie's consciousness that she has attained an intuitive grasp of cyclic things, including those polarities to which Madame Blavatsky paid such attention: love and hate, horror and beauty, life and death. A paradoxical closeness gathers all opposites. If one can read the signs, ageless human endeavor is apotheosized everywhere in the visible world. And as she sits at one of those still points, Virgie reads the message of her life: from music, from love, from longing, from travel, from the dead, from the skies. It is raining. The season is fall. Perhaps, she thinks, it is raining "on the everywhere" (*CS* 460). Mysteries in suspension converge, and through an act of profound simplicity, Virgie gathers in knowledge.

The end of any well-wrought fiction is a confluence of the repetitions out of which that fiction is woven, analogous, perhaps, to what Welty calls "the greatest confluence of all"—that which makes up the human memory—the individual human memory. Her own memory, she has written, "is the treasure most dearly regarded by me, in my life and in my work as a writer. Here time, also, is subject to confluence. The memory is a living thing—it too is in transit" (*OWB* 104).

In many discussions of Welty's work—as one can see, for example, in other essays in this collection—we hear of polarities, of dualities that swing back and forth, of paradoxes that refuse to resolve into absolute singularity, of spiralings down, of contradictions accepted and revealed as a source of power and knowledge. Welty's other, carefully set collections of stories, the individual stories themselves, and the novels all have ways of reminding us that she is deeply interested in things cyclic. She has perceived the complex fictional possibilities of the concept *cycle;* and as Faulkner, for example, pushed the meanings of the term *novel* by forcing his bold structures under that rubric (so that he, unlike Welty—and with economic motives, too—insisted that the seven-story cycles *The Unvanquished* [1938] and *Go Down, Moses* [1942] were novels), she has deliberately pushed, and we might even say transcended, the cycle of tales.

In her essay "Technique as Myth: The Structure of *The Golden Apples,"* Danièle Pitavy-Souques cites the restatement of a common formalist theorem in Jean Ricardou's *Problèmes du nouveau roman:* "Great narratives can be recognized in that the story they tell is nothing but the dramatization of their own function" (267). Pitavy-Souques uses this observation to support her argument that "the narratives that constitute *The Golden Apples* are dramatizations of the function of the myth of Perseus," a useful point I do not want to dispute entirely but to enlarge upon. The fact is that the cycle of Perseus is only one of many cycles that lie beneath the surface of the Morgana cycle; and it is *cycle,* as subject, as allusion, and as form, that is repeatedly drawn into the reader's presence by the stories.

We live, this resonant book seems to say, in ever-repeating cycles of time and memory, loss and recollection, in which humans love and lose and love again, and where understanding comes to the one who can stop the beat of time while it paradoxically beats all around her. Reading *The Golden Apples,* we begin as travelers held for a moment to hear a tale from Virgie's mother, Katie. We end as if sharing the memory and voice of Virgie, sitting and thinking under the great "public tree" (*CS* 461) at MacLain courthouse. There, in the rain, at the center of a world where many things fall apart, something still seems to hold. It is October, the month in which the book began. Possibly once again it is the eve of the Celtic New Year. Virgie has been through all the false comforts of a funeral. She has put her mother's house in order. She has visited the cemetery and seen the graves which make her angry or sad. Yet Virgie smiles to remember Mr. King MacLain's "hideous and delectable" defiance to death in the face he makes for her at her mother's funeral, "when they all knew he was next—even he" (*CS* 461). We are taken back to the scary fingers and curiously portentous Halloween masks of the MacLain twins in the first episode of the book when they frighten away their wandering father (*CS* 270–71).

The Golden Apples ends on a note of reconciliation, but the ending reflects neither an easy victory nor an easy acquiescence. Sitting beneath the axle tree of her turning world, her head filled with messages from the dead, Virgie Rainey reflects upon the endlessly cyclic nature of things, comprehends the union of opposites and the endless repetition of human endeavor, and accepts the burden of memory, which is the burden of knowledge. But knowledge is a burden only until it is completed. In Virgie's experience, her sudden grasp of things cyclic is a wisdom beyond rationality and a comfort, too. Though we do not witness such scenes, we may assume that Virgie's tale-telling mother, Katie, has told and retold the cycles of Morgana to her daughter, including, of course, some version of the book's primal story: that tale recounted in "Shower of Gold" about King's return on Halloween—which also happens to be the eve of the Celtic New Year. That fall day, Katie tells *us,* had a "two-way look"—the twins too, we know, are Janus-like, born on January first, New Year's Day (*CS* 267)— and like the day on which Virgie is able to grasp all the contrarities, rain is coming. The quick cycling of King's arrival and departure—"I'm going. You stay," he says to his masked twins (*CS* 272)—is compounded in confusion because the infant Virgie swallows a button. In the view of Miss Snowdie MacLain, at least, Katie and Virgie must take some blame: "she kind of holds it against me, because I was there that day when he come; and she don't like my baby any more" (*CS* 274). Perhaps Snowdie even suspects that Virgie is King's child and that the presence of Katie and Virgie, not the booger-dancing of the twins, sent King off on his way again. But Snowdie, in Katie Rainey's view, had never "got a real good look at life. . . . Not the kind of look I got, and away back when I was twelve year old or so. Like something was put to my eye" (*CS* 266).

A special sense of what it means "to get a real good look at life" is expressed in the final scene. "Passionate, recalcitrant, stubbornly undefeated by failure or hurt or disgrace or bereavement, all the while heedlessly wasting of her gifts," as Welty has commented, Virgie "knows to the last that there is a world that remains out there, a world living and mysterious, and that she is of it" (*OWB* 102). Knowledge comes when one can get a good look at life, which is exactly what the retrospective Virgie does under the tree at the MacLain courthouse. What she sees is metaphorically expressed in the story of Perseus, in the union of the contrarities, in the myths expressed by the wheeling constellations. Knowledge comes when the periodicity of the cycles can be held momentarily in suspension. As Welty writes in *One Writer's Beginning*, "The events of our lives happen in a sequence in time, but in their significance to ourselves they find their own order, a timetable not necessarily—perhaps not possibly—chronological . . . it is the continuous thread of revelation" (68–69).

Among Welty's antecedents in the making of cyclic literature are, as she who invokes *Tannhäuser* knew, the troubadours—and tradition even has it that some *kings* were troubadours—and the trouvères. The root word associates these singers with the verb *to find*, as well as with a verb meaning *user of tropes*. Welty certainly would have identified with the first and most common etymology; for as she says frequently, and perhaps best near the ending of *One Writer's Beginnings*, *The Golden Apples* fell into a pattern of confluences for her, and she simply discovered the relationships among characters, the connections between their lives and the domain of poetry and myth. But she might also associate herself easily with the root that makes a *trouvère* a user of tropes, a phrase that aptly describes one of the main features of her poetical prose.

In *The Golden Apples* it is not only the language that is metaphorical but the structure as well. Welty's book *represents* in every sense that all things are cyclic. For the living, all life is more radically linked with every day and every age that passes, so long as memory exists. As Welty has written in *One Writer's Beginnings*, "The memory too is in transit. But during its moment, all that is remembered joins, and lives—the old and the young, the past and the present, the living and the dead" (104). As a young piano student in the MacLain house where Miss Eckhart is a sojourner, a boarder, Virgie fiercely rejects the beat of the metronome that Miss Eckhart worships "as if it were the most precious secret in the teaching of music." This is the secret for which Virgie is not ready. Rejecting the metronome, the beat of time, Virgie forces her own will upon a piece of cyclic music, has "a little *Rondo* her way" (*CS* 294). But at the close of *The Golden Apples,* she is better able to comprehend the beat of time, and to accept that one does not exactly have one's way with the round of life, though acceptance does not mean defeat.

The mythological past and the personal past are not so different. Both can be revelations of the passing of time, seen not as chronology but as periodicity. In Virgie's vision, as in Welty's fiction, the mythological past and the personal past are linked, for the boundary between the everyday world and the world of the imagination is bridged repeatedly by the artist's vision and the ineluctable intertextuality of language. There are more than a few teachers of this wisdom, and so we need not believe that Welty had to imbibe it from Madame Blavatsky or Yeats—whose work is filled with similar vision—though she would have been interested in the weapons against a rigid materialism these writers provided. The gifts to genius fall only in fields that have been worked hard. Welty's luck was that her work on *The Golden Apples* fell, complexly, into nested cycles that encompassed image, allusion, character, setting, and form, cycles with which she had been familiar since her childhood and youth.

Let us not, then, worry about a label or genre for *The Golden Apples*. In writing about Willa Cather, Welty has observed that the pattern of a story may be the nearest thing to a "mirror image" of the artist's mind and heart. "Fictional patterns may well bite deeper than the events of a life will ever of themselves, or by themselves, testify to. The pattern is one of interpretation" (*Eye* 48). The pattern of *The Golden Apples* is cyclic in the most complex sense of that word. It rings with references to cyclic literature, music, cosmology. And in the end, it presents one woman's vision of a true dance of the elements, a union of all that humankind may hope to see and know. Perhaps all this is too ineffable to have a name.

RUTH M.

VANDE KIEFT

"WHERE IS THE VOICE COMING FROM?"

Teaching
Eudora Welty

In reviewing the singular delights and ardors of the 1987 Eye of the Storyteller conference in Akron, I have made what strikes me as an astounding discovery: as senior contributor and Welty scholar in this collection, I am almost certainly unique in never having heard of Eudora Welty nor having read a line of her fiction before I was required to teach it. That was at Wellesley College thirty-three years ago: the Modern Library edition of *A Curtain of Green* and *The Wide Net* was on a preselected reading list of an introductory literature course that also included works by Shakespeare, Milton, Donne, James, Ibsen, and Yeats, all great canonical writers I felt reasonably well prepared to teach. But teaching Welty seemed a rash and existential act, however necessary. Usually responses to literature are comprised of differentiable acts of first reading, reflecting, rereading and studying with fellow students under a teacher's guidance; writing papers and reading criticism; eventually, perhaps, writing for a graduate degree and with the hope of publication; and then, finally, teaching a writer's fiction by choice or special privilege. For me reading, interpreting, and teaching Welty's fiction were fused into a single, shared act, linking the public and private in my response, the puzzles and self-doubts and anxieties of performance with the pleasures and surprises of first readings, all welded in a sense of improvisation and urgency.

Those were, of course, the Arcadian days of a dominant literary pedagogy, the extension to the classroom of our own "close reading" shared with colleagues and friends, variously practiced but with a single commitment and implicit surrender to the text and the writer's imagined intention;

the golden days when teaching was privileged over publication in promotion and tenure decisions, and students were valued over administrators; before the days when one published or inevitably perished; might, indeed, perish *because* of publication.

What is required of us if we are to teach Eudora Welty's fiction effectively is some patient listening to a multitude of voices in order to hear where they are coming from, respond both justly and sympathetically, and adapt and appropriate discriminatingly to our teaching praxis. The voices that require our attentive listening and appraisal are Eudora Welty's, both in and out of her fiction (though mostly in), the voices of critics of her fiction, our own voices, and finally, the voices of our students. If I concentrate on the second of these categories, it is not because I do not think the author's voice to be of primary importance; but Welty's voice and intentions, like those of most fiction writers, are largely buried in her works—or rather, burning intensely in them: we perceive them through the experience of the stories.[1]

I focus chiefly on the voices of two recent critics because they seem to me crucial to the current practice of teaching Welty's fiction, influenced as it must be by new developments in post-modern, and especially feminist, critical theory. *We are* the teacher-critics, and I believe our function is extremely important to the future of Eudora Welty's place in the canon of southern and women's and American literature. Hence we should be wary, lest our voices become impediments rather than aids to understanding and appreciation for our students. Eudora Welty is often, and understandably, anxious about what we do. *She* is not accountable to us, but to herself and the stories; we are accountable to the stories, and we have a great responsibility to our students—so that they may share in our pleasure and understanding—to make her work part of their lives. Effective criticism and good teaching are not fixed, stable, certain; they are always developing, both questing and questioning, and rather elusive. Though my past work on Welty will probably be regarded as traditional-formalist,[2] I wish to assure my readers (or warn you, as the case may be) that my own voice no longer comes from the far right, if it ever did, and I have been attentive to voices coming from a variety of contemporary sources. I want to listen to a couple of current critical voices, to see what they have to offer that may broaden, stimulate, or further enlighten our reading of Welty's fiction and our classroom performance.

The first of these voices is that of Patricia Yaeger in an article first published in *PMLA,* and therefore of major importance as a "first" in Welty studies in that most prestigious publication in our profession. In the article, titled " 'Because a Fire Was in My Head': Eudora Welty and the Dialogic Imagination," a great many voices are heard to be speaking: Yaeger's; the voices of several modern feminist critics; the Russian critic Bakhtin; the

Irish poet W. B. Yeats and the voice of his alter ego, the wandering Aengus; Eudora Welty and her fictional character, Mattie Will Sojourner; the voice of Zeus; and the soundless voice of the ravished Leda. Let us try sorting them out.

Because she is writing feminist criticism, Yaeger first summons the voices of many of those critics, describing and applauding their notable attempts to clear the boards of masculine language and thought structures. But then she abandons them, perhaps because she finds none quite suitable, and turns to what she calls the "plagiarized" critical language of Bakhtin. (Plagiarism is here defined as showing "any complicity with masculine ideology, theatricality, or rhetorical style" [140].) Where is Bakhtin's critical voice coming from? He was a Russian who began his critical writing in the 1920s, whose voice was not heard in his own time, and whose work was promulgated first in Europe and later in America, in part for its political implications, which were democratic in a force state, though he himself was not politically active. He showed how the voices of fiction—in Dostoevsky, for example—were drawn from all strata of society, each carrying its own attitudes, assumptions, and social codes, energetically in dialogue with each other. An additional motive for the theories Bakhtin and his followers espoused was to upset the hegemony of the univocal lyrical poem, boosting fiction to a higher, more competitive place in the hierarchy of literary forms. Yaeger employs Bakhtin's terms, which seem highly appropriate to a writer whose imagination certainly seems dialogic. But the terms seem misapplied, for the next voice summoned is that of a strong-voiced lyric poet, Yeats, in his "Song of the Wandering Aengus" and "Leda and the Swan," rather than another or other prose or fictional voices, as in Bakhtin's own critical practice.[3] The dialogue which transpires, according to Yaeger, is that of the male poet (Yeats) and his poetic projection and alter ego, the wandering Aengus, and the female writer (Welty) in her fictional projection of the female alter ego, Mattie Will Sojourner, the glimmering girl changed to female muse and fantasizer; the dialogue is that between gynocentric and phallocentric discourse. As I see it, however, Yeats's language in the two poems is scarcely that of any class or social group or set of social codes, and the nature and terms of the two kinds of discourse do not seem comparable.

Yaeger shows, largely effectively, how Welty uses the tropes and language of Yeats's poem in *The Golden Apples,* extending the discovery of those uses already made by other critics. But in her concentration on the Yeats/Aengus tropes, especially the key phrase "Because a fire was in my head," Yaeger makes some rather serious mistakes. Yeats is working with the imaginary experience of his early verse, that of the Celtic twilight, in which he occupies a beautiful never-never land later abandoned for the rag-and-bone shop of his own heart. Yaeger seems to be making a jump out of the historical bounds and conditions of the fictional genre that Welty employs in *The Golden Apples,* namely (despite the use of an impressionistic fictional technique) those of an essentially realistic or representational way of looking at the world. Yaeger concentrates on the image of the "glimmering girl" Aengus seeks, equating "his discovery of [her] . . . with a capacity to conjure presence out of absence, closure out of uncertainty, eroticism out of ennui" (143). Thus Yaeger must make Mattie Will's encounter with King in the forest (in "Sir Rabbit") "a fantasy of love-making" (147), a fire in Mattie Will's head rather than also in King's highly inflammable loins, leading to the sexual act experienced, rather ambiguously enjoyed, immediately reflected upon, and long remembered in later years by Mattie Will.

One reason for Yaeger's mistake lies in her focusing more in her reading of "Sir Rabbit" on the hero Aengus than on the Zeus who lusted after mortal women. Another and more generalized difficulty comes from her assumptions regarding Morgana's embracing of the double standard in sexual conduct. The evidence is that Morgana women are not really in thrall to the men, not victims, as Yaeger finds them, of the closed-in communal mythos "which makes it natural for men to be boisterous, libidinal, and free-spirited like King, and for women to be pale, patient homebodies like Snowdie" (148). So far as I can see, the only free-spirited male in the stories is King, and he is driven and frantic; his twin sons Randall and Eugene MacLain seem as much victims of their differently dominating wives as they are victimizers. Old Lady Stark owns a good deal of the town: it is her property being trespassed on by hunters of birds and pretty young wives alike. Your Fate Raineys, Junior Holifields, and Wilbur Carmichaels are scarcely free-spirited but rather the dullest of mates and most ineffectual of protectors. Mattie Will's husband Junior would have assumed she was making up a story had she ever told him about the ambiguously sexual assault she suffered, but essentially enjoyed, of the MacLain twins—not that she *would* have told him. Both sexes treat their mates like children—but only the women seem really mature. No man in the stories possesses anything remotely comparable to the fortitude, passion, independence, even the heroism of character to be found in Miss Eckhart and her sometime pupil Virgie Rainey. The women of Morgana are scarcely dutiful wives, but often wanderers in fact as in fantasy; and there are all those orphans to prove it, starting with Easter, that most independent and adventuresome among them.

But since Yaeger's line of reasoning requires her to interpret Mattie Will's conduct in keeping with what she thinks is Morgana's code of female repression, Yaeger must consider the girl's encounter with King to be imaginary, despite the lack of evidence. There is no foolproof way of *demonstrating* that it is actual, except perhaps for the circumstantial evidence of all those potent appeals to Mattie Will's roused senses and sensibility at the times of her two sexual romps in the woods with the twins when they are all fifteen, and her later encounter with King some years after. But the coup de grâce of Yaeger's reading, it seems to me, is this: no girl fantasizing a sexual encounter with the King of the town is going to give him *brown teeth* and "a thatch of biscuit-colored hair" (*CS* 338), nor is she going to imagine the taste of starch, nor is she going to imagine coming upon and inspecting him later when he is open-mouthed, snoring, and thoroughly diminished. This is not the stuff of sexual fantasies. The whole episode is wonderfully visual and tactile, with many pretty pictures which do not lead the reader chiefly toward the battle of words Yaeger perceives the encounter to be (Yeats versus Welty); and Mattie Will's leaning over and inspecting King, bottom up like a little bird, and her plucking a feather out of the falling golden autumn light, seem not to suggest that Welty boldly seizes the male writer's phallic quill, but rather, that Mattie Will catches a trace of a fallen bird in hunting season. And from Welty's literary source, the white goose King has become soon turns, in this comic story of metamorphosis, into a large white Rabbit.

Yaeger does, however, call attention to the audacious thing Welty is doing in adapting the language of Yeats's sonnet, "Leda and the Swan," and turning it over to the Leda figure in her fictional account of the experience. Yet it seems to me that Welty's appropriation of Yeats's language is not an unqualified success. If this is a rhetorical battle of the sexes, I would have to admit that Welty seems to have lost the contest in the crucial moments of the sexual assault, when the reconstruction from Yeats's poetic language becomes something like translation. Yeats has all the advantage of excitement generated by his breathy language—"he holds her helpless breast against his breast"—and an overwhelming sense of portentousness with his compression of images of high sexual passion with those of prophesy, of history and destiny, the fateful Trojan War, as "a shudder in the loins engenders there / The broken wall, the burning roof and tower / and Agamemnon dead." Yeats's final indirectly rhetorical question of Leda, "Did she put on his knowledge with his power?", awe-stricken and probably to be answered in the affirmative, Welty renders in the declarative: "But he put on her, with the affront of his body, the affront of his senses too. No pleasure in that. She had to put on what he knew with what he did— maybe because he was so grand it was a thorn to him" (*CS* 338). Yaeger claims that Welty's incorporation of Yeats's poem in a prose text proves the poem can be altered—even violated—by a new prose context; by implication, that the purity and unified force of the lyric poem is radically disrupted.

To me, the effect here is exactly the reverse: the overwhelming power of the poem, living as it does in the heartland of "Leda and the Swan" mythic language territory, is not seriously affected by Welty's invasion. To me, the passage demonstrates the opposite of what Yaeger intends to prove, the superior power to move the reader (and hence overwhelm the story) possessed by a strong univocal poem. As readers of this passage we are brought sharply to the awareness of contrasts, for the swan in the poem is Zeus, king of the gods, omniscient and omnipotent; his rape of Leda is the beginning of an age, as was the annunciation to Mary of Christ's conception through the dove. Leda, Yeats suggests, is caught up into knowledge supernal and divine. Nothing remotely similar happens to Mattie Will. "The affront of [King's] sense" conveys little to me because I cannot easily imagine what knowledge it is that Mattie Will puts on from King which makes her feel it's "Like submitting to another way to talk," and giving her the power "to answer to his burden now, his whole blithe, smiling, superior existence" (*CS* 338). The meaning is obscure, but perhaps the suggestion is that *being* a legend, living up to it, feeling driven not only by explicit sexual needs and a superabundance of physical prowess but by the frantic, compulsive need to put it to the test—that *that* was King's burden, now understood in the sharing of the sexual act by Mattie Will Sojourner. And she *does know* that she *must submit* to this, for King *must have his way* with her, whether or not she happens to be willing. (Of course, she *is*.) But her new elevated knowledge seems not to last for long, and Mattie Will's final assessment of the experience reminds me of the comment the mother of a friend of mine habitually made after attending some local entertainment or other—"not much to it"—though justice, or charity, usually compelled her to add of one or another performer, "He done his part real good." The incident is comic, and thoroughly delightful in its own terms. The best part of the experience for Mattie Will seems, in the end, to have been the pleasure and pride of becoming a secret part of the legend of King and his exploits, with a reservation: that it is the *earlier* part of the legend-making pair of sexual encounters—the spring romp with the twins—that she remembers most fondly, almost maternally, associating the twins with "young deer, or even remoter creatures . . . kangaroos. . . . Mattie Will thought they were mysterious and sweet—gamboling now she knew not where?" (*CS* 341).

As should be apparent, though I found Yaeger's article demanding and provocative and it sent me back to the text (all to the good), I could not find much in it that might be adaptable to the classroom. I recognize it as a performance designed for literary professionals, not amateurs. Its language and vocabulary are not the primary ones of life and the common human experience Welty's stories confront us with (and we as teachers should want, I think, to confront our students with) but rather the secondary discourse of theory, thick in language and style, attenuated in meaning. In teaching fiction to undergraduates, especially nonmajors with minimal skills and experience in reading complex literature of any sort, theory and its enabling vocabularies have little or no place. (Upper-class English majors and graduate students can and must learn it; some may develop such a taste for it that it replaces literary texts as the subject of their most involving interest.) I am not opposed to the use of theory or special vocabularies in the classroom. Such terms as *metaphor* (or variants such as *image* or *trope*), *irony, narrative point of view,* and *closure* are indispensable to the understanding of fiction; in a course taught from a feminist vantage point, the terms *phallocentric* and *gynocentric* might be equally crucial. But I think these vocabularies should be kept minimal and functional, *aids* rather than impediments to understanding and pleasure in reading fiction.

There is another critical voice speaking about Welty's fiction from the same general direction as Yaeger's. It is of the critical left or avant-garde of post-modernism, and it speaks with accents more authentic, clear and discriminating, and by chance, or design, positioned by editor Albert Devlin in *Eudora Welty: A Life in Literature* adjacent to Yaeger's. The voice I refer to has, appropriately, a foreign accent, the unmistakably French one of Danièle Pitavy-Souques, in a remarkably stimulating essay titled "A Blazing Butterfly: The Modernity of Eudora Welty." Its significant parallels with Yaeger's essay consist in its relative density and difficulty of argument and the contemporaneity of critical stance and voices summoned. Pitavy-Souques is thoroughly familiar with post-modernism and the terms of deconstruction, though she uses them sotto voce. The differences are that while Yaeger begins with feminist and Bahktinian theories and seems to superimpose them on the text inappropriately, seems inattentive to the text and misinterprets what happens as well as the vision of Morgana life implied in the text, Pitavy-Souques keeps the stories primary in her interpretation, thus providing exciting new openings to understanding. Throughout, she never loses either the sense of delight in Welty's performance or pleasure at being on the receiving end of experiences Welty is offering in and through the stories. With Pitavy-Souques, seeing is believing instead of the reverse, or rather, in this case, seeing double, paradoxically and contradictorily, so that seeing double becomes also, in part, disbelieving. She is finding a new vocabulary for what I called in my critical study of Welty's fiction—perhaps too effortlessly or romantically—"the mysteries of Eudora Welty" (ch. 2). But because I recognize so clearly that it is the same writer, the same texts we are talking about, I welcome the opportunity to engage this critical voice.

While finding Welty's fiction essentially modern rather than post-modern, primarily because Welty never fails to achieve, in William Gass's phrase, " 'the full responsive reach of her readers' " (116), Pitavy-Souques finds much of what could be called post-modern fictional practice in several stories, including "A Still Moment," "Moon Lake," and "Old Mr. Marblehall." Another story, "A Memory," illustrates such current modes of perception as "the need to see the world familiarly, because of preoccupation with the self rather than with the world" (122). Pitavy-Souques shows how Welty's investigation of the familiar in "A Memory" leads her from the child's relative control of the dream to a confrontation of the "violence and rage and ugliness" (123) that exist and intrude on her carefully ordered universe. This is the child's recognition of the difference, the unaccountable, a reality of perception that she negates, disavows. The child is aware of "the presence of an absence" and suffers "a cleavage of the self," a "fracture" (124). These are all terms from deconstructive criticism, pointedly used, I think. Pitavy-Souques's excellent critique of "A Still Moment" makes me aware of how radically unstable Welty's texts so often are; how their unflinching gaze on human experience and on the creative process of painting or writing leaves us in a state so divided that anything like conventional closure is out of the question. Neither "A Memory" nor "A Still Moment" has it, nor does "Moon Lake."

Pitavy-Souques's reading of "Old Mr. Marblehall" controversially but persuasively makes the old man's double life entirely the product of fabulation, which, given what Pitavy-Souques describes as the stylized characterization, the lack of realism and sheer verbal exuberance of the text and frequent flight from probabilities, is far more credible to me than Yaeger's pushing of Mattie Will's experience in the same realm. The story radically questions the nature of reality—not only Mr. Marblehall/Grenada's, but anybody's. Mr. Marblehall, as Pitavy-Souques points out, provides himself with a past, a present, and a future—his is, accordingly, a self-endowed existence. Having discovered how to create experience, he endures secretly the private life he thinks he needs in order to acquire public importance—the power to shock people into envy and admiration. Either, both, or neither of his two households may exist, Pitavy-Souques suggests, since both are stylized and satirized, and the identical appearance of the two canny, uncanny little sons inclines the reader to think neither exists (132–33). As for Mr. Marblehall's dream of being a "blazing butterfly" ("which doesn't make sense," says the narrator), I have come to guess a possible source. Could it be Chaungtu's famous dream of being a butterfly, and then awakening to ponder the idea that perhaps he might be a butterfly dreaming he was a man? Whether butterfly or man, whether beautiful and blazing or dreary and ordinary, this one dreams his own imprisonment in confining nets: fantasy can be as confining as real life if we make it so.

These are fascinating insights and approaches I can use to refurbish my readings and introduce to a class without much cumbersome vocabulary, though there is no reason not to introduce the terms *post-modernism* and *deconstruction* along with as much of the aesthetics of post-modern fiction as time and the level of the class will allow. I would call attention at least to Welty's technique of stylization and the brilliant rhetoric of "Old Mr. Marblehall," showing Welty as a performer in fiction, she the puppeteer and we her knowing audience (the wonderfully intimate point of view pulls us in); she is completely successful in her risk-taking here, as also in "Powerhouse," another brilliant story which explores the nature of reality and fantasy. Welty's writing itself, Pitavy-Souques concludes, is the great blazing butterfly.

Coming from where she does, the European post-modern literary situation, and from the vantage point of a mature critic who has lived through the development of mid- and late-twentieth-century literary movements, Pitavy-Souques is in an excellent position to perceive what Welty has achieved by having an adventuresome fiction writer's imagination, and more unwittingly, perhaps, by absorbing much of the modern and post-modern attitudes and fictional techniques. However, my general enthusiasm about Pitavy-Souques's article does not extend to her reading of "Kin," which it seems possible she does not understand because she is French and does not perceive Welty's complex feelings about her native state, its people and places. Pitavy-Souques thinks that in "Kin" Welty treats "the myth of the Old South" as would an impressionist painter (134). Yet it does not seem to me that the impressionistic style of the story is used to treat anything so heavy sounding as "the myth of the Old South," but only one typical, middle-class, extended southern family, the "kin" of the southern girl gone north and returned for a visit. Pitavy-Souques finds that "For all its beauty and polished appearance this [southern] society is essentially racist, materialistic, frivolous and irresponsible" (134).

That seems an indictment far too severe for the largely appreciative tone of the story as experiences of Dicey, with her northern perspectives and complex sympathies, her eye for comedy and irony, unfold with the support of the implied author. From this perspective, though there is beauty, there is little polish of appearance in this southern society, certainly none of the aristocratic surfaces and manners the phrase suggests. Racist, yes, though the sound of Uncle Theodore's voice talking to "the little, low black cows" (CS 566) at the end of the story seems as harmonious with nature as that of old Phoenix talking to the birds and animals in "A Worn Path." But materialistic, frivolous, irresponsible? These harshly judging terms are surely not what Welty (through her narrator) intends for people who enjoy "wonderful black, bitter, moist chocolate pie under mountains of meringue, and black, bitter coffee" (CS 539), people who overeat on a Sunday afternoon, and love to make and hear banjo playing afterward. And what is materialistic or frivolous about enjoying fresh roses out of a garden? This is plenitude, southern style, rather than materialism, for Dicey is very much part of the old soft airs of Mingo . . . the interior airs that were always kitchenlike, of oil-lamps, wood ashes, and that golden scrapement off cake-papers—and outside, beyond the just-watered ferns lining the broad strong railing, the fragrances winding up through the luster of the fields and the dim, gold screen of trees and the river beyond, fragrances so rich I could almost see them, untransparent and Oriental. (*CS* 563)

This rich pleasure is as much aesthetic as materialistic; it is directly related to the very innocent delight shared by Dicey and her now ancient Uncle Felix (whose name means *happy*) as they looked together at pictures of exotic places with the stereopticon when she was a child; it is the delight and romance still burning brightly in the old man, once a serenader, as he writes his little love note—"River—Daisy—Midnight—Please" (*CS* 561)—perhaps confusing the names *Dicey* and *Daisy* (nearly identical in southern pronunciation), merging the two pretty young girls in his imagination. Nor are the portraits of Sister Anne and Great-grandmother Jerrold being satirically identified because of their common fraudulent frame and backdrop, the latter photographed and the earlier painted; for though Sister Anne *is* a bit of a fraud in her trying on of several faces for the Yankee photographer, her coy use of a fan, she is really, quite openly to Dicey's eyes, simply flirting unsuccessfully with him.

And the great-grandmother is not one of a series of old-fashioned portraits of the art of living in the South, all showing, as Pitavy-Souques says, how *made up* and inauthentic the legends were, exposing "Kin" as "fraud." The description of the *head* of the black-haired, opaque-eyed Evelina Mackail is unmistakably that of a strong-spirited pioneer woman who "had eaten bear meat, seen Indians, married into the wilderness at Mingo," held dying slaves in her arms (*CS* 561). Dicey feels a direct spiritual kinship with her, "her divided sister," who had felt "the wildness of the world," for both were "homesick for somewhere that was the same place" (*CS* 561). To me, this sounds like Eudora Welty's sense of kinship with her grandmother Eudora Carden Andrews, described in *One Writer's Beginning*. This woman, whose strong, authentic pioneer spirit and independence she felt directly transmitted to her through her mother—this feeling of kinship is what "Kin" is about. And although Sister Anne is guilty of great insensitivity to Uncle Felix, her failing is not shared by the rest of the family: they call her "common" (*CS* 566). The chief reaction of Dicey and Kate to her commonness is a fit of uncontrollable laughter. The story asks to be read with a smile of pleasure at its delicious comedy and the delight in its evocation of myriad and teeming sense impressions, for this is a Keatsian sensuousness, amoral, as inappropriate to condemn for its materialism, artificiality, and vanity as is Porphyro's exotic midnight feast for Madeline in "The Eve of St. Agnes." And yet Welty's final tribute in the story seems to be to the simple country people who gather on the porch after the picture taking, reluctant to go home after the day's excitement, their faces "like dark boxes of secrets and desires to [Dicey], but locked safely, like old-fashioned caskets for the safe conduct of jewels on a voyage" (*CS* 565). The story celebrates the enormous power of the human imagination to create a private world of secret excitement, of old or recent romance, which it takes only an itinerant photographer to set off. That romantic feeling is high in the narrator, Dicey, recently engaged to be married, and wafted away on thoughts of her love while she rides home at the very end. The final words of the story, "I thought of my sweetheart, riding, and wondered if he were writing to me" (*CS* 566), make this story's closure unified, organically whole, *romantic*—not a bit post-modern.

A southerner would not, I think, have seen in "Kin" a satirical exposure of a fraud, but on the other hand, a southerner might not be capable of discerning the modern psychic states Welty conveys so poignantly in some of her stories, nor appreciate, as does Pitavy-Souques, the variety of fictional techniques she uses so brilliantly. Southerners might tend to value Welty's most "southern" novels and stories, such as *The Ponder Heart* and *Losing Battles,* precisely because they understand them so well, and at the expense of Welty's more difficult, introverted fiction. What this demonstrates is the hazardous nature of interpretation and the need for each person who aspires to being an effective teacher-critic of Welty's fiction to know where his or her own voice is coming from. This is like repeating the Socratic maxim, "Know thyself," a good, durable maxim, along with that other, "Nothing too much." I'll now offer another, "Don't be afraid to change your mind"—or, more memorably phrased in Emerson's words, "A foolish consistency is the hobgoblin of little minds"—though to be sure, you must have a mind to change: one that is capable of beliefs held rather than opinions that change with trends.

Self-knowledge *should* lead to an awareness of where one's *own voice* is coming from, what one's own perspectives and prejudices are—regional, sexual, racial, generational—and therefore send out some warning signals about which stories one might teach most effectively and how to teach them and which ones might well be left alone. For me, the story "Where Is the Voice Coming From?" falls into the latter category, because I am unwilling to believe that a man cowardly enough to shoot his helpless victim in the back would be capable of thinking of that victim humanely, as he does: "Something darker than him, like the wings of a bird, spread on his back and pulled him down. He climbed up once, like a man under bad claws, and like just blood could weigh a ton as he walked with it on his back to better light" (*CS* 604). The killer seems suddenly too sensitive to his victim's vulnerability, the pathos of his ebbing life—whether for me to find him quite credible, or to feel free to hate him along with his deed, or what, I'm not sure—but it *feels* like a prejudice, and I think that might prevent me from teaching the story fairly.

Once aware of ourselves, I think we naturally teach to, or from, our strengths rather than our weaknesses, and choose those Welty stories (or novels) for classroom discussion that have most delighted, intrigued, or moved us, stories we greatly admire as works of fiction, believe we understand but know we'll never be in control of because we find them elusive and brimming with inexhaustible energy. Among these stories will usually be one or more of Welty's clear celebrations of life: "Powerhouse," "A Worn Path," "Livvie," or the one I usually start with, title story of the second collection, "The Wide Net." The story is difficult, but not daunting, richly evocative, and subtle. With the utmost delicacy the invisible narrator transports the reader into the heart of her Mississippi rural and small-town community. It is the golden season of changes: right there is sufficient cause for delight as the narrator lavishly shows autumn with the aid of Doc, a kind of subnarrator and director of ceremonies. The characters (mostly male) act, speak, quarrel, respond to nature and each other, eat and drink, dream, sleep, all the while engaging in a rather odd quest—a river dragging, for (of all unlikely things) a corpse—a suicide victim who never appears. The least experienced readers in the class will guess, early on, that the corpse will never be found, and their instinctive *feel* of the story as comic will lend the immediate self-confidence in their reading that students need in order to follow the progress of a Welty story. The stories always proceed from the external and literal to the internal (and often symbolic) from the lesser to the greater mystery, where the deepest meanings emerge.

At the center of "The Wide Net" is a young wife with a secret. Her husband goes in quest of that secret—and of her. He begins to find something about it in the depths of the Pearl River, from which he emerges after one long period of agonized and lonely submersion, holding a little green ribbon of plant, complete with its root. It is the mystery of his wife's great expectations, at once sobering and exhilarating. Here he comes to an awareness of the new and growing life within her, the mystery of change, of beginnings.

In teaching that story I try to impress on the students the prime requisites of a Welty reader: a willing imagination and sensitivity. I often quote to them Henry James's directive in *The Art of Fiction* to aspiring writers, "Try to be one of the people on whom nothing is lost": this counsel applies as well to aspiring readers. Sensitivity requires an alert passivity which is the power of absorption, and the flexibility to enter into the variety of mixed moods and nuances of thought and feeling with which Welty stories confront a reader.

From such a celebration of life as "The Wide Net" one may proceed in many possible directions: to the psychological intricacies of "A Memory," the tragedy of thwarted lives of "The Death of a Traveling Salesman" or "A Curtain of Green," the gossipy comedy and biting satire of "Petrified Man," the dark enigmas of "A Still Moment." Within the limits of the time allowed for study of Welty's fiction in any given class, I always try to give students a sense of the astounding *variety* to be found there. For a course in Southern Women's Literature I have used *Delta Wedding* on the whole successfully. Despite the subtleties of its manner, this novel engages the concerns and preoccupations of women of all ages and conditions as well as the life on the plantation. In teaching that novel, I have been helped by the insights of such feminist critics as Peggy Prenshaw and Louise Westling, whose mythic and archetypal approaches seem eminently appropriate and fruitful in the disclosure of the work's meaning, while Carol Manning's study has been helpful in its stress on the importance of Welty's use of a feminine story-telling tradition in the South.

Yet success in the classroom is always hazardous and never predictable, not even with that most famous of Welty's monologues, that triumph of her art in capturing the special delights of southern colloquial speech, "Why I Live at the P.O." Dramatic oral reading helps, but is no guarantee of success: less because of the teacher's own possibly recalcitrant accent or lack of dramatic talent than the occasional unsympathetic student who may demand to know, as one of mine once did, what was so funny about the story. I found that I could not tell her, whereupon my dismay and frustration infected the class, and seemed to ruin the story for everyone. (This particular student went on to get her Ph.D. in English, a decision I choose to think implies more about her and graduate education in English than my teaching of the story.) So there are no sure-fire stories, and even supposing there were, teachers of Welty's fiction, faithful to her spirit, ought to take risks, and not make a known thing of any story or approach to it. I have so far had no palpable success in teaching two of my favorite Welty stories, "A Still Moment" and "June Recital." Perhaps loving them so much and so complicatedly, I am despairing from the outset because of the immeasurable gap between the richness in these stories and what I as teacher might be able to convey or my students to perceive. But I keep trying, and learning to trust the stories more, to do the work that only they can do. One day I hope I shall have the courage to teach *The Optimist's Daughter*, though I cringe at the thought of an insensitive response, or worse, a "blank." Though that last *can* occur, it rarely does.

Having listened to some post-modern critical voices and to our own through the path of self-knowledge, let me turn briefly to the voices of our students. What a wonderful cacophonous chorus is there, especially where I teach at a New York City College, in which every class is a veritable

United Nations, students of all ages, races, national and ethnic origins, though with a common working-class social and economic status. Here is indeed your true democratic, American dialogic discourse! The most important initial thing to say is that we must *listen* to our students' voices carefully—become aware of how purely individual they can be if students are taught to find their deepest responses and articulate them. We must learn to cope with strong resistance to Welty's voice, clear up rudimentary confusions which may come from ignorance of the South, like that of a student who didn't know what a Confederate statue was, still less that there was one in the public square of a good many southern towns; or from their own life history, such as that of the student who thought Tom Harris of "The Hitch-Hikers" had a single problem: alcoholism. And having learned that Eudora Welty's literary agent, Diarmuid Russell, and Katherine Anne Porter, the southern writer who helped foster her early career, often found her work obscure, we should be patient with our students in their attempts to understand her sensitive and elusive art. It is a rare student who will like *all* of a great variety of the stories, though even more rare is a student who will like *none* of them.

I think we should teach Welty's fiction with the hope and intention of passing on to our students whatever it is that we have found in them most deeply enriching for our own lives. To me, the enormous gift of Welty's fiction has been the direct result of *her* own gift of "slipping into" people, of absorbing everything around her—nature, people (singly or in groups), places, art and music—catching and savoring the essences of everything. Sharing in that capacity is a most wonderful way of extending and enlarging oneself, and it is *that* I want to try to pass on to my students. Critical systems help us achieve the experience only when they open up what's there in the stories, not when they substitute themselves for the genuine life her fiction is vibrant with.

In every piece of interpretation or critique and in every classroom, there are at least two impulses at play in relation to a text. The one is analytical, it currently may also be deconstructive: we are putting ourselves at right angles to the text, with the aid of greater and lesser critics, ancient and modern, and thinkers assimilated by our age—Darwin, Marx, Freud, Nietzsche, Heidegger, feminist theorists, and others in many specialized fields. As we analyze for meaning, we can learn a great deal about a text in relation to such theorists. The human impulse to break down, to take things apart in order to discover what they're made of, is very strong. But because the motive of curiosity and the desire for knowledge in the impulse to break things down so often edges off into the unholy desire to dominate, even destroy, to satisfy our urge for power, it is something we must be especially wary of in dealing with works of art. Hawthorne explored some of these dangers in "The Artist of the Beautiful." It is not, after all, so very difficult to destroy one of those blazing butterflies, a Welty story, for ourselves and our students, in a single class hour.

The second impulse at play is that of appreciation, which puts us not in opposition to the text, at right angles, but in a parallel relationship to it. In an essay called "How I Write," Welty has spoken of the mysteries "rushing unsubmissively" (Brooks and Warren 547) through life which keep running through her fiction: we might think of ourselves, then, in reading and teaching her work, as running with the mysteries in parallel relationship to the stories. We are then responding in sympathy, with the "willing imagination" she asks for in a reader (548), *feeling* what the stories are asking us to, reacting to Welty's lyrical voice, and answering to that other strong impulse in us, the drive toward unity and harmony. We do *want* to see things holding together, even more perhaps than we want to see how they threaten to, and usually do, fall apart. But we should not force Welty's fiction into either extreme—either that of the unreconstructed piece of chaotic life, or that of an immaculate and self-contained well-wrought urn. If we keep the polarities of our critical approval always in lively relation to each other, again and again the superabundant and contagious life of the stories will connect with that of our students as we perform the tasks of our always risky and exciting vocation as teachers of literature.

NOTES

American Folk Art, Fine Art, and Eudora Welty: Aesthetic Precedents for "Lily Daw and the Three Ladies"

1. Theora Hamblett (1895–1977), lived in Oxford, Mississippi. Her bright colors and stylized designs resemble those of Grandma Moses, but the trees she loved to paint are done with a self-taught pointillist technique. William Ferris, whose interview of Mrs. Hamblett accompanies the publication of several of her paintings in *Local Color: A Sense of Place in Folk Art*, notes that her "stick-like human figures are overshadowed by the natural world" and that her "bursts of color and shapes . . . draw the viewer's eye to unexpected, sometimes frightening images" (xxiv). From the title of this study of Southern artists and their relation to their region, it is clear that, as Ferris remarks, it was "shaped by Eudora Welty's 'Place in Fiction' " (vii).

Some of Hamblett's paintings are held in the Center for Southern Folklore Archives in Memphis, Tennessee. See also Hamblett, Meek, and Haynie's *Dreams and Visions*. I am indebted to Professor James G. Watson, the University of Tulsa, for alerting me to the existence of Hamblett's work, and to Professor Thomas L. McHaney, Georgia State University, for assistance in locating the Hamblett materials.

2. Welty wrote the song, entitled "Fifty-Seventh Street Rag-Ballet," in collaboration with Hildegard Dolson during a summer in New York, for *What Year Is This?* The musical was never staged in full; the typescript is held in the Eudora Welty Collection in the Department of Archives and History in Jackson, Mississippi. See also Elizabeth Evans's *Eudora Welty*, 14–15; and Jane Reid Petty 34.

3. Barbara Groseclose notes that modern southern photographic artists, such as Eggleston, often assume a particular perspective that results in subjects that parallel those of "Faulkner, O'Connor, and especially Welty." She cites an Eggleston photograph in which "the viewpoint

that gives monumentality to a perky green and white tricycle is undercut by the rusted handlebars and muddy wheels" (223–24).

4. See also H. D. Vursell who calls "Asphodel" a ballet of a story [which is] choreographed (53). Welty's children's book, entitled *The Shoe Bird*, was adapted for the stage as *The Shoe Bird Ballet*.

5. My discussion of spatial form is indebted to Frank; Kestner, *The Spatiality of the Novel* 13–32; and Kestner, "Secondary Illusion: The Novel and the Spatial Arts." I am grateful to Professor Kestner for reading a draft of this essay. He is, of course, in no way responsible for my appropriation of his work.

6. Welty's centripetal form was pointed out by Alun R. Jones (182), though he does not note the accompanying centrifugal motion in Welty's patterning.

7. Tate qtd. by Chase ix, 4.

8. Marcel Proust, *Remembrance of Things Past*, vol. 5: *Sodom and Gomorrah*, qtd. in Bachelard xxviii–xxix. Bachelard asserts that, even in Proust's day, painters no longer considered the image as "a simple substitute for perceptible reality."

9. The concept of the "sacrifice of . . . the 'related' sides of situations" and of the necessity that the romancer "cut the cable" between the actual and the imaginary without our detecting it is that of Henry James, qtd. in Bell 8.

10. This sculpted wood figure is included in a current exhibit of American folk art at the Fenimore House Gallery, Cooperstown, New York, arranged by guest curators Suzette Lane and Paul D'Ambrosio, whose gallery note *Shifting Wind* emphasizes folk artists' lack of academic training and artistic self-consciousness.

11. Kenner is discussing *The Sound and the Fury*, but the caution about reductive analysis has been advanced about Welty by Vande Kieft ("Eudora Welty: Visited" 478), Kreyling, and others, and especially by Welty herself (*Conversations* 10, 66, 273).

12. See especially his murals *Joplin at the Turn of the Century, 1896–1906* (1972), reproduced in *Thomas Hart Benton* 25–26; and the *Harry S. Truman Library Mural* in Independence, Mo. (1961), reproduced in Benton's *An American in Art* 137. The latter work includes Benton's account of his long technical study of painting before developing the simple-appearing but sophisticated sculptural techniques that characterize his best-known paintings.

13. Some of Wyeth's most acclaimed paintings are of Christina Olson, whom the painter knew in Cushing, Maine. Although severely restricted by a childhood attack of polio, Christina is described as having "a force of character that would make any condescension to her paralysis an insult" (O'Doherty 34); see Corn 32–34; and reproduction plate of *Christina's World* (Corn 39).

Wyeth has said that his inspiration for the painting was the sight of Christina crawling across a field, a comment similar to Eudora Welty's description of the inception of "A Worn Path." Of the model for Phoenix Jackson, Welty says that she witnessed a "small, distant figure come out of the woods and move across the whole breadth of my vision and disappear into the woods" (*Conversations* 186).

14. The one-woman show, originally produced at the Chelsea Theater Center in 1981, was restaged by David Kaplan and Brenda Currin, and performed by Currin, opening at the Second Stage Theatre, off-Broadway in New York City, in July 1985. In the performance I viewed, the play opened with "Sister" at her ironing board in the "P.O." seen through a transparent curtain.

15. Muir's concept is an aspect of spatial form; see his *Structure of the Novel* 24. See also Mickelsen in Smitten and Daghistany 72.

16. Emile Borel (163–64) discusses "the idea that causality, which we presume to be based on time is in reality much more spatial, dependent on distance and our identity with a particular group of observers." Borel is cited by Kestner, who continues, "Thus, the position one chooses to take vis-à-vis a novel is critical to whether he perceives causality in the work at all" (*Spatiality* 17).

17. See especially Benton's murals of the 1930s, for example, *City Activities* (1930–31) and *Industrial Progress* (1933), reproduced in Baignell 74–75, 90–91.

"Contradictors, Interferers, and Prevaricators": Opposing Modes of Discourse in Eudora Welty's *Losing Battles*

1. On approaches to the novel as a text about language and storytelling, see, for example, Boatwright 4; Manning 137–62; Eisinger in Prenshaw (*Thirteen Essays*) 21; Messerli in Prenshaw (*Critical Essays*) 351; and Magee.

2. For instance, M. E. Bradford seems to suggest that the novel's sympathies and perspective lie largely with the Renfros and Beechams. Also favoring the side of the family is Messerli (363). In contrast, a good many early reviews tended to side with Miss Julia and her allies. See, for example, Louis D. Rubin, Jr., "Everything Brought Out in the Open"; and Gossett. A third group of critics suggests that both sides, as Kreyling has observed, "have their limitations" (151). See also Heilman; Stroup 47; Moreland 94; Moore; and Landess.

3. Culler 271. See also Johnson; and Felman.

4. Qtd. Devlin and Prenshaw 449. In that same interview Welty noted that during her Jackson childhood ". . . politics was everywhere . . ." (449).

5. See Faust, *A Sacred Circle;* and Faust, ed., *The Ideology of Slavery.* See also Michael O'Brien, ed.; and Gray.

6. See also Bakhtin's *Dialogic Imagination: Four Essays;* and his *Problems of Dostoevsky's Poetics.*

7. Mary Anne Ferguson (Prenshaw, *Critical Essays*) remarks upon Welty's affinity for what Bakhtin would describe as polyphony and multiplicity (315).

8. In a recent interview Welty took care to stress the importance of Vaughn Renfro for *Losing Battles* as a whole:

He thinks there's something else besides the voices he's heard all day. He feels that everything may have a voice. But he's *in* the world, he is in this strange, blue-lit night, and he feels— what I was trying to say—that there's so much more than what he's been listening to all day. I don't know whether I conveyed that. He is the introspective one; he's questioned so many things that the others don't, and he's also young enough not yet to have got that armor over him. I think I just tried to express an awareness that there was something over and beyond the circle of the family that was still capable of being understood. (Qtd. in Devlin and Prenshaw 443–44.)

The "Assault of Hope": Style's Substance in Welty's "The Demonstrators"

1. My treatment of style derives from numerous linguistic approaches to literary stylistics, notably those of Roger Fowler, *Linguistics and the Novel* and his earlier anthology, *Essays on Style and Language;* Ullmann, *Language and Style* and other works, including his *Meaning and Style: Collected Papers;* and collections such as that of Love and Payne, *Contemporary Essays on Style.* A useful introduction is G. W. Turner. For American fictional styles, the influential pioneering studies remain Bridgman, and Gibson.

2. The most perceptive analysis of Welty's style to date seems to me to be Fleischauer. In Dollarhide and Abadie, *Eudora Welty: A Form of Thanks,* Cleanth Brooks deals with Welty's representation of speech patterns. Other studies giving major attention to Welty's style are Vande Kieft, *Eudora Welty;* and Zelma Turner Howard, *The Rhetoric of Eudora Welty's Short*

Stories. I see some criticism which purports to be about Welty's style as dealing primarily with other narrative strategies such as point of view; for example, Kreyling's chapter on *Delta Wedding* (52–76); and Pollack. On the other hand, Yaeger's use of Bakhtin's notion of heteroglossia seems to me a fruitful approach to Welty's style.

3. "The Demonstrators" won first place in the O. Henry competition in 1968.

4. Joyce Carol Oates uses "The Demonstrators" as her chief example of Welty's habitual "delicate blending of the casual and the tragic," where "horror may evolve out of gentility" (71, 74). In her study questions for "The Demonstrators," McKenzie states that "the tone [a product of style] stands at odds with the subject matter" (262). Other good treatments of "The Demonstrators" include Vande Kieft's "Demonstrators in a Stricken Land," in McKenzie; Peggy Prenshaw's "Cultural Patterns in Eudora Welty's *Delta Wedding* and 'The Demonstrators,' " *Notes on Mississippi Writers;* Romines; and Devlin's *Eudora Welty's Chronicle*.

5. Welty comments on the story at some length in *Conversations*, 259–63.

6. Answering questions at Denison University, 16 Oct. 1976.

7. The ice pick is noted as found "in the grounds of the new $100,000 Negro school." In 1966, the anachronism of a segregated Negro school would have been an unpleasant but no doubt accurate reminder of why the political demonstrations took place.

Eudora Welty and the Dutiful Daughter

1. Elizabeth Lawrence, *Gardening for Love*. Eudora Welty introduced Lawrence to the Mississippi *Market Bulletin*, an occasion that led Lawrence to receive the *Market Bulletin* from most southern states. Here she found a lifeline for farmers as they advertised livestock and gear for sale and trade, for farmers' wives who advertised to sell and exchange flower seeds, cuttings, lore. Katie Rainey is reminiscent of such women, whose lists of flowers are sent frequently by mail to the *Market Bulletin*.

2. Simpson recounts her early married life in Paris when she was so acutely aware of the mother-daughter relationship she had been deprived of: "What struck me was the number of mothers and grown daughters walking arm in arm. Unhurriedly, yet purposefully, they made their way up the avenues, stopping to admire a display of leather goods in a shop window, picking up a package at a silversmith's, greeting another mother-and-daughter couple coming in the opposite direction, dropping into their favorite café for pastry and coffee, the whole time talking animatedly. This intimacy of mothers and daughters was also new to me" (11–12).

Sibyls in Eudora Welty's Stories

1. For essential background information on "Powerhouse," see Vande Kieft, *Eudora Welty:* "she wrote [the] story rapidly just after going to a dance where the Negro jazz musician, Fats Waller, played with his band" (23). The best discussions of "Powerhouse" are in Vande Kieft's book, esp. 81–84; Appel's *Season of Dreams* 148–64; and Stone. The jazz critic Whitney Balliett's essay on Fats Waller, which refers to Welty's story, is also recommended. Vande Kieft is especially prescient discussing why Welty does not reveal whether Powerhouse's wife is really dead, while Appel's is the fullest and most balanced reading the story has received; he stresses the various shifts in the story's point of view and demonstrates the tension between Powerhouse and his various audiences.

2. Such readings are offered in Appel, *Season of Dreams*, 93–99; Zelma Turner Howard, *Rhetoric*, 73–74; and St. George Tucker Arnold, Jr. Arnold speaks of a "savage matriarchal

deity to whom human sacrifices, often male infants, were dedicated in the dawn phases of human society," and calls Welty's women "avatars of the Terrible Mother" (22). Appel even goes so far as to call the rapist, Mr. Petrie, the "only free man": "with the arrest of the petrified man the women seem to have succeeded in subjugating the only free man in the story—but not quite, for Billy Boy remains to be vanquished" (97). One partial exception in Welty criticism is Vande Kieft, *Eudora Welty*, 62–65. For two articles cataloguing the presence of Medusa allusions in the story, see Helterman; and Walker. For more on Medusas, mirrors, and other relevant matters, see Gilbert and Gubar; Auerbach; McGann; Irigaray; and Cixous.

3. My understanding of advertising and the "male gaze" has been particularly influenced by Barthes, especially *Mythologies;* Berger; Mulvey; and Ewen's *Captains of Consciousness: Advertising and the Social Roots of the Consumer Culture,* a history of advertising in America focusing on the radical transformations that occurred between the 1920s and the 1950s. Boorstin's *The Americans: The Democratic Experience* and Marchand's *Advertising the American Dream* provide a general history of the development of advertising in America in the nineteenth and twentieth centuries. Ewen notes the influence on advertisers of social psychologists and their theories of female narcissism (180) but does not connect his discussion of advertising's treatment of women as sexual objects to male narcissism or rape fantasies.

4. Compare Ewen on the role played by mirrors in advertising in creating anxiety (177–83 and, in particular, 239, n121): "In an informal survey of *Ladies Home Journal* and *Saturday Evening Post* ads through the 1920s, I have found that between eight and ten ads per issue depict a woman at or looking into a mirror. Many of these ads are *not* for cosmetic products."

5. On the subject of advertising as a male-dominated field see esp. Marchand 1–51, 66–69.

6. For a concise history of Eudora Welty's critical reception, see Devlin, *Eudora Welty's Chronicle*.

7. Domenichino, "The Cumaean Sibyl," Pinacoteca Capitolina, Rome (c. 1620–23). See Spear plate 255 vol. 2 and 232–33 in vol. 1.

8. I thank my colleague William Turpin of Swarthmore's Department of Classics for translating and analyzing Domenichino's Greek text for me. Spear translates the phrase as follows, somewhat simplifying its ambiguous syntax: "There is only one God, infinite [and] unborn." He notes that the Cumaean sibyl is traditionally associated with this prophecy (1: 232). For two cogent discussions of the difference between the authority of oral speech versus the authority of written texts in the Western tradition, see Thoreau's distinction between the mother and the father tongue in his chapter on "Reading" in *Walden,* and Michel Foucault's *The Order of Things:* "[In the Renaissance, the spoken word] is stripped of all its powers; it is merely the female part of language, Vigenere and Duret tell us, just as its intellect is passive; Writing, on the other hand, is the active intellect, the 'male principle' of language. It alone harbours the truth" (38–39). Foucault, however, ignores the authority given in the Renaissance to God's spoken word. Derrida has written on the subordination problems created by adding a "supplement" to a prior text, as well as on the vexed relations between oral and written discourse (6–26, 141–64).

Domenichino's portrait of such sibylline powers is of course indebted to Michelangelo, whose five sibyls on the Sistine Chapel ceiling dramatize the contrast between the oral and the textual, the authority of inspiration versus the authority of tradition. The Cumaean sibyl is given special authority in Michelangelo's sequence because the contents of her prophetic song as recorded in Virgil's Fourth (Messianic) Eclogue were thought to foretell the coming of Christ and the founding of His church in Rome. The Cumaean sibyl thus anticipated the essentially oral moment of Christian revelation: her song was her strength, allowing her to contravene false prophets and centuries of written pagan law. Four works are especially relevant for a survey of the role sibyls have played in Western art: Charles de Tolnay 2: 57–62, 155–58; Wind; Schiller, esp. plates 33 and 51 and commentary 1: 19, 102–03; and Dotson. These critics—particularly de Tolnay and Dotson—disagree considerably about the meaning of Michelangelo's placement and posing of the Sistine sibyls, but all the commentators stress that from Augustine to Aquinas to the Neoplatonic philosophers of the Renaissance the sibyls were thought to be among the most privileged of the pagan prophets. Especially relevant for the reader of Welty's stories is this sentence by de Tolnay: "The motif of the turned-away head, covered by a head-cloth, is an old one in Italian art, used to express the mysterious Cassandra-like female character . . ." (157). Michelangelo's interpretation of the sibyls is revolutionary for the clarity with which it depicts the fact that the sibyls' authority comes from oral rather than written language: the first sibyl in the Sistine sequence, the Delphic oracle, hears the word of God directly; the last, from Libya, puts down a book and prepares to rise, as if in preparation for the Day of Judgment. Domenichino's more secularized sibyls are strongly influenced by Michelangelo's Sistine sibyls. The standard work on Domenichino is Spear; see 1: 191–92, 232–33 in particular, which discuss Domenichino's two most important sibyl paintings. Relevant early literary texts mentioning sibyls include Plato, *Phaedrus* 224B; Virgil, *Eclogues* IV, *Aeneid* III.443ff and VI.9ff; Ovid, *Metamorphoses* XIV.143ff; Dante, *Paradiso* XXXIII.66; and Milton, "Il Penseroso."

9. For this second Domenichino sibyl, in the Villa Borghese, Rome, dated 1616–17, see Spear, 2: plates 171–72 and 1: 191–92. Excellent discussions of "June Recital," "Music from Spain," and "The Wanderers" in the context of *The Golden Apples* include those by Vande Kieft, Appel, McHaney, Pitavy-Souques, Pugh, MacKethan, Rubin, and Yaeger.

10. My understanding of American sentimental romance and local color writing is especially indebted to Baym, Tompkins, Smith-Rosenberg, Donovan, Huf, Petry, Falk, McNall, Douglas, and Papashvily. More general studies by Gilbert and Gubar (cited in the text); Auerbach, DuPlessis, Moers, Homans, Showalter, Kristeva, Cixous, and Irigaray were also indispensable. Jennifer Lynn Randisi has recently published a study chronicling Welty's skepticism toward the sentimental romance as shown in her novels, and Devlin's *Eudora Welty's Chronicle* makes a similar point about Welty's novels. As useful as these two books are, neither one discusses Welty's stories within the context of the sentimental romance as interpreted by recent developments in feminist literary theory and historiography.

11. Women musicians are prominent in some nineteenth-century American women's fiction; perhaps the four most instructive examples are Margaret Huell in Elizabeth Stoddard's "Lemorne versus Huell" (1863); Salome Owen, the foil for the heroine in Augusta Evans's *Vashti* (1869); Candace Whitcomb in Mary Wilkins Freeman's "A Village Singer" (1891); and the music teacher, Mademoiselle Reisz, in Kate Chopin's *The Awakening*. Evans's handling of this character demonstrates how in sentimental romances such heroines provide cautionary, not potentially revolutionary, scenes of instruction. As Fletcher and Baym have shown, Salome devotes all her energy to a singing career but loses her voice on the night of her debut and spends the rest of her days doing penance for her sin of pride. Stoddard's and Wilkins Freeman's stories, on the other hand, are considerably more sardonic; Stoddard's recounts an independent woman's betrayal by an evil fairy godmother figure, while Wilkins Freeman's depicts the losing battle a church choir's premier soprano wages with her church's power structure.

How Not to Tell a Story: Eudora Welty's First-Person Tales

1. I have confined my discussion to first-person stories which are not parts of a larger unit, because I think that the stories' identities as aggressively self-sustained utterances are significant to my thesis. In addition to the three first-person stories discussed here, Welty wrote two others: "A Memory" and "Kin," both adolescent memory tales with protagonists who may bear some resemblance to the young Welty. Welty also uses first person for two of the

interconnected stories in *The Golden Apples* and for *The Ponder Heart*. The novella's narrator, Edna Earle, bears striking resemblances to Sister and Circe.

2. May also comments on the reversal of the sisters' positions ("Why Sister" 246), and provides a useful summary of the relatively scant comment on this story, as well.

3. For Welty herself, the hurried writing of this story, immediately after the murder of Medgar Evers in her "home town," was a compelling effort at the very communion which her character uses his monologue to deny. She wrote, "all that absorbed me, though it started as outrage, was the necessity I felt for entering into the mind and inside the skin of a character who could hardly have been more alien or repugnant to me. Trying for my utmost, I wrote it in the first person. . . . I'm not sure this story was brought off; and I don't believe that my anger showed me anything about human character that my sympathy and rapport never had" (*OWB* 39).

Realities in "Sir Rabbit": A Frame Analysis

1. Manz-Kunz argues, for example (90–93), that narrative technique and Mattie Will's obsession with King MacLain's legend evoke a fantasy. Skaggs argues in Prenshaw (*Critical Essays*) that accumulated evidence points to a rape fantasy produced by Mattie Will's boredom. Yaeger examines how Welty transforms Yeats's poetic images and themes to redefine the potential power of female, rather than male, imagination. Howard notes how Mattie Will's impression of King MacLain's grandeur mocks Yeats's version of the Zeus and Leda myth in *The Rhetoric of Eudora Welty's Short Stories* (63–64). Vande Kieft discusses this parody in *Eudora Welty* (114–15), and Manz-Kunz also addresses the parody in her discussion of this story. Finally, several writers consider how Mattie Will's perception of King MacLain contributes to the cycle's pattern of associating him with Zeus. Vande Kieft notes how this story emphasizes Zeus's comic, even absurdly human, qualities. Bryant points to the additional connection to the Celtic Aengus. Morris considers how the association contributes to the story's mythological purpose in "Zeus and the Golden Apples: Eudora Welty." Howard argues (*Rhetoric* 64) that with this story, nothing will harm King's mythic stature.

2. For a general description of Celtic mythology, particularly its Beltene and Samhain festivals, see "Celts," 2: 441 and "All Hallows Eve," 1: 109 in *Man, Myth, and Magic: The Illustrated Encyclopedia of Mythology, Religion and the Unknown,* 1st ed.; see also, "Celtic Mythology," *New Larousse Encyclopedia of Mythology,* 1968 ed. 236.

3. "Horns," *Man, Myth, and Magic,* 5: 1352.

4. "Oak," *Man, Myth, and Magic,* 8: 2033–35.

From Metaphor to Manifestation: The Artist in Eudora Welty's *A Curtain of Green*

1. I shall use the terms *author* and *artist* interchangeably. Although Welty's medium is writing, I believe her insights apply to other art forms as well.

2. Both Porter (xi–xxiii) and Carson recognize an autobiographical element in "A Memory" and discuss the girl as an artist. Carson makes passing mention of Mrs. Larkin as kin to "Hawthorne's and Poe's dark romancers" (421) and interprets Powerhouse as "the prototype for the artist-visionaries throughout Welty's fiction," reconciling "the dialectic of the primitive and the civilized in man" (427). Carson bases his analysis on a Coleridgean concept of the artist, whereas I find correspondences between Welty's fiction and her own essays on writing.

3. Welty deleted this passage, published in "Place in Fiction" in the January 1956 *South*

Atlantic Quarterly, when she prepared the essay for republication in *The Eye of the Story.* She may have felt that it had become dated; perhaps she regretted its tone of censure.

Of Suffering and Joy: Aspects of Storytelling in Welty's Short Fiction

1. These comments were made in a personal interview with Eudora Welty, Sept. 14, 1987.
2. The first draft is in the Mississippi Department of Archives and History, Jackson, Miss.
3. As discussed by Morin in "Le bon plaisir d'Edgar Morin" on the radio channel France-Culture, Sept. 12, 1987. (See also Morin 419–25.)

From Civil War to Civil Rights: Race Relations in Welty's "A Worn Path"

1. The earliest critical reference to the mythological phoenix is William Jones. Two interesting studies parallel Phoenix's physical description with other birds. See Donlan, who also interprets Phoenix's encounters with the small boy and the hunter as manifestations of the sun god Ra; and Nostrandt, who traces Phoenix as an inversion of an old Norse folktale in which a selfish woman is transformed into a woodpecker.

2. Almost all of these interpretations are implicit in Isaac's seminal (though too loosely argued) study of the story. Welker and Gower (203–06) make suggestive parallels to religious questers. The most detailed study of the Christian imagery, including specific analogues to the Passion Week, is Keys (354–56). Daly offers an existentialist interpretation which views Phoenix as less like Christ and Bunyan's Christian than Don Quixote. See also Trefman.

3. Welty, "And They Lived Happily Ever After" 3; *OWB,* esp. 8, 99. See also her *Conversations* interviews with Van Gelder, Buckley, Freeman, Gretlund, Maclay, Haller, and Jones (4, 107–08, 174, 224–25, 275, 313, and 324, respectively).

4. Hardy's treatment of blacks is difficult to understand because it is internally contradictory. Clearly he intends his treatment of Phoenix to be sympathetic (see also his comments on Welty's characters in the introduction and conclusion [221, 232]). Yet he confusingly refers to Phoenix's "outrageous request" that the white woman tie her shoes as an example of "the ways in which southern Negroes have learned to take subtle revenge on the 'superior race,' to exploit, for their own material or psychological advantage, the weaknesses of white pride" (228–29).

5. Welty's "Must the Writer Crusade?" (*Eye* 146–58) is her most thorough discussion of what she considers the author's appropriate role in regard to morality and reforming society. For specific comments on race, see her *Conversations* interviews with Clemons, Bunting, Kuehl, Buckley, Walker, Ferris, Freeman, Gretlund, Royals and Little, Brans, and Jones (31, 48, 83–84, 99–103, 136–37, 166, 182–84, 225, 259, 299–300, and 337, respectively), as well as the preface to *The Collected Stories of Eudora Welty* (x–xi). In the Brans interview, she remarks that making Phoenix black was not a deliberate decision, such as "I am now going to write about the black race. I write about all people." She continues somewhat facetiously, "I think all my characters are about half and half black and white." Later in the same interview, however, she admits that only a black person "would be in such desperate need and live so remotely away from help and . . . have so far to go" (*Conversations* 300). She also notes that Phoenix is a common black name (*Conversations* 51); see also Freeman's interview (*Conversations* 188). Davis (5) interestingly notes the irony in the practice of slaveholders who named slaves and other chattel for classical personages. Within a larger cultural context,

he sees this practice in Welty's fiction as "both a constant reminder of the past and a testament to the capacity to turn derision into dignity."

6. See also Vande Kieft, *Eudora Welty* (rev. ed., 140); and Moss (147–49) which asks some very difficult questions about the race issues in the story, especially regarding those readers who have been searching to find illiberal racial attitudes.

7. See Bartel; Feld 64–65; and Robinson 24. For dissenting views, see Cooley (23) and Hardy (226).

8. This scene is analyzed in great detail by Robinson (25–26).

9. Ardolino (8) relates the dove symbolism with Song of Solomon 2:10–13; Welker and Gower (204–05) also notes New Testament birds to which Welty may have been alluding. Throughout Welty's fiction birds seem to be signs of beneficence. See, for example, the scene in "Keela, The Outcast Indian Maiden" in which at the moment when Little Lee Roy recognizes Steve, "a sparrow alighted on his child's shoe" (*CS* 43), and the conclusion of "The Demonstrators" in which Dr. Strickland watches the hen and the cock and peacefully recalls how his estranged wife's "eyes would follow the birds when they flew across the garden" (*CS* 621), as well as "A Pageant of Birds."

10. Casty (6) captures the dualism of the hunter well, seeing him as exemplifying "the imperfect mixture that is mankind." See also Moss 149–50 and Robinson 24–27. Cooley lamentably claims that the "white reader may identify himself with the hunter" (24). Recent studies of race relations in Welty's fiction, particularly Vande Kieft on "The Demonstrators" and "Where Is the Voice Coming From?" and Coulthard's study of "Keela, The Outcast Indian Maiden," represent perceptive and balanced treatments of the complex and tragic issue of racism.

11. Hardy (227–29) presents the most scathing interpretation of their actions. See also Appel, *A Season of Dreams* 16; and Cooley 24. Welker and Gower (205) offer a necessary corrective that "all Christians, through Grace, are 'charity cases'"; the "obstinate case," they further argue, suggests Original Sin, "the nature of the human condition."

Falling into Cycles: *The Golden Apples*

1. For the Ellmann and Feidelson anthology, Eliot wrote a note on his piece, dated January 1964: "To say that the novel ended with Flaubert and James was possibly an echo of Ezra Pound and is certainly absurd" (681). In a good essay, "Traditionalism and Modernism in Eudora Welty," in Prenshaw's *Critical Essays,* Eisinger puts Welty between the early and late modernists and calls *The Golden Apples* a novel (17).

2. See esp. Bakhtin's *Problems of Dostoevsky's Poetics* and "Epic and Novel" in Holquist's edition of Bakhtin, *The Dialogic Imagination.*

3. Welty's memories include a special regard for the moon during her childhood and her father's putting her eye to the family telescope in the front yard (*OWB* 10). Star maps published for amateur observers of the night sky show that Welty's references to the heavens are correct for the time-settings of her stories. Barton and Barton's *Guide to the Constellations,* first issued in 1928, is a popular example of such charts prepared for the home astronomer. Issued in 1928 and revised in 1935 and 1943, and written for the common reader and amateur astronomer, it has a section on the mythology behind major constellation names, and the account of the myths pays a great deal of attention to the role of Perseus, including his rescue of Cassiopeia's daughter Andromeda, the killing of Medusa, and the stealing of the golden apples. In the lyrical ending to *The Golden Apples* Welty's reference to "the stroke of the leopard" (*CS* 461) cites an animal not found by that name among the constellations, though there is Camelopardalis (giraffe), and both Leo Minor (small lion) and Lynx in addition to Leo. Since she seemed to know the heavens well, it may be that Welty deliberately used

license, translating Leo minor or Lynx into "leopard" to help the rhythm or power of her sentence.

4. In his talk at the Eye of the Storyteller Conference in Akron (1987), Michael Kreyling quoted a letter from Welty to her agent Diarmuid Russell, the son of AE, in which she appears to make a lighthearted transference of the experience with Yeats, claiming that she came across an open book of AE's poems in the library and knew then that Diarmuid would become her agent.

5. In the 1948 biography of Yeats, Ellmann mentions de Jubainville in the same phrase with Max Müller and Sir James G. Frazer and points out that the interests of these investigators of the origins of myth and religion were similar to Madame Blavatsky's, though she reached her conclusions by a different avenue (57).

"Where Is the Voice Coming From?": Teaching Eudora Welty

1. Harriet Pollack has effectively summarized Welty's stated intentions in an exploration of reader response to Welty's fiction.

2. My relation to the writer and her work in writing my critical study, *Eudora Welty,* is set forth at some length in "Eudora Welty: Visited and Revisited."

3. Suzanne Ferguson's essay in this volume would seem better suited to illustrations of Bakhtin's theory and practice concerning intertextuality and the dialogic imagination than Yaeger's. Ferguson shows how the story includes a heroic romantic rhetoric "highly orna-mented" and "the bare, figure-poor lexicon" of the bleak, horrible facts; the rhetoric of the small-town journalese with all its innuendo of social commentary; the dialect of black speakers over against that of the educated white doctor—all these are redolent of social codes, attitudes and norms, different vocabularies jostling against each other—closer to Bakhtin's essential meaning than Yaeger seems to come.

WORKS CITED

Appel, Alfred. "Powerhouse's Blues." *Studies in Short Fiction* 2 (1965): 221–34.
———. *A Season of Dreams: The Fiction of Eudora Welty*. Baton Rouge: Louisiana State UP, 1965.
Ardolino, Frank R. "Life Out of Death: Ancient Myth and Ritual in Welty's 'A Worn Path.' " *Notes on Mississippi Writers* 9 (1976): 1–9.
Arnold, Marilyn. "When Gratitude Is No More: Eudora Welty's 'June Recital.' " *South Carolina Review* 13.2 (1981): 62–72.
Arnold, St. George Tucker, Jr. "Mythic Patterns and Satiric Effect in Welty's 'Petrified Man.' " *Studies in Contemporary Satire* 4 (1977): 21–27.
Auerbach, Nina. *Women and the Demon: The Life of a Victorian Myth*. Cambridge: Harvard UP, 1982.
Babcock, Barbara A., ed. *The Reversible World: Symbolic Inversion in Art and Society*. Ithaca: Cornell UP, 1978.
Bachelard, Gaston. *The Poetics of Space*. Trans. Maria Jolas. Boston: Beacon, 1969.
Baignell, Matthew. *Thomas Hart Benton*. New York: Abrams, 1975.
Bakhtin, M. M. *The Dialogic Imagination: Four Essays*. Trans. Caryl Emerson and Michael Holquist. Ed. Michael Holquist. Austin: U of Texas P, 1981.
———. *Problems of Dostoevsky's Poetics*. Trans. and ed. Caryl Emerson. Vol. 8 of *Theory and History of Literature*. Minneapolis: U of Minnesota P, 1984.
Balliett, Whitney. "Fats." *Jelly Roll, Jabbo, and Fats: Nineteen Portraits in Jazz*. New York: Oxford UP, 1983. 85–96.
Bartel, Roland. "Life and Death in Eudora Welty's 'A Worn Path.' " *Studies in Short Fiction* 14 (1977): 288–91.
Barthes, Roland. *Mythologies*. Trans. Richard Howard. New York: Hill and Wang, 1957.
Barton, Samuel G., and William H. Barton. *A Guide to the Constellations*. New York and London: McGraw, 1943.

Baym, Nina. *Woman's Fiction: A Guide to Novels by and about Women in America, 1820–1870*. Ithaca: Cornell UP, 1978.

Bell, Michael Davitt. *The Development of American Romance: The Sacrifice of Relation*. Chicago: U of Chicago P, 1980.

Benjamin, Walter. "The Storyteller." *Illuminations*. Trans. Harry Zohn. Ed. Hannah Arendt. New York: Schocken, 1968. 83–109.

Benton, Thomas Hart. *An American in Art: A Professional and Technical Autobiography*. Kansas City: UP of Kansas, 1969.

———. *Thomas Hart Benton: A Personal Commemorative*. Joplin, MO: Joplin Council for the Arts, 1973.

Berger, John. *Ways of Seeing*. New York: Viking, 1973.

Bloom, Harold, ed. *Eudora Welty*. New York: Chelsea, 1986.

Boatwright, James. "Speech and Silence in *Losing Battles*." *Shenandoah* 25 (1974): 3–14.

Boorstin, Daniel. *The Americans: The Democratic Experience*. New York: Random, 1973.

Borel, Emile. *Space and Time*. 1926. New York: Dover, 1960.

Bradford, M. E. " 'Looking Down from a High Place': The Serenity of Miss Welty's *Losing Battles*." Desmond 103–09.

Bridgman, Richard. *The Colloquial Style in America*. New York: Oxford UP, 1966.

Brookes, Stella Brewer. *Joel Chandler Harris: Folklorist*. Athens: U of Georgia P, 1967.

Brooks, Cleanth. "Eudora Welty and the Southern Idiom." Dollarhide and Abadie 3–25.

Brooks, Cleanth, and Robert Penn Warren. *Understanding Fiction*. New York: Appleton, 1959.

Brooks, Peter. *Reading for the Plot*. 1984. New York: Vintage, 1985.

Bryant, J. A. "Seeing Double in *The Golden Apples*." *Sewanee Review* 82 (1974): 300–15.

Carson, Gary. "Versions of the Artist in *A Curtain of Green:* The Unifying Imagination in Eudora Welty's Early Fiction." *Studies in Short Fiction* 15 (1978): 421–28.

Casty, Alan. *Instructor's Guide to "The Shape of Fiction": Stories for Comparison*. Lexington, MA: Heath, 1967.

Cather, Willa. *Obscure Destinies and Literary Encounters*. New York: Knopf, 1932.

———. *The Song of the Lark*. 1915. Lincoln: U of Nebraska P, 1978.

———. *Youth and the Bright Medusa*. New York: Knopf, 1920.

Chase, Richard. *The American Novel and Its Tradition*. New York: Doubleday-Anchor, 1957.

Chekhov, Anton. *The Tales of Chekhov*. Trans. Constance Garnett. 1916. New York: Ecco, 1984–87.

Chopin, Kate. *The Awakening*. 1899. New York: Avon, 1972.

Cixous, Helène. "The Laugh of the Medusa." Trans. Keith and Paula Cohen. *Signs: A Journal of Women in Culture and Society* 1 (1976): 875–93.

Conrad, Joseph. Preface. *Nigger of the "Narcissus."* London: Dent, 1960.

Cooke, Rose Terry. *"How Celia Changed Her Mind" and Selected Stories*. Ed. Elizabeth Ammons. New Brunswick: Rutgers UP, 1986.

Cooley, John R. "Blacks as Primitives in Eudora Welty's Fiction." *Ball State University Forum* 14 (1973): 20–28.

Corcoran, John X. W. P. "Celtic Mythology." *New Larousse Encyclopedia of Mythology.* 2nd ed. Hong Kong: Hamlyn, 1968.

Corcoran, Neil. "The Face That Was in the Poem: Art and 'Human Truth' in 'June Recital.'" *Delta* 5 (1977): 27–34.

Corn, Wanda, ed. *The Art of Andrew Wyeth.* Boston: Little, 1973.

Cornell, Brenda G. "Ambiguous Necessity: A Study of *The Ponder Heart*." Prenshaw, *Critical Essays* 208–19.

Coulthard, A. R. " 'Keela, The Outcast Indian Maiden': A Dissenting View." *Studies in Short Fiction* 23 (1986): 35–41.

Culler, Jonathan. *On Deconstruction: Theory and Criticism after Structuralism.* Ithaca: Cornell UP, 1982.

Daghistany, Ann, and J. J. Johnson. "Romantic Irony, Spatial Form and Joyce's *Ulysses*." Smitten and Daghistany 48–60.

Daly, Saralyn R. " 'A Worn Path' Retrod." *Studies in Short Fiction* 1 (1964): 133–39.

Dante Alighieri. *The Divine Comedy: Paradiso.* Trans. John D. Sinclair. New York: Oxford UP, 1961.

Davidson, Abraham A. *The Story of American Painting.* New York: Abrams, 1974.

Davis, Charles E. "Eudora Welty's Blacks: Name and Cultural Identity." *Notes on Mississippi Writers* 17.1 (1985): 1–8.

Dazey, Mary A. "Phoenix Jackson and the Nice Lady: A Note on Eudora Welty's 'A Worn Path.'" *American Notes and Queries* 17 (1979): 1–8.

de Jubainville, H. d'Arbois. *The Irish Mythological Cycle and Celtic Mythology.* Trans. Richard Irvine Best. 1903. New York: Lemma, 1970.

Derrida, Jacques. *Of Grammatology.* Trans. Gayatri Chakravorty Spivak. Baltimore: Johns Hopkins UP, 1976.

Desmond, John F., ed. *A Still Moment: Essays on the Art of Eudora Welty.* Metuchen, NJ: Scarecrow, 1978.

de Tolnay, Charles. *Michelangelo. Volume II: The Sistine Ceiling.* Princeton: Princeton UP, 1945.

Devlin, Albert J. *Eudora Welty's Chronicle: A Story of Mississippi Life.* Jackson: UP of Mississippi, 1983.

———. "Jackson's Welty." *Southern Quarterly* 20 (Summer 1982): 54–91.

———, ed. *Welty, A Life in Literature.* Jackson & London: UP of Mississippi, 1987.

Devlin, Albert J., and Peggy Whitman Prenshaw. "A Conversation with Eudora Welty, Jackson, 1986." *Mississippi Quarterly* 39 (1986): 431–54.

Dollarhide, Louis, and Ann J. Abadie, eds. *Eudora Welty: A Form of Thanks.* Jackson: UP of Mississippi, 1979.

Donlan, Dan. " 'A Worn Path': Immortality of Stereotype." *English Journal* 62 (1973): 549–50.

Donovan, Josephine. *New England Local-Color Literature: A Woman's Tradition.* New York: Ungar, 1983.

Doolittle, Hilda [H. D.]. *Trilogy.* New York: New Directions, 1973.

Dotson, Esther Gordon. "An Augustinian Interpretation of Michelangelo's Sistine Ceiling." Pts. 1 and 2. *Art Bulletin* 61 (1979), 2:223–56, 3:405–29.

Douglas, Ann. *The Feminization of American Culture.* New York: Knopf, 1977.

DuPlessis, Rachel Blau. *Writing beyond the Ending.* Bloomington: Indiana UP, 1985.

Eisinger, Chester E. "Traditionalism and Modernism in Eudora Welty." Prenshaw, *Critical Essays* 3–25.

Eliot, T. S. "*Ulysses,* Order and Myth." *Dial* 75 (1923): 480–83. (Rpt. in Ellmann and Feidelson 679–81.)

Ellmann, Richard. *Yeats: The Man and the Masks.* New York: Macmillan, 1948.

Ellmann, Richard, and Charles Feidelson, eds. *The Modern Tradition.* New York: Oxford UP, 1965.

Evans, Augusta [Wilson]. *St. Elmo.* New York: Grosset and Dunlap, 1866.

———. *Vashti; or, "Until Death Us Do Part."* New York: Carleton, 1869.

Evans, Elizabeth. *Eudora Welty.* New York: Ungar, 1981.

Ewen, Stuart. *Captains of Consciousness: Advertising and the Social Roots of the Consumer Culture.* New York: McGraw, 1975.

Falk, Robert P. "The Rise of Realism, 1871–91." *Transitions in American Literary History.* Ed. Harry Hayden Clark. 1954. Durham: Duke UP, 1967. 381–442.

Faust, Drew Gilpin, ed. *The Ideology of Slavery: Proslavery Thought in the Antebellum South, 1830–1860.* Baton Rouge: Louisiana State UP, 1981.

———. *A Sacred Circle: The Dilemma of the Intellectual in the Old South, 1840–1860.* Baltimore: Johns Hopkins UP, 1977.

Feld, Bernard David. *The Short Fiction of Eudora Welty.* Diss. Columbia U, 1978. Ann Arbor: UMI, 1984.

Felman, Shoshana. "Turning the Screw of Interpretation." *Literature and Psychoanalysis: The Question of Reading Otherwise.* Ed. Felman. Baltimore: Johns Hopkins UP, 1982. 94–207.

Ferguson, George. *Signs and Symbols in Christian Art.* New York: Oxford UP, 1954.

Ferguson, Mary Anne. "*Losing Battles* as a Comic Epic in Prose." Prenshaw, *Critical Essays* 305–24.

Ferris, William. *Local Color: A Sense of Place in Folk Art.* Ed. Brenda McCallum. New York: McGraw, 1982.

Fleischauer, John. "The Focus of Mystery: Eudora Welty's Prose Style." *Southern Literary Journal* 5.2 (1973): 64–79.

Fletcher, Marie. "The Southern Heroine in the Fiction of Representative Southern Women Writers, 1850–1960." Diss. Louisiana State U, 1963.

Foucault, Michel. *The Archaeology of Knowledge and the Discourse on Language.* Trans. A. M. Sheridan Smith. New York: Pantheon, 1972.

———. *Discipline and Punish: The Birth of the Prison.* Trans. A. M. Sheridan. New York: Pantheon Books, 1977.

———. *The Order of Things: An Archaeology of the Human Sciences.* New York: Random, 1970.

———. "The Subject and Power." *Michel Foucault: Beyond Structuralism and Hermeneutics.* Ed. Hubert L. Dreyfus and Paul Rabinow. 2nd ed. Chicago: U of Chicago P, 1983. 208–26.

Fowler, Roger. *Essays on Style and Language*. London: Routledge, 1966.
———. *Linguistics and the Novel*. London: Methuen, 1977.

Frank, Joseph. *The Widening Gyre: Crisis and Mastery in Modern Literature*. 1945. New Brunswick: Rutgers UP, 1963.

Frazer, Sir James G. *The Golden Bough*. 3rd ed. 12 vols. London: Macmillan, 1907–15.

Gardner, Helen. *Gardner's Art through the Ages*. 1926. Ed. Horst de la Croix and Richard G. Tansey. New York: Harcourt, 1975.

Geertz, Clifford. " 'From the Native's Point of View': On the Nature of Anthropological Understanding." *Local Knowledge: Further Essays in Interpretive Anthropology*. New York: Basic, 1983.

Gibson, Walker. *Tough, Sweet, and Stuffy; an Essay on Modern American Prose Styles*. Bloomington: Indiana UP, 1966.

Gilbert, Sandra M., and Susan Gubar. *The Madwoman in the Attic: The Woman Writer and the Nineteenth-Century Literary Imagination*. New Haven: Yale UP, 1979.

Gilligan, Carol. *In a Different Voice: Psychological Theory and Women's Development*. Cambridge: Harvard UP, 1982.

Goffman, Erving. *Frame Analysis: An Essay on the Organization of Experience*. New York: Harper, 1974.

Gossett, Louise Y. "Eudora Welty's New Novel: The Comedy of Loss." *Southern Literary Journal* 3.1 (1970): 122–37.

Gray, Richard. *Writing the South: Ideas of an American Region*. New York: Cambridge UP, 1986.

Groseclose, Barbara. "Photography and the (New) South." *Literature and the Visual Arts in Contemporary Society*. Ed. Suzanne Ferguson and Barbara Groseclose. Columbus: Ohio State UP, 1985.

Hamblett, Theora, Ed Meek, and William S. Haynie. *Dreams and Visions*. Oxford: UP of Mississippi, 1975.

Hardy, John Edward. "Eudora Welty's Negroes." *Images of the Negro in American Literature*. Ed. Seymour L. Gross and John Hardy. Chicago: U of Chicago P, 1966. 221–32.

Hawthorne, Nathaniel. *Tales and Sketches*. New York: Library of America, 1982.

Heilman, Robert B. "*Losing Battles* and Winning the War." Prenshaw, *Critical Essays* 269–304.

Helterman, Jeffrey. "Gorgons in Mississippi: Eudora Welty's 'Petrified Man.' " *Notes on Mississippi Writers* 7 (1974): 12–20.

Highet, Gilbert. "The Human Comedy." *Times Literary Supplement* 29 October 1954: 685.

———. "Laugh and Grow Thin." *Harper's* 208 (1954): 97.

Homans, Margaret. *Bearing the Word: Language and Female Experience in Nineteenth-Century Women's Writing*. Chicago: U of Chicago P, 1986.

Howard, Zelma Turner. *The Rhetoric of Eudora Welty's Short Stories*. Jackson: UP of Mississippi, 1973.

Howell, Elmo. "Eudora Welty's Negroes: A Note on 'A Worn Path.' " *Xavier University Studies* 9 (1970): 28–32.

Huf, Linda. *A Portrait of the Artist as a Young Woman: The Writer as Heroine in American Literature.* New York: Ungar, 1983.

Irigaray, Luce. *Speculum of the Other Woman.* Trans. Gillian C. Gill. Ithaca: Cornell UP, 1985.

Issacs, Neil D. "Life for Phoenix." *Sewanee Review* 71 (1963): 75–81.

Johnson, Barbara. *The Critical Difference: Essays in the Contemporary Rhetoric of Reading.* Baltimore: Johns Hopkins UP, 1980.

Jones, Alun R. "The World of Love: The Fiction of Eudora Welty." *The Creative Present: Notes on Contemporary American Fiction.* Ed. Nona Balakian and Charles Simmons. Garden City: Doubleday, 1963.

Jones, William M. "Welty's 'A Worn Path.'" *Explicator* 15 (1957). Item 57.

Kaftal, George. *Iconography of the Saints in Tuscan Painting.* Florence: Sansoni, 1952.

Kenner, Hugh. *A Homemade World.* New York: Knopf, 1975.

Kestner, Joseph A. "Secondary Illusion: The Novel and the Spatial Arts." Smitten and Daghistany 100–28.

———. *The Spatiality of the Novel.* Detroit: Wayne State UP, 1978.

Keys, Marilynn. " 'A Worn Path': The Way of Dispossession." *Studies in Short Fiction* 16 (1979): 354–56.

Kreyling, Michael. *Eudora Welty's Achievement of Order.* Baton Rouge: Louisiana State UP, 1980.

Kristeva, Julia. *Desire in Language: A Semiotic Approach to Literature and Art.* Trans. Thomas Gora, Alice Jardine, and Leon S. Roudiez. Ed. Leon S. Roudiez. New York: Columbia UP, 1980.

Lacan, Jacques. "La chose freudiènne." *Ecrits.* Paris: Seuil, 1966.

———. *Ecrits, a Selection.* Translated by Alan Sheridan. London: Tavistock, 1977.

———. *Ecrits II.* Paris: Seuil, 1966.

Landess, Thomas H. "More Trouble in Mississippi: Family vs. Antifamily in Miss Welty's *Losing Battles.*" *Sewanee Review* 79 (1971): 626–34.

Lane, Suzette, and Paul D'Ambrosio. *A Shifting Wind: Views of American Folk Art.* Cooperstown: New York State Historical Association, 1986.

Lawrence, Elizabeth. *Gardening for Love.* Durham: Duke UP, 1987.

Love, Glen, and Michael Payne. *Contemporary Essays on Style.* Chicago: Scott Foresman, 1969.

MacCana, Proinsias. *Celtic Mythology.* 2nd ed. New York: Peter Bedrick Books, 1985.

MacEwen, Gwendolyn. "Dark Pines under Water." *Magic Animals.* Toronto: Macmillan, 1974.

McGann, Jerome J. "The Beauty of the Medusa: A Study in Romantic Literary Iconology." *Studies in Romanticism* 11 (1972): 3–25.

McHaney, Thomas L. "Eudora Welty and the Multitudinous Golden Apples." *Mississippi Quarterly* 26 (1972): 589—624.

McKenzie, Barbara, ed. *The Process of Fiction.* 2d ed. New York: Harcourt, 1974.

MacKethan, Lucinda H. "To See Things in Their Time: The Act of Focus in Eudora Welty's Fiction." *American Literature* 50 (1978): 258–75.

McNall, Sally Allen. *Who Is In The House? A Psychological Study of Two Centuries of Women's Fiction in America, 1795 to the Present.* New York: Elsevier, 1981.

Magee, Rosemary M. "Eudora Welty's *Losing Battles:* A Patchwork Quilt of Stories." *South Atlantic Review* 49.2 (1984): 67–79.

Man, Myth, and Magic: The Illustrated Encyclopedia of Mythology, Religion and the Unknown. 1st ed. New York: Cavendish, 1983.

Manning, Carol. *With Ears Opening like Morning Glories: Eudora Welty and the Love of Storytelling.* Westport: Greenwood P, 1985.

Manz-Kunz, Marie Antoinette. *Eudora Welty: Aspects of Reality in Her Short Fiction.* Bern: Franke, 1971.

Marchand, Roland. *Advertising the American Dream: Making Way for Modernity, 1920–1940.* Berkeley: U of California P, 1985.

Markale, Jean. *Women of the Celts.* 1972. Trans. A. Mygind, C. Hauch, and P. Henry. London: Gordon Cremonesci, 1975.

May, Charles E. "Le Roi Mehaigné in Welty's 'Keela, The Outcast Indian Maiden.' " *Modern Fiction Studies* 18 (1973): 559–66.

———. "Why Sister Lives at the P.O." *Southern Humanities Review* 12 (1978): 243–49.

Messerli, Douglas. " 'A Battle with Both Sides Using the Same Tactics': The Language of Time in *Losing Battles.*" Prenshaw, *Critical Essays* 351–66.

Mickelson, David. "Types of Spatial Structure in Narrative." Smitten and Daghistany 63–78.

Miller, Sue. *The Good Mother.* New York: Dell, 1986.

Milton, John. "Il Penseroso." *Complete Poems and Major Prose.* Ed. Merritt Y. Hughes. New York: Odyssey, 1957. 72–76.

Moers, Ellen. *Literary Women.* New York: Doubleday, 1975.

Moore, Carol A. "The Insulation of Illusion and *Losing Battles.*" *Mississippi Quarterly* 26 (1973): 651–58.

Moreland, Richard C. "Community and Vision in Eudora Welty." *Southern Review* 18 (1982): 84–99.

Morin, Edgar. *La Methode.* Vol. 2 of *La Vie de la Vie.* Paris: Seuil, 1980.

Morris, Harry C. "Eudora Welty's Use of Mythology." *Shenandoah* 6 (1955): 33–40.

———. "Zeus and the Golden Apples: Eudora Welty." *Perspective* 5 (1952): 190–99.

Moss, Grant, Jr. " 'A Worn Path' Retrod." *CLA Journal* 15 (1971): 144–52.

Muir, Edwin. *The Structure of the Novel.* London: Hogarth, 1928.

Müller, Max. *Comparative Mythology.* London, 1856.

Mulvey, Laura. "Visual Pleasure and Narrative Cinema." *Art after Modernism: Rethinking Representation.* Ed. Brian Wallis. New York: Godine, 1984. 361–73.

New Larousse Encyclopedia of Mythology. London: Hamlyn, 1968.

Nostrandt, Jeanne R. "Welty's 'A Worn Path.' " *Explicator* 34 (1976). Item 33.

Oates, Joyce Carol. "The Art of Eudora Welty." Bloom 71–74.

O'Brien, Michael, ed. *All Clever Men, Who Make Their Way: Critical Discourse in the Old South.* Fayetteville: U of Arkansas P, 1982.

O'Brien, Sharon. "Mothers, Daughters, and the 'Art Necessity': Willa Cather and the Creative Process." *American Novelists Revisited: Essays in Feminist Criticism.* Ed. Fritz Fleishmann. Boston: Hall, 1982. 265–98.

O'Doherty, Brian. "A Visit to Wyeth Country." Corn. 14–44.

Opitz, Kurt. "Eudora Welty: The Order of a Captive Soul." *Critique* 7 (1965): 79–91.

Ostriker, Alicia. *Stealing the Language: The Emergence of Women's Poetry in America.* Boston: Beacon, 1986.

Ovid. *Metamorphoses.* Trans. Rolfe Humphries. Bloomington: Indiana UP, 1955.

Papashvily, Helen Waite. *All the Happy Endings: A Study of the Domestic Novel in America, The Women Who Wrote It, The Women Who Read It, In the Nineteenth Century.* New York: Harper, 1956.

Petry, Alice Hall. "Universal and Particular: The Local-Color Phenomenon Reconsidered." *American Literary Realism, 1870–1910* 12 (1979): 111–26.

Petty, Jane Reid. "The Town and the Writer: An Interview with Eudora Welty." *Jackson Magazine* September 1977: 28+. (Rpt. in Prenshaw, *Conversations* 200–10.)

Pitavy-Souques, Danièle. "A Blazing Butterfly: The Modernity of Eudora Welty." *Mississippi Quarterly* 39.4 (1986): 537–60. (Rpt. in Devlin 113–38.)

———. "Technique as Myth: The Structure of *The Golden Apples.*" Prenshaw, *Critical Essays* 258–68. (Rpt. in Prenshaw, *Thirteen Essays* 146–56; and Bloom, *Eudora Welty* 109–18.)

———. "Watchers and Watching: Point of View in Eudora Welty's 'June Recital.'" Trans. Margaret Tomarchio. *Southern Review* 19 (1983): 483–509.

Plato. *Dialogues of Plato.* Trans. Benjamin Jowett. Ed. William Chase Green. New York: Liveright, 1932.

Polk, Noel. "A Eudora Welty Checklist." *Mississippi Quarterly* 26 (Fall 1973): 662–93.

———. "Water, Wanderers, and Weddings: Love in Eudora Welty." Dollarhide and Abadie 95–122.

———. "Welty, Eudora: 1909–." *Lives of Mississippi Authors, 1817–1967.* Ed. James B. Lloyd. Jackson: UP of Mississippi, 1981. 459–64.

Pollack, Harriet. "Words between Strangers: On Welty, Her Style, and Her Audience." *Mississippi Quarterly* 39 (1986): 481–506. (Rpt. in Devlin, *A Life* 54–81.)

Porter, Katherine Anne. *The Collected Stories of Katherine Anne Porter.* New York: Harcourt, 1965.

———. Introduction. *A Curtain of Green and Other Stories.* By Eudora Welty. 1936. New York: Harcourt, 1979. xi–xxiii.

Prenshaw, Peggy Whitman, ed. *Conversations with Eudora Welty.* Jackson: UP of Mississippi, 1984.

———. "Cultural Patterns in Eudora Welty's *Delta Wedding* and 'The Demonstrators,'" *Notes on Mississippi Writers* 3 (1970): 51–70.

———, ed. *Eudora Welty: Critical Essays.* Jackson: UP of Mississippi, 1979.

———, ed. *Eudora Welty: Thirteen Essays.* Jackson: UP of Mississippi, 1983.

———. "Woman's World, Man's Place: The Fiction of Eudora Welty." Dollarhide and Abadie 46–77.

Pritchett, V. S. "Bossy Edna Earle Had a Word for Everything." *New York Times Book Review* 10 January 1954: 5.

Pugh, Elaine Upton. "The Duality of Morgana: The Making of Virgie's Vision, The Vision of *The Golden Apples*." *Modern Fiction Studies* 28 (1982): 435–51.

Rabuzzi, Kathryn Allen. *The Sacred and the Feminine: Toward a Theology of Housework*. New York: Seabury, 1982.

Randisi, Jennifer Lynn. *A Tissue of Lies: Eudora Welty and the Southern Romance*. Washington: UP of America, 1982.

Ricardou, Jean. *Problèmes du nouveau roman*. Paris: Seuil, 1967.

Robinson, David. "A Nickel and a Dime Matter: Teaching Eudora Welty's 'A Worn Path.'" *Notes on Mississippi Writers* 19 (1987): 23–27.

Romines, Ann. "The Power of the Lamp: Domestic Ritual in Two Stories by Eudora Welty." *Notes on Mississippi Writers* 12 (1979): 1–16.

Rosenberger, Coleman. "Eudora Welty Tells a Wise and Comic Story of a Mississippi Town." *New York Herald Tribune Book Review* 10 January 1954: 1.

Ross, Anne. "Celts." *Man, Myth, and Magic: The Illustrated Encyclopedia of Mythology, Religion, and the Unknown*. New York: Cavendish, 1983.

Rourke, Constance. *The Roots of American Culture and Other Essays*. Ed. Van Wyck Brooks. 1942. Westport: Greenwood, 1980.

Royals, Tom, and John Littler. "A Conversation with Eudora Welty." Prenshaw, *Conversations* 259–63.

Rubin, Louis D., Jr. "Art and Artistry in Morgana, Mississippi." *Missouri Review* 4 (1981): 101–16. (Rpt. in Rubin, Louis D., Jr. *A Gallery of Southerners*. Baton Rouge: Louisiana State UP, 1982. 49–66.)

———. "Everything Brought Out in the Open: Eudora Welty's Losing Battles." *Hollins Critic* 7(1970): 1–12.

Sarton, May. *Recovering*. New York: Norton, 1978.

———. *A World of Light*. Film transcribed in *May Sarton: A Self-Portrait*. Ed. Marita Simpson and Martha Wheelock. New York: Norton, 1982.

Schiller, Gertrud. *Iconography of Christian Art*. Trans. Janet Seligman. 2 vols. Greenwich: New York Graphic Society, 1971.

Shinn, Thelma J. *Radiant Daughters: Fictional American Women*. Contributions in Women's Studies, Number 66. New York: Greenwood, 1986.

Showalter, Elaine. *The Female Malady: Women, Madness, and English Culture, 1830–1980*. New York: Pantheon, 1985.

Shweder, Richard A. "Anthropology's Romantic Rebellion against the Enlightenment, or There's More to Thinking than Reason and Evidence." *Culture Theory: Essays on Mind, Self, and Emotion*. Ed. Shweder and Robert A. Levine. New York: Cambridge UP, 1984. 27–66.

Simpson, Eileen. *Orphans*. New York: Weidenfeld, 1987.

Skaggs, Merrill Maguire. "Morgana's Apples and Pears." Prenshaw, *Critical Essays*. 220–41.

Smith-Rosenberg, Caroll. *Disorderly Conduct: Visions of Gender in Victorian America*. New York: Knopf, 1985.

Smitten, Jeffrey, and Ann Daghistany, eds. *Spatial Form in Narrative*. Ithaca: Cornell UP, 1981.

Solomon, Barbara H., ed. *Short Fiction of Sarah Orne Jewett and Mary Wilkins Freeman*. New York: Signet, 1979.

Spear, Richard E. *Domenichino*. 2 vols. New Haven: Yale UP, 1982.

de Staël, Anne Louise Germain. *Corinna; or, Italy*. Philadelphia: Fry and Krammerer, 1808.

Stoddard, Elizabeth. *The Morgesons and Other Writings, Published and Unpublished*. Ed. Lawrence Buell and Sandra A. Zagarell. Philadelphia: U of Pennsylvania P, 1984.

Stone, William B. "Eudora Welty's Hydrodynamic 'Powerhouse.' " *Studies in Short Fiction* 11 (1974): 93–96.

Stroup, Sheila. " 'We're All Part of It Together': Eudora Welty's Hopeful Vision in *Losing Battles*." *Southern Literary Journal* 15.2 (1983): 42–58.

Sypher, Wylie. "The Meanings of Comedy." *Comedy*. 1956. Baltimore: Johns Hopkins UP, 1980. 191–255.

Terdiman, Richard. *Discourse/Counter-Discourse: The Theory and Practice of Symbolic Resistance in Nineteenth-Century France*. Ithaca: Cornell UP, 1985.

Thoreau, Henry. *Walden and Civil Disobedience*. Ed. Owen Thomas. New York: Norton, 1966.

Tiegreen, Helen Hunt. "Mothers, Daughters, and One Writer's Revisions." *Mississippi Quarterly* 39 (Fall 1986): 205–26.

Todorov, Tzvetan. "Literary Genres." *Encyclopedic Dictionary of the Sciences of Language*. Trans. Catherine Porter. Baltimore: Johns Hopkins UP, 1979.

Tompkins, Jane F. *Sensational Designs: The Cultural Work of American Fiction, 1790–1860*. New York: Oxford UP, 1985.

Trefman, Sara. "Welty's 'A Worn Path.' " *Explicator* 24 (1966). Item 56.

Trilling, Diana. "Fiction in Review." *Reviewing the Forties*. New York: Harcourt, 1978.

Turner, G. W. *Stylistics*. Harmondsworth: Penguin, 1973.

Turner, Victor. *Dramas, Fields, and Metaphors*. Ithaca: Cornell UP, 1974.

———. *The Ritual Process*. Ithaca: Cornell UP, 1969.

Ullmann, Stephen. *Language and Style*. Oxford: Blackwell, 1964.

———. *Meaning and Style: Collected Papers*. New York: Barnes, 1973.

Vande Kieft, Ruth. "Demonstrators in a Stricken Land." McKenzie 342–49.

———. *Eudora Welty*. 1962. Rev. ed. Boston: Twayne, 1987.

———. "Eudora Welty: The Question of Meaning." *Southern Quarterly* 20 (1982): 24–39.

———. "Eudora Welty: Visited and Revisited." *Mississippi Quarterly* 39 (1986): 455–79. (Rpt. in Devlin, *A Life* 27–53.)

Vasse, Denis. *Le Poids du réel*. Paris: Seuil, 1983.

———. *Le Temps du désir, la souffrance*. Paris: Seuil, 1966.

Virgil. *Eclogues, Georgics, Aeneid*. Trans. H. R. Fairclough. Rev. ed. 2 vols. Loeb Classical Library. Cambridge: Harvard UP, 1974.

Vursell, H. D. "The Best American Short Stories, 1943." *Tomorrow* 3 Nov. 1943: 53.

Walker, Robert C. "Another Medusa Allusion in Welty's 'Petrified Man.' " *Notes on Mississippi Writers* 9 (1979): 10.

Warren, Robert Penn. "The Love and Separateness in Miss Welty." *Kenyon Review* 6 (1955): 34–40.

Welker, Robert L., and Hershel Gower, eds. *Study Guide to "The Sense of Fiction."* Englewood Cliffs: Prentice-Hall, 1966.

Welty, Eudora. *The Bride of the Innisfallen.* New York: Harcourt, 1955.

———. *The Collected Stories of Eudora Welty.* New York: Harcourt, 1980.

———. *Conversations with Eudora Welty.* Ed. Peggy Whitman Prenshaw. Jackson: UP of Mississippi, 1984.

———. *A Curtain of Green.* Garden City, N.Y.: Doubleday, 1941.

———. *Delta Wedding.* New York: Harcourt, 1946.

———. "Department of Amplification." *New Yorker* 24 (1 January 1949): 50–51.

———. *The Eye of the Story: Selected Essays and Reviews.* New York: Random, 1978.

———. "How I Write." *Virginia Quarterly Review* 31 (Winter 1955): 240–51. (Rpt. in Brooks and Warren 545–53.)

———. *Losing Battles.* New York: Random, 1970.

———. *One Time, One Place: Mississippi in the Depression: A Snapshot Album.* New York: Random, 1971.

———. *One Writer's Beginnings.* Cambridge: Harvard UP, 1984.

———. *The Optimist's Daughter.* New York: Random, 1972.

———. *The Ponder Heart.* New York: Harcourt, 1954.

———. "The Reading and Writing of Short Stories." *Atlantic Monthly* 183 (19 Feb. 1949): 54–58.

———. *The Robber Bridegroom.* New York: Harcourt, 1970.

———. *The Shoe Bird.* New York: Harcourt, 1964.

———. " 'The Surface of Earth.' " *New York Times Book Review* 20 July 1975: 24–25.

———. "And They Lived Happily Ever After." *New York Times Book Review* 10 Nov. 1963: 3.

———. *The Wide Net.* New York: Harcourt, 1943.

Westling, Louise. *Sacred Groves and Ravaged Gardens: The Fiction of Eudora Welty, Carson McCullers, and Flannery O'Connor.* Athens: U of Georgia P, 1985.

Wharton, Edith. *Age of Innocence.* New York: Grosset, 1920.

———. *The House of Mirth.* New York: Scribner's, 1905.

Wilden, Anthony. *Speech and Language in Psychoanalysis: Jacques Lacan* (Baltimore: Johns Hopkins UP, 1968).

Wind, Edgar. "Michelangelo's Prophets and Sibyls." *Proceedings of the British Academy* 51. London: Oxford UP, 1965. 47–84.

Yaeger, Patricia S. " 'Because a Fire Was in My Head': Eudora Welty and the Dialogic Imagination." *PMLA* 99 (1984): 955–73. (Rpt. in Devlin, *A Life* 139–67. Rev. and rpt. in *Mississippi Quarterly* 39.4 [1986]: 561–86.)

Yeats, W. B. *The Collected Poems of W. B. Yeats.* New York: Macmillan, 1956.

CONTRIBUTORS

Marilyn Arnold is professor of English and dean of graduate studies at Brigham Young University. Her articles on twentieth century American literature have been published in such journals as *South Carolina Review, Southern Literary Journal, Mississippi Quarterly, Research Studies,* and *Western American Literature*. She has written two books on Willa Cather and is working on a third, as well as a book on Eudora Welty.

Cheryll Burgess is a doctoral candidate at Cornell University, where she holds a Jacob K. Javits Fellowship. Her dissertation explores the representation of nature in the fiction of Sarah Orne Jewett, Willa Cather, and Eudora Welty. In addition to her work on Welty, she has presented papers on Cather and is organizing an association of persons interested in ecological issues in literature.

Nancy Butterworth is director of the Writing Center at the University of South Carolina. She has written on Flannery O'Connor and Faulkner's *Go Down, Moses*. She has co-written with her husband, A. Keen Butterworth, the annotations for *A Fable*.

Susan V. Donaldson teaches American literature at the College of William and Mary. She has written on Nathanael West, William Faulkner, Eudora Welty, and the Mississippi painter Walter Anderson. She is finishing a book on writers and painters of the modern South.

Elizabeth Evans has taught at the Georgia Institute of Technology since 1964. She is the author of books on Eudora Welty and on Thomas Wolfe. Her critical study of May Sarton appeared in 1989, published by Twayne.

Suzanne Ferguson is professor of English and dean of Humanities and Social Sciences at Case Western Reserve University. She has written extensively on Randall Jarrell, beginning with *The Poetry of Randall Jarrell* (1971). Her recent work has been on the theory and history of the short story and on relations between modern poetry and painting.

Jan Nordby Gretlund is associate professor of American literature at Odense University, Denmark. He is a contributor to the annual *American Literary Scholarship* and editor of the newsletter for the Forum for Southern Studies in Europe. He has written essays on Ralph Ellison, Barry Hannah, Madison Jones, Walker Percy, Katherine Anne Porter, and Eudora Welty and he co-edited *Realist of Distances: Flannery O'Connor Revisited*.

Daun Kendig is an associate professor in the Department of Speech Communication at St. Cloud State University, where she teaches literature in performance. Her recent work deals with narrative and performance theory.

Thomas McHaney teaches and directs the graduate program in English at Georgia State University. He has written critical, bibliographical, and textual work on William Faulkner and other southern writers. His short stories have appeared in numerous literary magazines and four of his plays have been produced in Atlanta.

Danièle Pitavy-Souques is professor of North American Literature at the University of Franche-Comté (Besançon), France. She is Director of the Centre for Canadian Studies at the University of Burgundy in Dijon. Her special fields of research are Eudora Welty, the South, and women writers of the United States and Canada. She has had numerous publications in Europe and the U.S. and is presently working on two books on Eudora Welty.

Noel Polk is professor of English at the University of Southern Mississippi. He has edited works of William Faulkner and is currently working on a Eudora Welty bibliography.

Ann Romines teaches American literature and women's studies at George Washington University. She has written essays on Eudora Welty, Mary Wilkins Freeman, Sarah Orne Jewett, and Willa Cather. She is completing a book on American women writers and domestic ritual and beginning a feminist reading of the Little House books of Laura Ingalls Wilder.

Peter Schmidt teaches American literature at Swarthmore College. He is the author of *William Carlos Williams: The Arts and Literary Tradition,* and editor of *William Carlos Williams Review*. In addition to articles on Welty, he has also written about Charles Simic and Michael Hamburger.

Dawn Trouard is an associate professor teaching modern and southern fiction at the University of Akron. A native of New Orleans, she has published essays on William Styron, William Faulkner, F. Scott Fitzgerald, and Mary McCarthy.

Ruth Vande Kieft, professor of English at Queens College, City University of New York, is the author of the first full-length study of Eudora Welty's fiction, *Eudora Welty.* She introduced and edited a widely used and often reissued collection of Welty's stories, *Thirteen Stories,* in 1965. Her critical writings include articles on William Faulkner, Flannery O'Connor, and other fiction writers.

Carey Wall, professor of English at San Diego State University, has written articles on William Faulkner, Mark Twain, Henry Green, and Eudora Welty, and on the American musical as a vehicle mediating business culture's inflection of our social relations. She is working on a book about Welty, for which this volume's essay on "June Recital" sets the tone.

Ruth Weston is assistant professor of English at Oral Roberts University. A poet and feminist critic, she has written articles on Alice Walker, Cynthia Asquith, Mary Stewart, and Welty. She is completing a book on Welty.

INDEX

"Acrobats in a Park," 145
Allegory, 45, 157, 160
American visionary painters, 5; Magic
  Realist tradition, 8
Anderson, Sherwood, 175
Andrews, Eudora Carden, 199
Appel, Alfred, Jr., on "June Recital," 167,
  171
Archive, 153
Arnold, Marilyn, social cruelty in "June
  Recital," 15, 27; social structure in
  "June Recital," 18–19
Artist figure, xiii, 133–41, 143–44,
  150,179
Atlanta Journal and Constitution, 107
"At the Landing," 89, 143; compared to
  "The Demonstrators," 51, 54; isolation,
  115; journey, 149; joy, 148–49;
  suffering, 143
Austen, Jane, 133

Babcock, Barbara, 18, 26
Bakhtin, Mikhail, x, xi, 42, 174, 191, 192
Beethoven, Ludwig van, 144, 176
Benjamin, Walter, 35
Benton, Thomas Hart, 8, 11
Blavatsky, Madame [Helena], 181–82,
  183, 186, 189
Bonnefoy, Yves, 149
Brecht, Bertolt, 121
Breughel, Pieter, visual imagination, 3
"Bride of the Innisfallen, The," 116; jour-
  neys, 147–48; joy, 148; margins, 147;
  optimism, 116; role of place, 159; suffer-
  ing, 145–46
*Bride of the Innisfallen, The, and Other
  Stories,* xiii, 145; changes for *CS,* 148;
  place, 153, 158, 162; published, 153; suf-
  fering, 143
Brookes, Stella, 167
Brooks, Peter, 142
"Burning, The," 78, 153

Cather, Willa, 90, 91–92, 175, 189;
  pattern in the stories, 189; view of
  artists, 133, 175; Welty's admiration for,
  7, 13
Cézanne, Paul 5
Chaungtu, 197
Chekhov, Anton, xii, 107–18; absence of
  sentimentality, 117; characterization,
  108, 109–10, 111, 113; compared to
  Welty, 107–18; compression, 109, 118;
  didacticism, 111–13, 116; fictional
  topics, 107, 108; humor in, 113;
  isolation, 114–15; narrators, 110–11;
  possibility and waste, 116, 117; the real,
  119; similarities between Russian and
  southern talkers, 33
Chopin, Kate, 57, 90
"Circe," 153, 159; first-person narrative,
  94–95, 100–104; language in 101, 103;
  male hero, 101, 102; role of time, 102–
  4; sibyl, 78; stages of suffering, 145,
  146
"Clytie," 89; as grotesque, 7, 82; "mad-
  house," 82, 127; sibyl, 78
Coleridge, Samuel Taylor, 165
Collected Stories of Eudora Welty, 148;
  preface, 16
Communitas, in "June Recital," 17, 19,
  20, 22–26, 29, 31
Conversations with Eudora Welty, on
  Chekhov and Steinbeck, 113; on
  "Circe," 146; on Fats Waller, 138; on
  folk art, 3; on *GA,* 173, 174, 176; on
  LB, 32, 33, 34; misremembers slapping
  episode in "June Recital," 26; on Miss
  Eckhart, 21; on myth, 127; reflecting
  violence, 34; similarities between folk
  and literary art, 5; similarities between
  Russian and southern talkers in
  Chekhov, 33; skepticism, 43; on "A
  Worn Path," 167, 170
Cooley, John R., 166, 171